Death & Discrimination

Racial Disparities in Capital Sentencing

Samuel R. Gross & Robert Mauro

NORTHEASTERN UNIVERSITY PRESS
Boston

Northeastern University Press

Library of Congress Cataloging in Publication Data
Gross, Samuel R.
   Death & discrimination.
   Includes index.
   1. Capital punishment—United States.   2. Race discrimination—United States.   3. United States—Race relations.   4. Afro-American criminals—Civil rights.   I. Mauro, Robert.   II. Title.   III. Title: Death and discrimination.
HV8699.U5G76   1989   364.6'6'0973   88-25269
ISBN 1-55553-040-0 (alk. paper)

Designed by Mike Fender

Composed in Caslon 224 by Grafacon, Inc., Hudson, Massachusetts. Printed and bound by The Maple Press Co., York, Pennsylvania. The paper is Sebago Antique, an acid-free sheet.

.MANUFACTURED IN THE UNITED STATES OF AMERICA
93   92   91   90   89   5   4   3   2   1

*To Rina Mauro, to Phoebe C. Ellsworth,
and to the memory of Nora Faine Gross*

Contents

Foreword

Having had the privilege of working in the 1960s with Norman Amaker, Anthony Amsterdam, Jack Greenberg, Michael Meltsner, and others associated with the NAACP Legal Defense and Educational Fund, I became more precisely aware—legally and statistically—of the character and amount of racial discrimination in death penalty sentences. I also became much more sensitive than I had been previously to the many different levels of legal and statistical sophistication used in analyzing what at first appears to be a relatively simple working hypothesis: blacks, compared to whites, are disproportionately sentenced to death. The classic scientific requirement of holding constant as many relevant variables as possible, or to use the more commonly worded phrase, "all other things being equal," loomed especially large in examining the basic hypothesis.

From my contact with these brilliant, socially conscious lawyers, I also learned that the logic and language of the law and of social science have a relatively small degree of overlap, like a Venn diagram showing two circles with only a small section of interaction between them. The disparity between the two mind-sets increases from direct examination to cross-examination, from lower court opinions to those of the United States Supreme Court. And, until the last moment under direct examination, I learned to use the relatively benign and factual phrase "racially dispropor-tionate sentencing" instead of the more emotionally laden "racial discrimination in sentencing," which requires "intent" when bound to the Fourteenth Amendment.

Having learned these and other lessons of legal research on race and the penalty of death, I came to this volume by Samuel Gross and Robert Mauro with sharpened claws of critical analytic sensitivity and found the reward of reading similar to the delight a mathematician finds in the elegance of a particular proof. This work is the most comprehensive, thoroughly documented, carefully analyzed I have yet en-countered on the topic of racial disparities in capital sen-tencing. Their review of the literature, through text and notes, is complete; their reasoning and conclusions are compelling; their analyses of Supreme Court opinions and of statistical evidence in their own study of sentencing under post-*Furman* death penalty laws in eight states and in review of the statistics from *Maxwell v. Bishop* to *McCleskey v. Kemp* are as compact and solid as the tightly fitted layers of a heavy onion.

Particularly informative for social scientists are the legal discussions and interpretations of the Eighth and Fourteenth Amendments. Equally valuable for lawyers are the statistical interpretations of multiple regression, multiple logistic (or "logit") regression, and other techniques. I can think of no other book or article that helps more than *Death and Discrimination* to reduce the logical and linguistic gap between legal and social science thinking and research.

MARVIN E. WOLFGANG

Preface

When we began this project in 1980, it seemed a straightforward task. Eight years earlier, in the landmark case of
Furman v. Georgia (408 U.S. 238 [1972] the Supreme
Court had declared all existing capital punishment laws in
the United States unconstitutional and had vacated all death
sentences then in effect. The basis for this decision (as
best it can be deciphered) was the Court's conclusion that
the use of the death penalty under these pre-*Furman* laws
was "arbitrary" (meaning that there were no adequate legitimate distinctions between cases that received death
sentences and those that did not) and "discriminatory"
(meaning that death sentences were imposed in part on
the basis of impermissible distinctions, in particular race).
Four years later, in *Gregg v. Georgia* (428 U.S. 153 [1976])
the Court reversed its apparent course and approved several
new death penalty statutes (and by implication, dozens of
similar ones) on the ground that they promised to eliminate
the arbitrariness and the discrimination that had troubled
the Court in 1972. By 1980 several of these new laws had
been in effect for five years or longer, and hundreds of
new death sentences had been pronounced. The time seemed
right to try to determine whether the new capital sentencing

schemes did in fact cure the problems that led to the *Furman* decision.

In one respect, we were right. It was a good time to investigate the effects of the post-*Furman* reforms on capital sentencing in the United States. With regard to the scope of the task, however, we were off by quite a bit. Like many empirical research projects, this study took on a life of its own and grew beyond our original vision both in scope and in detail. In addition, soon after we started our work the issue of racial discrimination in capital sentencing became a major focus in the long-running constitutional controversy over the use of the death penalty in America. In the process, the empirical studies on this issue—including our own—became the central elements in a series of legal cases, culminating in 1987 in the Supreme Court's decision in *McCleskey v. Kemp* (107 S.Ct. 1756 [1987]. As a result, we extended our work to include a description and critique of the courts' use of this research, and of their treatment of the underlying legal issues. The end result is this book.

Part One describes the background of the issues we explore. In Chapter 1 we introduce the legal and empirical questions, and in Chapter 2 we summarize and evaluate the research on discrimination in capital sentencing that preceded our own.

Part Two contains the core of the book, an empirical study of death sentencing patterns in eight states from 1976 through 1980. In Chapter 3 we describe the sources of our data and the methods that we used to analyze them. In Chapter 4 we describe in detail our findings for the three states in our sample that had the largest numbers of death sentences in the period we studied: Georgia, Florida, and Illinois. In this chapter we also describe our findings on the effect of appellate review on racial patterns in capital sentencing in two states, Georgia and Florida. Chapter 5 contains a brief review of our findings for the other five states in the study. (These findings are displayed in detail in Appendix 2.) And in Chapter 6 we consider and reject several alternative explanations that could account for our findings in the absence of racial discrimination, and we discuss the relationship between our findings and other related recent research.

Part Three is addressed to the causes and consequences of racial discrimination in capital sentencing. In Chapter 7 we discuss possible psychological explanations for the racial patterns that we found. In Chapter 8 we describe the legal context of this issue prior to the *McCleskey* case. And finally, in Chapters 9, 10, and 11, we discuss the *McCleskey* case itself, in the lower federal courts and in the Supreme Court, and its implications.

In a word, these implications are grim. The Supreme Court has more or less acknowledged that race continues to play a major role in capital sentencing in America; in any event, this is an undeniable fact. But the Court has decided to do nothing about this form of discrimination and to refuse to hear future claims based on it. We think we can explain why the Court reached this conclusion, but we cannot justify it. Whatever the reasons for the Supreme Court's decision in *McCleskey,* it is wrong.

This should not be the end of the story. Recently, Representative John Conyers, chairman of the Subcommittee on Criminal Justice of the House Judiciary Committee, responded to *McCleskey* by introducing a bill in Congress that both outlaws racial discrimination in capital sentencing and specifies a method of proving a violation of its provisions (H.R. 4442, 100th Congress, introduced April 21, 1988). Perhaps Congress will enact this bill or some similar law. Perhaps other legislatures or executives will attempt to address this problem now that the courts will not touch it. If not, someday perhaps the Supreme Court itself will overrule its own misguided decision. It is no small comment on our society that we openly and consciously tolerate a system in which race frequently determines whom we execute and whom we spare. Let us hope that this soon becomes a thing of the past.

June 1988
                                        Samuel R. Gross
                                    Ann Arbor, Michigan

                                        Robert Mauro
                                    Eugene, Oregon

Acknowledgments

Most studies of archival data depend on the assistance and generosity of many people, and this one is no exception. We are grateful in particular to Carol Palmer, formerly of the NAACP Legal Defense and Educational Fund, Inc., for her excellent and dedicated work collecting the data on death row inmates on which our research is based, and to William Bowers and Glenn Pierce, whose wisdom and experience were put repeatedly at our disposal. Without them this study could not have been conducted. We are likewise grateful to David Baldus, George Woodworth, and Charles Pulaski, and to Richard Berk, for permitting us to cite unpublished data and for their thoughtful comments on drafts of various portions of this book. John Boger, Richard Brody, and Tanya Coke of the NAACP Legal Defense and Educational Fund provided advice and information that were essential to the completion of this work.

Numerous colleagues helped our work with thoughtful comments on earlier versions of various parts of this book. A complete list would be embarrassingly long, but even an abbreviated one must include Hugo Bedau, William Cohen, Thomas Grey, Jerold Israel, Yale Kamisar, John Kaplan, Randall Kennedy, Michael Laurence, Richard Lempert, Robert Mnookin, Eric Multhaup, Frederick Schauer and

Robert Weisberg. Joseph Kadane and Lincoln Moses gave us excellent advice on statistics, Marty Mador provided essential help in organizing our computerized data, and Patrick Adair, Connie Beck, Kenneth Diamond, Kenneth Dintzer, Bryan Ford, Martin Koloski, and David Sprayberry were invaluable as research assistants. Countless drafts of the elements of this book, and (worse) uncountable tables were typed and retyped with precision and care by Judy Dearing, Moana Kutsche, and Marcea Metzler. Finally, Phoebe Ellsworth, a most valued colleague, provided regular aid and advice from start to finish.

The research reported in this book was supported in part by the Edna McConnell Clark Foundation, and by the Stanford Legal Research Fund made possible by a bequest from the Estate of Ira S. Lillick and by gifts from Roderick E. and Carla A. Hills and other friends of Stanford Law School. Earlier versions of portions of this book appeared previously in: Samuel R. Gross and Robert Mauro, *Patterns of Death: An Analysis of Racial Disparities in Capital Sentencing and Homicide Victimization,* 37 Stanford Law Review 27 (1984); and Samuel R. Gross, *Race and Death: The Judicial Evaluation of Evidence of Discrimination in Capital Sentencing,* 18 U.C. Davis Law Review 1275 (1985). We thank the publishers of these journals for their permission to republish those articles in this form.

PART ONE

1 | Introduction: Arbitrariness and Discrimination

Homicides are common in America; death sentences are very rare. By FBI estimates, 101,960 nonnegligent criminal homicides were committed in the United States in the five-year period from the beginning of 1976 through the end of 1980,[1] and 96,170 arrests were made for these homicides.[2] In that same period, 1011 death sentences were pronounced by American courts,[3] a ratio of nearly 100 to 1. Some of these homicides were committed in states without active death penalties, but only a small minority,[4] and some of the suspects arrested for these homicides were never convicted. The most relevant proportion may be hard to define and its exact size may be impossible to calculate, but the basic pattern is clear: among those hundred thousand homicides, death sentences were highly uncommon events. In this book we examine patterns of capital sentencing in this period in several states to determine whether race was a factor that caused some killers to be sentenced to death while the vast majority were not.

There is nothing wrong, in the abstract, with the fact that the death penalty is rarely imposed. At the opposite extreme, the general use of the death penalty as the punishment for over 20,000 homicides a year, or any number approaching that, would be unthinkable. In 1935, 199 people

3

were executed in the United States, the highest total since accurate records have been kept.[5] In the past decade, a similar number have been sentenced to death annually, but far fewer have been executed.[6] We are not likely to return to the 1935 execution rate in the near future, if ever, and even that rate would be extremely selective.[7] It seems inevitable that we will continue to impose the death penalty as we have in the past, winnowing a small set of capital cases from a vastly larger number of homicides.

Some steps in this winnowing process are relatively easy. The death penalty, like any other criminal sanction, is available only in cases in which suspects have been apprehended and convicted; only about half of all homicides fall in this category.[8] Moreover, many homicide convictions are for manslaughter rather than for murder, and among murderers only some are found guilty of capital murder under the laws of the relevant jurisdictions.[9] Actual numbers are hard to come by, but these restrictions undoubtedly reduce the pool of possible capital homicides considerably. They do not, however, determine who is sentenced to death. If only one homicide defendant in ten is legally eligible for the death penalty, only about one capital-eligible murderer in ten actually receives it.[10] This further selection is accomplished by a process that is anything but obvious, by actors vested with wide discretion. Two discretionary choices are particularly important: the decision by the prosecutor to seek the death penalty, and the decision by the sentencing judge or jury to impose it.

In practice, this discretionary use of the death penalty creates two moral and legal dangers: arbitrariness and discrimination. When a handful of cases is selected from a large mass, there is a risk that the selection will not be based on any consistent normative criteria—that those chosen for execution will be indistinguishable from the rest on any legally appropriate basis—or, worse, that they will be distinguished only by legally improper criteria—

poverty, powerlessness, or race. Walter Berns, an articulate advocate for capital punishment, has summarized the problem well: however strongly one may favor the death penalty in principle, its propriety in practice "depends on our ability to restrict its use to the worst of our criminals and to impose it in a nondiscriminatory fashion."[11]

The problems of arbitrariness and discrimination in the imposition of the death penalty have been the focus of a large body of litigation on the constitutionality of capital punishment. In 1972, in *Furman v. Georgia*,[12] the Supreme Court held that all death penalty statutes then in force were unconstitutional in that they violated the Eighth Amendment prohibition of cruel and unusual punishments.[13] There was no opinion of the Court in *Furman*; each of the nine justices wrote separately, concurring in or dissenting from the Court's judgment. All the justices in the majority were concerned about the arbitrary or the discriminatory nature of the death penalty, but their analyses of these problems varied. Two—Justice Brennan[14] and Justice Marshall[15]—concluded that the death penalty is an inherently cruel and unusual punishment. Justice Brennan relied in part on the infrequency of the death penalty as evidence that it had been imposed arbitrarily by what amounted to "little more than a lottery system."[16] Justice Marshall, on the other hand, based his decision in part on evidence that capital punishment had been used discriminatorily against defendants who were poor, powerless, or black.[17] The other three members of the majority, Justices Douglas,[18] Stewart,[19] and White,[20] each stated that capital punishment was unconstitutional as it was then employed in the United States. Justice Douglas concluded that the capital sentencing laws before the Court were "pregnant with discrimination,"[21] and that such discrimination violated the Eighth Amendment ban on cruel and unusual punishments. Justices Stewart and White focused on the arbitrariness with which the death penalty had been imposed. Justice Stewart complained that those actually sentenced to death were "a capriciously selected random handful"[22] taken from the vast number of those eligible; Justice White found "no meaningful basis for distinguishing the few cases in which [the death penalty] is imposed from the many cases in which it is not."[23]

The legal significance of the decision in *Furman* is probably best understood by examining the opinions of the two justices in the majority who decided the case on the narrowest constitutional grounds, Justices Stewart and White. The death penalty statutes that were condemned in *Furman* were all of the same general type: they permitted juries to impose capital punishment for murder or for rape but did not require them to do so, and they offered the juries no guidance in making this decision. Both justices found that this type of statute created a constitutionally unacceptable risk that the death penalty would be imposed arbitrarily, but they did not find that the use of the death penalty was inevitably arbitrary, nor that it was inherently unconstitutional on any other ground.[24]

Most states responded to *Furman* by enacting new death penalty statutes that were designed to avoid the problems identified by Justices Stewart and White. In 1976, the Supreme Court announced that some states had succeeded and some had failed. Capital punishment could be constitutionally imposed, at least in principle, under laws that guided and restricted the discretion of the sentencer, typically by providing statutory lists of aggravating and mitigating factors that must be considered in passing judgment.[25] Under such schemes, the Court stated, "[n]o longer can a jury wantonly and freakishly impose the death sentence; it is always circumscribed by the legislative guidelines."[26] On the other hand, laws that made the death penalty mandatory for certain crimes were held unconstitutional,[27] in part because mandatory capital sentencing, by ignoring the unique facts of each case, did not meet the constitutional "need for reliability in the determination that death is the appropriate punishment in a specific case,"[28] and in part because such sentencing schemes did not promise to eliminate the "arbitrary and wanton jury discretion"[29] condemned in *Furman*.

The 1976 capital punishment cases did not settle the constitutional problems that plague the administration of the death penalty. On the contrary, *Furman* became the fountainhead of an expanding swamp of uncertain rules and confusing opinions.[30] In the past fifteen years *Furman* has been cited as authority for every death penalty decision by the Supreme Court, regardless of content, and by every dissent from each of these decisions. A certain amount of ambiguity is a feature of many legal opinions, but this is something different, a case that is not so much a precedent as a Rorschach test.[31] Against this background it may be foolhardy to argue that *Furman*'s prohibition of arbitrariness in capital sentencing has any particular meaning, especially because (as we shall see) recent litigation on racial discrimination in the use of the death penalty has cast doubt on whether that rule has survived with any practical force at all.[32] For the moment, however, we will take the Court's statements of continuing adherence to *Furman* at face value, and assume that it is possible to derive a consistent and meaningful description of "arbitrariness" from *Furman* and the cases following it. Given that assumption, we can identify a few points of reference with reasonable clarity. Three of these points help define the legal issues that we address in this book:

1. Any system that imposes the death penalty "arbitrarily" violates the Eighth Amendment prohibition of cruel and unusual punishments.[33]

2. The guided discretion statutes that were considered by the Supreme Court in 1976 were approved because they "*promised* to alleviate" the arbitrariness condemned in

Furman.[34] The final constitutional judgment on these statutes, and others like them, will depend on whether their performance fulfills their promise.[35]

3. "Arbitrariness," in this context, means (at least) two different things: (a) the random or "capricious" use of the death penalty,[36] or (b) the imposition of the death penalty based on the presence or absence of a legally irrelevant factor, such as race.[37] These two forms of arbitrariness correspond to two modes of proof that there is "no *principled* way to distinguish"[38] "the few cases in which [the death penalty] is imposed from the many cases in which it is not."[39] If, after searching, no principled distinctions can be found between the two sets of cases, that would constitute indirect evidence that the choice is not based on legal principles. The strength of such evidence will depend on how thoroughly the range of appropriate legal principles has been searched. On the other hand, if a legally irrelevant factor were shown to influence the outcome, that would constitute a direct demonstration that principled considerations do not solely determine who is sentenced to death and who is not, since an *un*principled distinction has captured a share of that power.

The major portion of this book is a report on an empirical study that examines one aspect of the Eighth Amendment prohibition of arbitrariness in the use of the death penalty— the possibility of racial discrimination. Specifically, we have attempted to determine whether there has been racial discrimination in the imposition of the death penalty under several state statutes that were written in response to *Furman* with the aim of reducing or eliminating arbitrariness in capital sentencing. But racial discrimination is not just a species of "arbitrariness" that is unconstitutional in capital sentencing; it is also, and primarily, the major target of the equal protection clause of the Fourteenth Amendment. The imposition of *any* criminal sanction is unconstitutional if it is motivated by racial considerations.[40] These two constitutional objections to racial discrimination in capital sentencing overlap but are not congruent. "Discrimination" is a purposeful act. To prove a violation of the equal protection clause, one must show that the responsible person or institution acted with discriminatory "intent" or "purpose,"[41] although in some cases such intent may be inferred from "a clear pattern, unexplainable on grounds other than race."[42] "Arbitrariness," however, is not the description of an affirmative act; it is a wholly negative legal concept, the absence of a legitimate justification for an action or a pattern of actions. Not surprisingly, none of the Supreme Court opinions that condemn arbitrariness in the imposition of the death penalty suggests that intent is relevant to the issue.[43]

The research that is reported here is but one of several recent studies of racial discrimination in capital sentencing. Since this study first appeared in 1984,[44] there has been a spate of litigation on this issue, culminating in the case of *McCleskey v. Kemp*,[45] which focused on a comprehensive and extraordinarily detailed study of the death penalty in Georgia by David Baldus, George Woodworth, and Charles Pulaski.[46] In *McCleskey* the Supreme Court held that statistical evidence of racial discrimination—the type of evidence presented here—is intrinsically insufficient to establish an unconstitutional pattern of capital sentencing, either under the Eighth Amendment or under the Fourteenth.[47] This decision may have ended the legal battle over racial discrimination in the use of the death penalty by putting the question beyond the reach of the courts, but it has not ended the moral debate. Indeed, the *McCleskey* decision and the litigation leading up to it provide a useful focus for a discussion of the Supreme Court's role in that debate. They highlight two perennial problems in the peculiar arena of constitutional litigation on capital punishment: the troubled relationship between social scientific data and judicial policy, and the federal courts' continuing devotion to a fiction of their own invention—the fiction of the efficacy of the procedural reforms in capital sentencing that were initiated by the Supreme Court's decision in *Furman*.

Notes

1. FEDERAL BUREAU OF INVESTIGATION, UNIFORM CRIME REPORT, CRIME IN THE UNITED STATES 41 (1980) [hereinafter cited as UCR].
2. *See id.* at 173 (1976); *id.* at 172 (1977); *id.* at 186 (1978); *id.* at 188 (1979); *id.* at 191 (1980). The "clearance rate" for homicides— the percentage of cases that result in arrests—is higher than that for other categories of crime, but not as high as the total number of arrests suggests. In the period under consideration, the clearance rate averaged 75 percent. *Id.* at 161 (1976); *id.* at 161 (1977); *id.* at 176 (1978); *id.* at 178 (1979); *id.* at 181 (1980). The number of homicide arrests reflects the fact that in over 10 percent of the cases two or more suspects were arrested. *See, e.g., id.* at 8 (1980).
3. Greenberg, *Capital Punishment as a System*, 91 YALE L.J. 908, 936 (1982). The total reported here excludes 114 cases in which the death penalty was reimposed on defendants whose previous death sentences had been reversed or vacated by the courts; it includes a handful of cases in which defendants were sentenced to death for crimes that did not involve homicide, usually rape. *See* Coker v. Georgia, 433 U.S. 584, 595–98 (1977). Both the homicide rate and the death-sentencing rate that are reflected in these figures were fairly constant. In 1972 the Supreme Court declared all existing death penalty laws unconstitutional. Furman v. Georgia, 408 U.S. 238 (1972). In the first year or two after *Furman* few death sentences were returned, reflecting the fact that most states had no effective death penalty laws in place. From 1974 through 1980, however, the capital sentencing rate has been relatively stable, averaging about 210 per year: 1974, 190; 1975, 285; 1976, 266; 1977, 167; 1978, 219; 1979, 156; 1980, 203. Greenberg, *supra,* at 936. (These totals do not include cases in which previous death penalties were reimposed.)
4. Most states moved swiftly to reenact death penalty statutes in the wake of *Furman*. By June 1976 at least thirty-five of the fifty states had enacted new capital punishment laws. Gregg v. Georgia, 428 U.S. 153, 179–80 (1976). In the years following *Gregg* a number of these statutes were declared unconstitutional, and several new ones were enacted or reenacted. *See generally* Greenberg, *supra* note 3 (discussing patterns in decisions concerning capital punishment). Because of the complexity of these events, it is difficult to determine precisely how

many homicides were committed in jurisdictions that had death penalty laws in effect at the time of the killing, but an example is suggestive: in 1980, FBI estimates suggest that 80 percent of criminal homicides were committed in death penalty states. UCR, *supra* note 1, at 48–59 (1980). (The jurisdictions with death penalty laws in effect in 1980 were Alabama, Arizona, Arkansas, California, Colorado, Connecticut, Delaware, the District of Columbia, Florida, Georgia, Idaho, Illinois, Indiana, Kentucky, Louisiana, Maryland, Mississippi, Missouri, Montana, Nebraska, Nevada, New Hampshire, New Mexico, North Carolina, Oklahoma, Oregon, Pennsylvania, South Carolina, South Dakota, Tennessee, Texas, Utah, Virginia, Washington, and Wyoming.)

5. Greenberg, *supra* note 3, at 925; *see also Furman,* 408 U.S. 238, 291–93 (1972) (Brennan, J., concurring).

6. As of December 1987, 93 people had been executed since the *Furman* decision in 1972. Eleven of them refused to pursue available post-conviction remedies to review the legality of their sentences; the remainder were executed involuntarily, after exhausting all available avenues of review. NAACP Legal Defense and Educational Fund, Death Row U.S.A. (December 20, 1987) (unpublished document) [hereinafter cited as Death Row U.S.A.]. Only eleven people were executed from January 1977, when the first post-*Furman* execution took place, through the end of 1983. From 1984 through 1986, however, the execution rate hovered steadily around twenty per year, and twenty-five people were executed in 1987; *id.* There is speculation that the rate may now increase, *see, e.g.,* Taylor, *Foes' Hopes Dashed: Justices Not Swayed by Study Citing Role of Victim's Color,* N.Y. Times, April 23, 1987, at 1, but it is not clear whether that is true, and if so how high it will go. *See* pp. 217–24 *infra.*

7. Even before *Furman,* the number of executions lagged far behind the number of death sentences. *See Furman,* 408 U.S. 238, 291–93 (1972) (Brennan, J., concurring). William Bowers has documented the long-term trend in legal executions in the United States: the number of executions was stable from the 1890s through the 1920s (averaging about 1150 per decade), rose sharply during the 1930s to a total of 1670 for that decade, and then declined steadily and rapidly to a total of 191 executions in the 1960s. W. BOWERS, LEGAL HOMICIDE: DEATH AS PUNISHMENT IN AMERICA, 1864–1982, at 49–58 (1984). Greenberg argues that while the public supports the death penalty in principle, it would not tolerate large numbers of executions, and that the level of support for the death penalty would decrease as the execution rate increased. Greenberg, *supra* note 3, at 924–25. This remains to be seen.

8. This is a rough estimate, obtained by multiplying the clearance

rate for homicides by the conviction rate for those charged with homicide. *See, e.g.*, UCR, *supra* note 1, at 161, 217 (1976); *id.* at 161, 216 (1977).

9. Typically, modern capital sentencing statutes provide that a murder may be punishable by death if it involves one or more "aggravating circumstances." The current Georgia statute is a good example. A murder is a capital offense in Georgia if: (a) it was committed by a person with a record of conviction for a capital felony; (b) it was committed in the course of another capital felony, aggravated battery, kidnapping, rape, burglary, or arson; (c) the offender knowingly created "a great risk of death to more than one person in a public place"; (d) the murder was committed for pecuniary gain; (e) the victim was a judicial officer or prosecutor killed for reasons connected with his office; (f) the murder was committed for hire; (g) the murder was "outrageously or wantonly vile, horrible or inhuman"; (h) the victim was a peace officer killed in line of duty; (i) the murderer was a prisoner or an escaped prisoner; or (j) the murder was committed to prevent a lawful arrest or incarceration. GA. CODE ANN. § 17-10-30(b) (1982) (amending GA. CODE ANN. § 27-2534.1(b)) (1978); *see* p. 6 and note 25 *infra*. The death penalty statutes of the eight states that are discussed in this study are cited in App. 1 *infra*.

10. Thorsten Sellin has estimated the risk of a death sentence for various categories of homicide defendants using official data from several states for varying periods, almost all prior to 1970. He finds substantial variations from one place and time to another, but concludes that, in general, about one-fourth of all willful homicide defendants were prosecuted for capital murder. About half of those defendants, or fewer, were convicted of capital murder, and only a small (but highly variable) fraction of those convicted of capital murder were sentenced to death. T. SELLIN, THE PENALTY OF DEATH 35–53, 69–74 (1980).

11. Berns, *Defending the Death Penalty*, 26 CRIME & DELINQ. 503, 511 (1980).

12. 408 U.S. 238 (1972).

13. One year earlier, in McGautha v. California, 402 U.S. 183 (1971), the Court had held that the death penalty statutes of Ohio and California— which were essentially indistinguishable from those in *Furman*—did not violate the Fourteenth Amendment requirement of due process of law. The Eighth Amendment holding in *Furman* was justified in large part by the observation that "the penalty of death differs from all other forms of criminal punishment, not in degree but in kind. It is unique in its total irrevocability." 408 U.S. at 306 (Stewart, J., concurring).

14. *Furman*, 408 U.S. at 257–306.

15. *Id.* at 314–74.

16. *Id.* at 293.
17. *Id.* at 364–66.
18. *Id.* at 240–57.
19. *Id.* at 306–10.
20. *Id.* at 310–14.
21. *Id.* at 257.
22. *Id.* at 309–10.
23. *Id.* at 313.
24. *Id.* at 306–8, 310–11, 314.
25. Proffitt v. Florida, 428 U.S. 242, 247–60 (1976); Gregg v. Georgia, 428 U.S. 153, 188–195 (1976); *see* note 9 *supra.* Jurek v. Texas, 428 U.S. 262 (1976), approved a somewhat different scheme. Under the Texas law, the jury, after finding the defendant guilty of capital murder, must answer three statutory questions: (a) whether the defendant killed deliberately, (b) whether the defendant is likely to be violent in the future, and (c) (if raised by the evidence) whether the killing was unreasonable in response to provocation by the victim. If the answers are all affirmative, the judge must impose the death penalty. TEX. CODE CRIM. PROC. ANN. art. 37.071 (Vernon Supp. 1975–76) (current version at TEX. CODE CRIM. PROC. ANN. art. 37.071 (Vernon 1981)).
26. *Gregg,* 428 U.S. at 206–7 (plurality opinion).
27. *See* Roberts v. Louisiana, 428 U.S. 325 (1976); Woodson v. North Carolina, 428 U.S. 280 (1976); *see also* Roberts v. Louisiana, 431 U.S. 633 (1977) (*Roberts II*).
28. *Woodson,* 428 U.S. at 305 (plurality opinion).
29. *Id.* at 303 (plurality opinion); *see also Roberts,* 428 U.S. at 334–35. The plurality was concerned that under mandatory capital sentencing schemes jury discretion would be exercised de facto through the power of jury nullification, and that such discretion would be utterly unguided.
30. In Lockett v. Ohio, 438 U.S. 586 (1978), Chief Justice Burger acknowledged that "[t]he signals from this Court have not . . . always been easy to decipher." *Id.* at 602 (plurality opinion). Unfortunately, *Lockett* itself is a good example of this problem. The Court held that despite the constitutional requirement that discretion in capital sentencing be limited and guided, a capital sentencer must be able to give "independent mitigating weight," *id.* at 605, to "any aspect of a defendant's character or record and any of the circumstances of the offense that the defendant proffers as a basis for a sentence less than death," *id.* at 604 (footnote omitted). But what, if any, are the limits to this new requirement of open-ended mitigation? And does it create another form of unguided discretion in capital sentencing? *See id.* at 622 (White, J., concurring in part, dissenting in part, and concurring in the judgment).

("Today it is held, again through a plurality, that the sentencer may constitutionally impose the death penalty only as an exercise of his unguided discretion after being presented with all circumstances which the defendant might believe to be conceivably relevant to the appropriateness of the penalty. . . .") Perhaps these questions are not even meaningful, in view of later Supreme Court decisions continuing to uphold death sentencing statutes, such as those of Texas, that are plainly inconsistent with the holding in *Lockett*. See Hertz & Weisberg, *In Mitigation of the Penalty of Death: Lockett v. Ohio and the Capital Defendant's Right to Consideration of Mitigating Circumstances*, 69 CALIF. L. REV. 317, 328–41 (1981).

Other cases are equally puzzling. In Godfrey v. Georgia, 446 U.S. 420 (1980), for example, the Court found that, contrary to its earlier assumption in *Gregg*, the Georgia Supreme Court had not adopted a sufficiently narrow construction of the aggravating circumstance that a murder "was outrageously or wantonly vile, horrible or inhuman" to avoid the Eighth Amendment problem of arbitrariness. But rather than hold that this aggravating factor is unconstitutionally vague, the Court merely held that the statutory construction was unconstitutional *in Godfrey's case*, leaving the implications of the opinion for other cases unclear and undecided. *Id*. at 432–33; see also Bullington v. Missouri, 451 U.S. 430 (1981) (imposition of death sentence after reversal of life sentence violates double jeopardy in view of trial-like penalty proceeding, but no indication if such trial-like proceedings are constitutionally mandatory).

In Zant v. Stephens, 462 U.S. 862 (1983), the Court held that juries and judges could rely in part on nonstatutory *aggravating* circumstances when they impose sentences of death, and it found no fault in a Georgia sentencing procedure under which (as now interpreted), "the finding of an aggravating circumstance does not play any role in guiding the sentencing body in the exercise of its discretion, apart from its function of narrowing the class of persons convicted of murder who are eligible for the death penalty." *Id*. at 2741; see also Barclay v. Florida, 463 U.S. 939 (1983). These holdings (together with *Lockett*) seem to complete the dismantling of most of the procedural restrictions that were imposed on capital sentencing by *Gregg* and the other 1976 death penalty cases. *See Zant*, 462 U.S. at 910–14 (Marshall, J., dissenting). But the Court claims to reaffirm *Furman* and *Gregg*, interpreting them in a new light. The Georgia and Florida statutes that were considered in 1976 were upheld for two reasons: because they "circumscribe the class of persons eligible for the death penalty," *id*. at 878, and because they provide for "mandatory appellate review of each death sentence to avoid arbitrariness and to assure proportionality," *id*. at 890 (footnote omitted); *see also*

Barclay, 463 U.S. at 960 (Stevens, J., concurring). All other features of these statutes are constitutionally optional. For an excellent discussion of the implications of *Barclay* and *Zant,* and of the general pattern in Supreme Court decisions on the death penalty since 1972, see Weisberg, *Deregulating Death,* 1983 SUP. CT. REV. 305 (1984).

But are narrowing and proportionality review constitutionally necessary for the imposition of capital punishment, or merely sufficient as used in Georgia and Florida? This question was partially answered by Pulley v. Harris, 465 U.S. 37 (1984), in which the Court held that statewide proportionality review is not a constitutional requirement for capital sentencing. *See* ch. 4, pp. 70–77 and notes 42–76. *Harris* poses a basic question: What procedural requirements, if any, are necessary to satisfy the Court's current interpretation of the Eighth Amendment prohibition of arbitrary capital sentencing? If this issue is resolved with reasonable clarity—by no means a foregone conclusion—new ones may well take its place. These questions, however, are only marginally relevant here, since our focus is not on capital sentencing *procedures* but on the *outcomes* that they produce.

31. *See generally* Weisberg, *supra* note 30.

32. *See* ch. 10, pp. 159–211.

33. *Zant,* 462 U.S. 874; *Gregg,* 428 U.S. at 188; *Furman,* 408 U.S. 238 (1972).

34. *Zant* v. Stephens, 456 U.S. 410, 413 (1982) (per curiam) (emphasis added). *Compare Gregg,* 428 U.S. at 201 (approving an open-ended aggravating factor on the assumption that the Georgia Supreme Court would sufficiently narrow its construction and application), *with Godfrey,* 446 U.S. 420 (1980) (invalidating this same statutory provision in a particular case because the Georgia courts failed to construe it narrowly).

35. *Zant,* 456 U.S. at 413 (per curiam).

36. *Gregg,* 428 U.S. at 188 (plurality opinion), 220–21 (White, J., concurring); *Furman,* 408 U.S. at 309–10.

37. *Furman,* 408 U.S. at 310 (Stewart, J., concurring), 249–51 (Douglas, J., concurring), 364–66 (Marshall, J., concurring); *see also Zant,* 462 U.S. 862, 885 (1983); GA. CODE ANN. § 17-10-35(c)(1) (1982) (cited as GA. CODE ANN. § 27-2537(c) in *Gregg,* 428 U.S. at 166–67 (plurality opinion), 212 (White, J., concurring)); Spinkellink v. Wainwright, 578 F.2d 582, 613 n.38 (5th Cir. 1978), *cert. denied,* 440 U.S. 976 (1979); *cf.* Enmund v. Florida, 458 U.S. 782, 798 (1982) (Constitution mandates that sentences focus on "relevant facets of the [defendant's] character and record. . . .") (citation omitted).

38. *Godfrey,* 446 U.S. at 453 (emphasis added); *see also Gregg,* 428 U.S. at 313 (White, J., concurring).

39. *Furman,* 408 U.S. at 313 (White, J., concurring).

40. Wayte v. United States, 470 U.S. 598, 608 (1985) (dictum); Oyler v. Boles, 368 U.S. 448, 456 (1962) (dictum); Ah Sin v. Wittman, 198 U.S. 500 (1905); Yick Wo v. Hopkins, 118 U.S. 356 (1886).

41. Village of Arlington Heights v. Metropolitan Hous. Dev. Corp., 429 U.S. 252, 264–65 (1977); Washington v. Davis, 426 U.S. 229 (1976); cf. Oyler v. Boles, 368 U.S. 448, 456 (1961) (selectivity in enforcement of habitual criminal statute does not violate equal protection clause absent discriminatory intent).

42. Village of Arlington Heights v. Metropolitan Hous. Dev. Corp., 429 U.S. 252, 266 (1977).

43. See, e.g., Godfrey, 446 U.S. at 427–33 (plurality opinion); Gregg, 428 U.S. at 188–95 (plurality opinion); Furman, 408 U.S. at 306–10 (Stewart, J., concurring), 310–14 (White, J., concurring).

44. Gross & Mauro, Patterns of Death: An Analysis of Racial Disparities in Capital Sentencing and Homicide Victimization, 37 STAN. L. REV. 27 (1984).

45. McCleskey v. Zant, 580 F. Supp. 338 (N.D.Ga. 1984), aff'd sub nom McCleskey v. Kemp, 753 F.2d 877 (11th Cir. 1985) (en banc), aff'd, 478 U.S. ____, 107 S.Ct. 1756 (1987).

46. Baldus, Woodworth, & Pulaski, Discrimination and Arbitrariness in Georgia's Charging and Sentencing System: A Preliminary Report (July 29, 1983) (unpublished manuscript, College of Law, University of Iowa) [cited with the permission of the authors; hereinafter cited as the Baldus study]. This study was presented in evidence and its findings were described in detail to the district court in McCleskey, 580 F.Supp. 338. Some of the results of the Baldus study have already appeared in print in Baldus, Pulaski, & Woodworth, Comparative Review of Death Sentences: An Empirical Study of the Georgia Experience, 74 J. CRIM. L. & CRIMINOLOGY 661 (1983); Baldus, Woodworth, & Pulaski, Monitoring and Evaluating Contemporary Death Sentencing Systems: Lessons from Georgia, 18 U.C.D. L. REV. 1375 (1985); and Baldus, Pulaski, & Woodworth, Arbitrariness and Discrimination in the Administration of the Death Penalty: A Challenge to State Supreme Courts, 15 STETSON L. REV. (1986). Other findings will appear in a forthcoming book (1989).

47. McCleskey, 107 S.Ct. 1756 (1987).

2 | Previous Research on Race and Capital Sentencing

A. The Pre-*Furman* Era

Historically, the most striking racial pattern in the use of the death penalty in America has been the disproportionate execution of blacks. This pattern existed as far back as the Civil War,[1] although accurate figures are available only for the past half-century. Of 3984 people lawfully executed since 1930, 2113 were black,[2] over half of the total and almost five times the proportion of blacks in the population as a whole.[3] But this disproportion, while striking, does not demonstrate that there has been racial discrimination in the administration of the death penalty. The great majority of death sentences since 1930 have been imposed for homicide,[4] and the black homicide rate in that period has been several times higher than the white homicide rate.[5] The disparity in death sentences and executions could simply reflect the disparity in homicides.

A number of published studies suggest that racial discrimination did in fact exist in the imposition and execution of the death penalty for homicide prior to *Furman*.[6] In a detailed study of racial differences in the use of the death penalty, Harold Garfinkel collected data on more than 800 homicide cases that occurred in ten North Carolina counties

17

from 1930 through 1940.[7] Garfinkel found that white defendants who had been charged with first-degree murder were somewhat more likely to receive death sentences than black defendants, although the difference in proportions disappeared when he compared the ratios of death sentences to all homicide indictments rather than to first-degree murder indictments only. On the other hand, he found strong and stable disparities in death-sentencing rates by the race of the victim: defendants who killed whites were more likely to be sentenced to death than those who killed blacks. Moreover, when he controlled for the race of the victim, the impact of the race of the defendant changed. In both white-victim and black-victim cases, black defendants were substantially more likely to get death sentences than white defendants. The overall distribution of death sentences by race of defendant in Garfinkel's data appears to be the product of two separate patterns: white defendants were more likely to kill white victims, and all defendants who killed white victims were more likely to be sentenced to death than those who killed black victims.[8]

Thorsten Sellin summarizes reports of the South Carolina and Arkansas attorneys general that show that in the early part of this century black defendants in murder cases were much more likely to be convicted than white defendants.[9] Similarly, William Bowers found that blacks who had been sentenced to death from 1864 through 1967 were more likely to be executed without an appeal than whites, particularly in the South.[10] In addition, several pre-*Furman* studies examined racial patterns in the commutation of death sentences, and some, but not all, found that among death row prisoners, whites were more likely to have their death sentences commuted than blacks.[11] These studies, unfortunately, are of limited value because they do not contain data on the race of the victims.[12] If the true racial patterns for capital appeals and commutations were similar to those observed by Garfinkel for capital sentencing, then the absence of information on the victims' race might have obscured the existence or the magnitude of disparities based on the race of the defendants.

The most sophisticated study of capital sentencing prior to *Furman* was conducted in 1969 as a special project of the *Stanford Law Review*.[13] This study analyzed data on numerous variables for each of 238 cases between 1958 and 1966 in which California juries decided whether to impose the death penalty on defendants who had been convicted of first-degree murder. The study found that neither the race of the defendant nor the race of the victim was associated with capital sentencing.[14] The economic status of the defendant, however, did make a difference: controlling for many other variables, blue-collar defendants were considerably more likely to receive death sentences than white-collar defendants.[15]

One final pre-*Furman* study deserves mention. Zimring, Eigen, and O'Malley collected data on the first 204 homicides reported to the Philadelphia police in 1970.[16] This sample includes only three death sentences, far too few to permit any reasonable conclusions about the use of the death penalty as a unique punishment, but the data are suggestive. Among black defendants convicted of felony murder, 65 percent of those with white victims were sentenced to death or life imprisonment, compared to 25 percent of those with black victims, and all three death sentences were given to blacks convicted of killing whites even though only a fifth of all the homicides studied had that racial combination.[17] Zimring et al. describe this as a "paradox": "those who are least likely to be killed are most protected by sentencing policy."[18]

In a review of this literature, Gary Kleck summarizes and criticizes the studies of racial discrimination in the use of the death penalty prior to *Furman*.[19] On the basis of this review and some additional data on homicide, capital sentencing, and execution rates, Kleck reaches two general conclusions that are relevant to this inquiry. First, black defendants have not generally been discriminated against in the use of the death penalty, except in the South; elsewhere, black defendants have been, on the whole, less likely to receive the death penalty than white defendants.[20] And second, the death penalty is less likely to be imposed for homicides with black victims than for homicides with white victims.[21] Indeed, Kleck suggests that the apparently lenient treatment of black homicide defendants outside the South might be explained by the fact that they "commit predominantly intraracial crimes . . . with black victims, [which] are considered by [the] predominantly white social-control agents to be less serious offenses, representing less loss or threat to the community than crimes with white victims."[22]

B. Post-*Furman* Studies

A number of studies have examined the possibility of racial discrimination in capital sentencing after *Furman*. In this section we discuss those that were available in 1984, before the initial publication of our own study. In chapter 6 we discuss more recent research on racial discrimination in capital sentencing.[23]

The most extensive of these was conducted by William Bowers and Glenn Pierce, who examined death sentencing patterns in Florida, Georgia, Texas, and Ohio, from the effective date of each state's post-*Furman* death penalty statute through 1977.[24] Bowers and Pierce relied primarily on comparisons between the characteristics of all reported homicides, and of those homicides that resulted in death sentences. In each state, they found that courts were more likely to impose death sentences for homicides with white victims than for those with black victims, and that blacks who killed whites were more likely to receive death sentences than whites who killed whites. In three of the states— Florida, Georgia, and Texas—Bowers and Pierce were able to control for the commission of another felony in the course of the homicide, and they found that this factor did not explain the racial patterns in sentencing. The magnitude of the disparities between whites who killed whites and blacks who killed whites were reduced considerably when the felony circumstance of the homicide was introduced as a control variable, but the disparities by the race of the victim remained large. These findings are consistent with data reported earlier by Marc Riedel, who compared the racial composition of death rows across the nation the year before and three and one-half years after the *Furman* decision.[25] Riedel focused on the continuing overrepresentation of blacks on death row; in light of the high black homicide rate, this disproportion constitutes weak evidence of discrimination, as we have noted. But Riedel also reports more detailed data from a subsample of post-*Furman* cases in six states, and these data show large disparities by the race of the victim: 87 percent of the death sentences were for white-victim homicides and 45 percent were for the killing of whites by blacks,[26] while slightly fewer than 50 percent of all homicide victims in the country in that period were white, and only a small minority of those white victims were killed by blacks.[27]

Four recent studies have examined capital sentencing under Florida's post-*Furman* death penalty statute. Hans Zeisel, using data that overlap with those reported by Bowers and Pierce but that also include more recent cases, concludes that Florida has discriminated against the killers of white victims.[28] Steven Arkin, in a more detailed study of first-degree murder prosecutions in Dade County, Florida, from 1973 through 1976, found that black defendants accused of killing white victims were more likely to receive death sentences than other defendants, although the small size of his sample—ten death penalties in all—precludes a definite conclusion on the existence of racial discrimination.[29] Michael Radelet analyzed a set of data on all murder indictments in twenty Florida counties in 1976 and 1977.[30] He found that death sentences were more likely in white-victim cases than in black-victim cases, but that the race of the defendant had no independent effect on capital sentencing. The vast majority of the death sentences in Radelet's data, thirty-nine out of forty-two, were imposed for "non-primary homicides"—cases in which the defendant and the victim were strangers or only slightly acquainted—but the racial pattern of death sentencing remained substantially the same when he considered such homicides separately. Radelet also found that the racial disparities in sentencing could be traced, primarily, to the level of the homicide indictments chosen by prosecutors. This dovetails with the finding by Radelet and Pierce that the official *descriptions* of homicides by prosecutors were affected by racial considerations.[31] Radelet and Pierce examined data on a sample of approximately 1400 homicides in thirty-two Florida counties between 1973 and 1977, and compared initial police reports describing killings as "felony," "possible felony," and "nonfelony" homicides to descriptions of the same homicides in court records. They found that homicides with white victims, and in particular homicides with white victims and black suspects, were disproportionately likely to be "upgraded" to a more aggravated description, and disproportionately unlikely to be downgraded to a less aggravated description, as the cases moved into the judicial system.

Finally, Jacoby and Paternoster examined records of all reported homicides in South Carolina that could have been prosecuted as capital murders from June 8, 1977 (the effective date of the current death penalty statute), through November 30, 1979;[32] Paternoster later extended that research to include all potentially capital murders in South Carolina through the end of 1981.[33] In each case the researchers found that prosecutors sought the death penalty more often in white-victim cases than in black-victim cases, but that the race of the defendant had no significant additional impact on prosecutorial charging practices.

C. Summary and Criticism

In sum, there is a considerable body of earlier published research on racial patterns in capital punishment, and most of it indicates that racial factors have been influential in determining who has been sentenced to die and who has been executed. These studies, like most empirical research, have limitations. In this case, the conclusions that can be drawn from them are limited by the nature of the studies in two respects: first, by the lack of data on potentially important variables, and second, by the use of samples of cases that were created by discretionary and potentially biasing selection processes in the criminal justice system.

All these studies lack data on some variables that might be associated with capital sentencing. This is particularly true of studies that examine only the defendant's race and the outcome of the case, but it is true even of the *Stanford Law Review* study, which is conspicuous for the relative completeness of its data. The possibility that such omitted variables might explain or change observed patterns in the data is endemic to research of this type—indeed, it may be inevitable—but it does not, in itself, call the conclusions of a study into question. Caution is warranted, however, when there are specific empirical or theoretical reasons to believe that some omitted variable is necessary to understand the true relationship between observed variables. Two such considerations are apparent in this context. First, studies that do not include data on the race of the *victim* may overlook actual sentencing disparities by the race of the *defendant* within each race-of-victim category. Such disparities might be obscured by disproportionate capital sentencing for the killers of white victims, in combination with the fact that most white victims are killed by whites. Second, studies that do not control for the defendant's criminal record may exaggerate capital sentencing disparities that disfavor black defendants. Criminal record is an important determinant of capital sentencing, and black offenders are more likely than white offenders to have serious criminal records;[34] in the absence of a control for the defendant's record, a study may erroneously attribute some of the effect of that variable to the defendant's race.[35]

Many of the studies of capital sentencing examine sets of homicides that were created by discretionary processes of selection within the criminal justice system. For example, studies of commutation practices are necessarily restricted to those rare sets of cases in which death sentences were given. Racial factors may have influenced these prestudy selection processes; if they did, this may create two types of problems. First, such studies obviously cannot detect the discrimination at the earlier, unexamined stages of the criminal justice process. Second, and more troublesome, racial discrimination at these earlier stages of the system could mask or alter the appearance of the racial patterns at the later stages that are studied. This problem is known as sample selection bias.[36]

An example based on the studies that we have mentioned may be useful to illustrate how sample selection bias can operate. The Arkin study starts with the set of first-degree murder indictments that were sought by prosecutors in Dade County in 1973–1976.[37] If prosecutors discriminated against black defendants when they brought these charges, and the studies by Radelet and Pierce suggest that they might have,[38] then this sample will be ill assorted in some particular racial direction. For example, the prosecutors might have brought first-degree murder charges in black-victim cases only when the crime was uncommonly heinous. In the resulting sample of first-degree murder cases, black-victim homicides would be, on the whole, substantially more aggravated than white-victim homicides. If the study found that the same proportions of black-victim and white-victim cases received death sentences, the finding would appear to reflect evenhanded sentencing. But this appearance would be misleading. In reality, the courts would have discriminated against defendants who killed white victims by treating their cases as harshly as the more aggravated black-victim cases. The same problem can also occur within a study that includes a succession of selection stages that are examined separately. For example, Radelet's finding that there was relatively little racial discrimination in capital prosecutions once the prosecutor chose the level of the charge may have been an artifact of sample selection bias caused by the discrimination that he detected at the charging stage itself.[39]

Sample selection bias can have various effects.[40] It can create a false appearance of discrimination, or it can change the apparent magnitude of a real discriminatory practice. The most likely effect in this context, however, is the one illustrated: discrimination of a particular type at an early stage of the criminal justice process may conceal, or partially conceal, discrimination of the same type at a later stage. The danger of sample selection bias is minimized in studies that use data sets that have not been presifted by any discretionary selection process. Studies that examine all reported homicides for a period of time in a given jurisdiction may be essentially immune to this problem.[41] At the other end of the continuum, studies that are restricted to a single decision point late in the criminal justice process—studies of jury sentencing[42] and commutation practices,[43] for example—are especially prone to the biasing effects of sample selection.

Sample selection bias is caused by the fact that the decisionmakers in the criminal justice system may rely in part on information that is not available to the researcher. In the example given earlier, we assumed that sentencing rates are based in part on the "heinousness" of the homicides, and that the biased selection process has created a skewed sample in which "heinousness" is associated with the race of the victim. But if the researcher could observe and measure the "heinousness" of the cases, then he or she could control for the weight that the sentencers gave to this factor. This means that the danger of sample selection bias can be reduced by obtaining detailed data on the nonracial factors that might have been considered, and by controlling for their effects.[44] The problem cannot be eliminated, however, except in the unlikely situation in which the researcher has adequate information to predict the outcomes of individual cases with a high degree of accuracy.

Despite these limitations, it is possible to draw some important conclusions from this body of research. The studies are informative and, on the whole, consistent. The limited inconsistencies in their findings are not necessarily the result of methodological shortcomings, since racial factors may have different effects on capital sentencing at different times and in different places. Kleck concluded that the available research on the pre-*Furman* period demonstrates that there was discrimination against black defendants in the use of the death penalty in the South but does not show such discrimination elsewhere,[45] and we are inclined to agree. More detailed research may eventually reveal whether there was discrimination by race of defendant in capital sentencing outside the South prior to 1972. The evidence from the early post-*Furman* studies is ambiguous on this issue and does not suggest any particular hypothesis. Bowers and Pierce[46] found evidence of discrimination by race of defendant, but Radelet[47] and Jacoby and Paternoster[48] did not; all these post-*Furman* studies focused on southern states, and two of them examined data on Florida but reached opposing conclusions.

There is considerably more agreement on the effect of the victim's race on capital sentencing. Kleck found a general national pattern of disproportionate leniency toward criminals who victimized blacks in the pre-*Furman* era, especially with respect to capital sentencing.[49] The early post-*Furman* studies continue to show this pattern: each has found that black-victim homicides are less likely to receive death sentences than white-victim homicides. With the exception of the data on Ohio that Bowers and Pierce analyze, however, all these studies concern capital sentencing in southern states. Therefore, as we undertook our own research we expected to find disproportionate capital sentencing in white-victim cases in the post-*Furman* period, but this prediction was stronger for the South than for the rest of the country.

Notes

1. W. BOWERS, EXECUTIONS IN AMERICA 165–66 (1974). Before the Civil War several southern states had statutes that explicitly discriminated against blacks by making some types of conduct punishable by death only if the defendant was black, or the victim was white, or both. *See* Bowers & Pierce, *Arbitrariness and Discrimination under Post-*Furman *Capital Statutes,* 26 CRIME & DELINQ. 563, 575 (1980).

2. BUREAU OF JUSTICE STATISTICS, NAT'L PRISONER STATISTICS, U.S. DEP'T OF JUSTICE, CAPITAL PUNISHMENT, 1979, at 18 (1980) [hereinafter cited as NAT'L PRISONER STATISTICS]. These figures have been updated to include ninety executions that have taken place between the end of 1979 and December 20, 1987. *See* NAACP Legal Defense and Educational Fund, Death Row U.S.A. (May 1, 1987) (unpublished document) [hereinafter cited as Death Row U.S.A.].

3. These figures do not include illegal executions by lynch mobs, mostly of blacks. By one estimate, in the past century lynchings have claimed about half as many lives as judicially authorized executions. H. BEDAU, THE DEATH PENALTY IN AMERICA 3 (3d ed. 1982).

4. Most of the death sentences for nonhomicidal crimes were for rape. The racial disparity in capital sentencing is even more extreme for rapes than for homicides: Nearly 90 percent of those executed for rape since 1930 were black. NAT'L PRISONER STATISTICS, *supra* note 2, at 18; *see also* Furman v. Georgia, 408 U.S. at 364 (Marshall, J., concurring).

5. *See, e.g.,* FEDERAL BUREAU OF INVESTIGATION, UNIFORM CRIME REPORT, CRIME IN THE UNITED STATES 21 (1934) [hereinafter cited as UCR]; *id.* at 95, 101 (1960); *id.* at 13 (1980).

6. For a review of the published literature on this issue, see Dike, *Capital Punishment in the United States, Part II: Empirical Evidence,*

13 CRIM. JUST. ABSTRACTS 426, 441–47 (1981). In addition, a number of studies contain compelling evidence of racial discrimination in the use of the death penalty for rape in the pre-*Furman* era. Partington, *The Incidence of the Death Penalty for Rape in Virginia*, 22 WASH. & LEE L. REV. 43 (1965); Wolfgang & Riedel, *Race, Judicial Discretion, and the Death Penalty*, 407 ANNALS 119 (1973); Wolfgang & Riedel, *Rape, Race, and the Death Penalty in Georgia*, 45 AM. J. ORTHOPSYCHIATRY 658 (1975); Fla. Civil Liberties Union, Rape: Selective Electrocution Based on Race (1964) (unpublished manuscript). These studies describe a powerful pattern of discrimination against black men charged with raping white women. A recent study has found a similar pattern of discrimination for noncapital sentencing for rape in "a large midwestern city" from 1970 through 1975. LaFree, *The Effect of Sexual Stratification by Race on Official Reactions to Rape*, 45 AM. SOC. REV. 842 (1980). See also infra pp. 111–12.

7. Garfinkel, *Research Note on Inter- and Intra-Racial Homicides*, 27 SOC. FORCES 369 (1949). A portion of Garfinkel's data is also reported in Johnson, *The Negro and Crime*, 217 ANNALS 93, 98–100 (1941), together with more limited but consistent data from Georgia and Virginia.

8. A retabulation of a portion of Garfinkel's data reveals the following pattern:

RACIAL COMBINATION	Percentage of Death Sentences	
	1st-DEGREE MURDER INDICTMENTS	ALL HOMICIDE INDICTMENTS
Black kills white	43%	29%
White kills white	15%	7%
Black kills black	5%	3%
White kills black	0%	0%

Garfinkel, *supra* note 7, at 371 tables 2, 3; *see* Bowers & Pierce, *supra* note 1, at 578.

9. T. SELLIN, THE PENALTY OF DEATH, at 56–58 (1980).

10. W. BOWERS, LEGAL HOMICIDE: DEATH AS PUNISHMENT IN AMERICA, 1864–1982, at 73–87 (1984).

11. Racial disparities in commutations were found in Ohio Legislative Service Commission, *Capital Punishment, Staff Research Report No. 46* (1961); Johnson, *Selective Forces in Capital Punishment*, 36 SOC. FORCES 165, 166–67; Wolfgang, Kelly, & Nolde, *Comparison of the Executed and the Commuted Among Admissions to Death Row*, 53 J. CRIM. L., CRIMINOLOGY & POLICE SCI. 301 (1962). See generally T. SELLIN, *supra* note 9, at 64–65. Racial disparities were not found in Bedau, *Capital Punishment in Oregon 1903–1964*, 45 OR. L. REV. 1, 11–12 (1965); Bedau, *Death Sentences in New Jersey 1907–1960*, 19 RUTGERS L. REV. 1, 40–46 (1964).

12. A study by Edwin Wolf suffers from the same defect. Wolf found that black defendants convicted of capital murder in New Jersey from 1937 through 1961 were more likely to receive death sentences than white defendants, and that this difference could not be explained by the higher proportion of black defendants convicted of felony murder. Wolf, however, did not control for the race of the victim, although he does make a passing reference to some incomplete data that suggest that this factor might have played an important role in capital sentencing in New Jersey. Wolf, *Abstract of Analysis of Jury Sentencing in Capital Cases: New Jersey: 1937–1961*, 19 RUTGERS L. REV. 56, 64 n.17 (1964). In addition, one study, Johnson, *supra* note 11, contains data on the race of the victim in capital rape cases, but not homicide, and Johnson, *supra* note 7, at 100, table 2, reports some incomplete data on commutations that suggest that the victim's race did indeed influence the likelihood of a commutation in North Carolina from 1933 through 1939.

13. *A Study of the California Penalty Jury in First-Degree Murder Cases*, 21 STAN. L. REV. 1297 (1969) [hereinafter cited as *Stanford Law Review* study]. The data that were collected for the *Stanford Law Review* study were later reanalyzed in Baldus, Pulaski, Woodworth, & Kyle, *Identifying Comparatively Excessive Sentences of Death: A Quantitative Approach*, 33 STAN. L. REV. 1 (1980).

14. *Stanford Law Review* study, *supra* note 13, at 1368–76. The apparent conflict between the *Stanford Law Review* study and the other studies cited concerning racial effects on capital sentencing may reflect an actual difference in the jurisdictions examined. It may also, however, be the result of the methodological problem of "sample-selection bias" in the Stanford study, which might have obscured real racial effects in capital sentencing in California. *See* text accompanying notes 36–44 *infra*.

15. *Stanford Law Review* study, *supra* note 13, at 1376–79.

16. Zimring, Eigen, & O'Malley, *Punishing Homicide in Philadelphia: Perspectives on the Death Penalty*, 43 U. CHI. L. REV. 227 (1976).

17. *Id.* at 232–33.

18. *Id.* at 233 (footnote omitted).

19. Kleck, *Racial Discrimination in Criminal Sentencing: A Critical Evaluation of the Evidence with Additional Evidence on the Death Penalty*, 46 AM. SOC. REV. 783 (1981).

20. *Id.* at 798; *see also* Hagan & Burmiller, *Making Sense of Sentencing: A Review and Critique of Sentencing Research*, in RESEARCH ON SENTENCING: THE SEARCH FOR REFORM 2: 1, 31 (A. Blumstein, J. Cohen, S. Martin, & M. Tonry, eds., 1983) (noting studies that find racial discrimination in southern sentencing). Kleck's exception threatens to swallow his rule. Historically, 60 percent of all executions in America

have occurred in the southern states, NAT'L PRISONER STATISTICS, *supra* note 2, at 9—including 87 of the 93 executions since *Furman,* Death Row U.S.A., *supra* note 2, (December 20, 1987)—and over half of the nearly two thousand prisoners under sentence of death at the end of 1987 were in the South. *Id.* To say that there has been no racial discrimination in capital sentencing, except in the South, is a bit like saying that there is no housing discrimination in a metropolitan area, except in the major residential district. *See* G. MYRDAL, AN AMERICAN DILEMMA: THE NEGRO PROBLEM AND MODERN DEMOCRACY 554 (1944) ("The South makes the widest application of the death penalty, and Negro criminals come in for much more than their share of the executions.") (Footnotes omitted.)

21. Kleck, *supra* note 19, at 799.

22. *Id.* at 800.

23. *Infra* pp. 99–103.

24. *See* Bowers & Pierce, *supra* note 1.

25. Riedel, *Discrimination in the Imposition of the Death Penalty: A Comparison of the Characteristics of Offenders Sentenced Pre-*Furman *and Post-*Furman, 49 TEMP. L.Q. 261 (1976).

26. *Id.* at 285–86 tables 7, 10.

27. *See, e.g.,* UCR, *supra* note 5, at 17 (1974); *id.* at 17 (1975).

28. Zeisel, *Race Bias in the Administration of the Death Penalty: The Florida Experience,* 95 HARV. L. REV. 456, 459–60, 466 (1981).

29. Note, *Discrimination and Arbitrariness in Capital Punishment: An Analysis of Post-*Furman *Murder Cases in Dade County, Florida, 1973–1976,* 33 STAN. L. REV. 75 (1980). The reported data also show an overall disparity in capital sentencing by race of victim, but Arkin does not discuss it. *Id.* at 88–89. Indeed, the disparity by race of victim appears to be greater than Arkin reports: only one of the 138 black-victim cases in his sample resulted in a death penalty, and the defendant who was convicted in that case was also sentenced to death two additional times for killing two white victims, apparently in the same proceeding. *Id.* at 90 n.95. Thus, every death sentence in Arkin's sample was given to a defendant who killed, and who received a death sentence for killing, at least one white victim. Arkin counts each of these three death sentences separately; this classification, and that of other multiple homicides in his data, is puzzling in light of his recognition that in cases of multiple killings by a single defendant "the outcome of one case may have affected the outcome of [the others]." *Id.* at 86 n.84. In the empirical analyses reported here, we classified such multiple homicides as single homicidal incidents with multiple victims. *See* ch. 3, p. 38.

30. Radelet, *Racial Characteristics and the Imposition of the Death Penalty,* 46 AM. SOC. REV. 918 (1981).

31. Radelet & Pierce, *Race and Prosecutorial Discretion in Homicide Cases*, 19 LAW & Soc. REV. 587 (1985).

32. Jacoby & Paternoster, *Sentencing Disparity and Jury Packing: Further Challenges to the Death Penalty*, 73 J. CRIM. L. & CRIMINOLOGY 379 (1982).

33. Paternoster, *Race of Victim and Location of Crime: The Decision to Seek the Death Penalty in South Carolina*, 74 J. CRIM. L. & CRIMINOLOGY 754 (1983); Paternoster, *Prosecutorial Discretion in Requesting the Death Penalty: A Case of Victim-Based Racial Discrimination*, 18 LAW & Soc. REV. 437 (1984).

34. Kleck, *supra* note 19, at 786–88; *see Stanford Law Review* study, *supra* note 13, at 1326–35.

35. Kleck, *supra* note 19, at 788.

36. Klepper, Nagin, & Tierney, *Discrimination in the Criminal Justice System: A Critical Appraisal of the Literature*, RESEARCH ON SENTENCING, *supra* note 20, at 2: 55, 57; RESEARCH ON SENTENCING, *supra* note 20, at 1: 102–8; *see* Thomson & Zimgraff, *Detecting Sentencing Disparity: Some Problems and Evidence*, 86 AM. J. Soc. 869, 873 n.6 (1981).

37. Note, *supra* note 29.

38. Radelet, *supra* note 30; Radelet & Pierce, *supra* note 31.

39. Certain statistical techniques enable a researcher to estimate the effects of sample selection bias and to control for them when the prior selection stage is included in the study (for example, the Radelet illustration), but not when it is omitted (for example, the Arkin illustration). *See* Berk, *An Introduction to Sample Selection Bias in Sociological Data*, 48 AM. Soc. REV. 386 (1983).

40. *See* RESEARCH ON SENTENCING, *supra* note 20, at 1: 103–7.

41. *See, e.g.*, Bowers & Pierce, *supra* note 1; Jacoby & Paternoster, *supra* note 32; Zeisel, *supra* note 28; Zimring, Eigen, & O'Malley, *supra* note 16.

42. *See, e.g.*, *Stanford Law Review* study, *supra* note 13; Wolf, *supra* note 12.

43. *See, e.g.*, Bedau, *Death Sentences in New Jersey 1907–1960*, *supra* note 11, at 7; Bedau, *Capital Punishment in Oregon 1903–1964*, *supra* note 11, at 6; Johnson, *supra* note 7, at 100; Wolfgang, Kelly, & Nolde, *supra* note 11, at 307.

44. *See* RESEARCH ON SENTENCING, *supra* note 20, at 1: 107–8.

45. Kleck, *supra* note 19, at 788.

46. Bowers & Pierce, *supra* note 1.

47. Radelet, *supra* note 30.

48. Jacoby & Paternoster, *supra* note 32; Paternoster, *supra* note 33.

49. Kleck, *supra* note 19, at 799.

PART TWO

3 | Data and Methods

This study examines sentencing under post-*Furman* death penalty laws in eight states: Arkansas, Florida, Georgia, Illinois, Mississippi, North Carolina, Oklahoma, and Virginia. The primary data were the Supplementary Homicide Reports (SHRs) that local police agencies file with the Uniform Crime Reporting section of the FBI.[1] These reports include case-by-case data on each reported homicide. In 1976, the FBI expanded the SHR format to include information on the suspected killer as well as information on the victim and the circumstances of the killing. An SHR now includes data on (1) the sex, age, and race of the victim or victims; (2) the sex, age, and race of the suspected killer or killers; (3) the date and place of the homicide; (4) the weapon used; (5) the commission of any separate felony accompanying the homicide; and (6) the relationship between the victim(s) and the suspected killer(s). Our study is based on this expanded SHR format; it covers all homicides that were reported to the FBI from these states for the period from January 1, 1976, through December 31, 1980, or for the portion of that period during which the state in question had a capital sentencing statute in force.[2] Our major aim in selecting states was to include those with large numbers of death sentences in the relevant period, but our choice was also guided by the availability of data.[3] The eight states that we studied returned 379 death sentences in this five-year period, more than one-third of the national total of 1011.

The SHR data on reported homicides were analyzed in conjunction with death penalty data gathered by the NAACP Legal Defense and Educational Fund (LDF) as part of its regular census of death-sentenced inmates in the United States, *Death Row U.S.A.*[4] For this study, LDF added several items to its normal survey to correspond to items on which the FBI gathers data. LDF was able to collect sufficiently complete data on the following variables: (1) the race of the defendant, (2) the race of the victim, (3) the sex of the victim,[5] (4) the use of a gun, (5) the commission of a separate felony in conjunction with the homicide, (6) the number of victims, (7) the relationship of the defendant to the victim(s), and (8) the location of the homicide.

Death Row U.S.A., which has become the standard reference source for current data on death row inmates,[6] includes individual information on every death-sentenced inmate in the country. The FBI's national homicide data are, likewise, the best available, but the problems of compiling that data set are considerably greater. Most homicides that are known to the police are reported to the FBI, but not all.[7] Moreover, some homicides, although reported to the FBI, are not included in the SHRs because the available data are insufficiently detailed.[8] On the whole, however, the SHRs are an excellent source of data on reported homicides. Some homicides, of course, are never reported to any police agency, although this is far less common for homicides than for other crimes.[9] This type of undercoverage is not relevant to the present study. Unreported homicide cases never enter the criminal justice system, are never subjected to the sequence of decisions that may result in the imposition of the death penalty, and are not part of the universe of cases under consideration.

A different problem is posed by killings that are reported in SHRs but for which significant items of information are missing. Usually the missing information concerns the characteristics of the suspected killer; for example, while the race of the victim was reported in 99.7 percent of the homicides from Georgia, the race of the suspected killer was reported in only 82.9 percent. Such information is generally missing because the suspected killer was never apprehended or otherwise identified. Inevitably, our analysis is restricted to cases for which we have complete data on the critical variables we consider. For the most part, this restriction is simply a reflection of the focus of our research: suspects who were never identified, like homicides that were never reported, are outside the scope of this investigation.

To eliminate SHR cases with unknown suspects, we constructed a data set restricted to cases for which the age of the suspect was reported. Within this data set we have virtually complete information on the race and sex of the suspects. We also eliminated from this data set a small number of cases in which the suspects were known to be juveniles.[10]

We discuss two racial groups, whites and blacks. Until 1980, the FBI data did not distinguish Spanish ancestry as a racial or ethnic category. Unfortunately, this failure to identify Hispanics separately may mask some racial patterns in our data, especially in Florida, where the Hispanic population is relatively large.[11] A very small number of cases involving Asian or American Indian defendants or victims have been removed from any tabulations that include the racial characteristics of the defendants or of the victims, respectively, from all regression analyses, and from tabulations involving our scale of aggravation.[12]

The unit of analysis used throughout our research is the "homicidal act," which we define as the participation of an individual in an action that causes the death of another person or persons. Thus, if two people kill a single victim they have committed two homicidal acts, but if one person kills two victims in a single incident he has committed only one homicidal act, albeit a much more aggravated one. For simplicity, we refer to homicidal acts as "homicides." The number of homicides, thus defined, does not correspond exactly either to the number of victims or to the number of killers, but the three figures are closely linked since the great majority of criminal homicides are single killings by single killers.

A few multiple homicides in our data included both black and white victims. If a homicide with multiple victims included at least one white victim, we classified it as a "white-victim" homicide; correspondingly, if it included no white victims and at least one black victim we classified it as a "black-victim" homicide. The reason for this choice is plain. We have hypothesized that the killing of white victims is punished more harshly than the killing of black victims, but even in the context of this hypothesis we are unwilling to entertain the possibility that a defendant who kills a white victim might be treated with uncommon leniency if he also kills a black person. For similar reasons, we classified multiple homicides that included both male and female victims as "female-victim" homicides.[13]

To conduct this research, we merged the SHR and the death row data sets. In doing so, we tentatively assumed that each homicide that resulted in a death sentence had been reported to the FBI. This assumption cannot be directly verified, since the SHRs do not include the names of the victims or those of the suspected killers, but it seems reasonable to suppose that those cases that were successfully prosecuted to judgments of death are not likely to be among the minority of homicides that were not reported. Therefore, to remove duplications, we attempted to match each death row case with an SHR case that had identical information on every item in our data. Often more than one SHR case would correspond to a given death row case; however, since this matching was done only for the purpose of analyzing data on variables that were reported in both sources, it did not matter whether a particular death row case was identified with a unique SHR case. For a minority of death row cases we could not locate any SHR case that matched on all items. After searching the SHR records, we were generally able to identify the missing case, either as a case in the SHR files that matched the death row case in all respects except for the absence of one or more items of information about the suspect—typically, the suspect's race—or as a case for which one item had been erroneously reported to the FBI. In both situations, we corrected the SHR files to correspond to the more recent information on the death-sentenced inmates. In a few cases no close match could be found. In these instances, we concluded that the death row case had never been reported to the FBI, and we created a new SHR file to correspond to the death row case. The impact of all these corrections on the overall homicide statistics in each state was trivial.

We report a large amount of data, more, perhaps, than some readers may want to see. We have tried to ease the shock by dividing the eight states into two groups: those with high numbers of death sentences and those with fewer death sentences. The death-sentencing patterns of the three states with the largest numbers of death sentences—Georgia, Florida, and Illinois—are described jointly in the body of the book; the data on the remaining five states—Arkansas, Mississippi, North Carolina, Oklahoma, and Virginia—are described briefly in the main text, and are displayed in tabular form in Appendix 2.

Notes

1. The SHR data were obtained from the FBI on magnetic tape.
2. *See* App. 1 *infra* for the actual dates that were covered for each state.
3. At the time we conducted our study, Pennsylvania, for example, did not house death-sentenced prisoners in any special unit or units of the state prison system. As a result, we could not obtain complete information on all prisoners under sentence of death in that state. In addition, we chose to avoid a few states with large Hispanic populations because of the lack of SHR data on Spanish ancestry of victims and killers in pre-1980 homicides. *See* note 11 *infra*.
4. Unless another source is cited, all homicide and sentencing statistics reported in this article are derived from these two sets of data.
5. Our entire sample includes only four women who were sentenced to death (two in Georgia and one each in Florida and Oklahoma), which represents slightly more than 1 percent of the total. By way of comparison, women accounted for about 14 percent of homicide arrests in the United States from 1976 through 1980. FEDERAL BUREAU OF INVESTIGATION, UNIFORM CRIME REPORT, CRIME IN THE UNITED STATES 184 (1976), 183 (1977), 197 (1978), 199 (1979), 203 (1980) [hereinafter cited as UCR]. This disparity is interesting in itself, and it may indicate discrimination against male defendants, *see* T. SELLIN, THE PENALTY OF DEATH, at 66–68 (1980), but it makes the sex of the defendant useless as an analytic variable in a study that focuses on racial discrimination.

On occasion in this book, we refer to death row inmates, or to convicted murderers, using masculine pronouns. This does not reflect obedience to an archaic linguistic convention but rather the fact that with rare exceptions all such people are men.

6. *See, e.g.,* McCleskey v. Kemp, 107 S.Ct. 1756, 1771 n.23 (1987); Enmund v. Florida, 458 U.S. 782, 795 nn.18–19 (1982); *id.* at 818 n.34 (O'Connor, J., dissenting); Godfrey v. Georgia, 446 U.S. 420, 439 nn.7–8 (1980) (Marshall, J., concurring); H. BEDAU, THE DEATH PENALTY IN AMERICA, at 64 tables 2, 3, 5 (3d ed. 1982); Gillers, *Deciding Who Dies,* 129 U. PA. L. REV. 1, 2 n.2 (1980); Greenberg, *Capital Punishment as a System,* 91 YALE L. J. 909 n.7 (1982).
7. Over the five-year period covered by this study, the FBI estimates that the reporting rates were nearly 100 percent for Florida, Illinois, North Carolina, Oklahoma, and Virginia; 95 percent for Arkansas; 92 percent for Georgia; and 74 percent for Mississippi. *See* App. 1 *infra*.
8. For detailed information on the reporting rates for each state, see App. 1 *infra*. The proportion of reported homicides included in the SHRs is quite high in each of these states except Mississippi: over 98

percent in Florida, Illinois, North Carolina, and Virginia; over 90 percent in Arkansas and Oklahoma; 72 percent in Georgia; and 60 percent in Mississippi. These proportions were obtained by dividing the number of victims reported in the SHRs for each state by the estimated total of homicides for that state, as reported by the UCR. The major effect of the underreporting in Mississippi, and to a lesser degree in Georgia, is that the death-sentencing rates in those states will be inflated somewhat for every category of homicide.

9. *See* F. ZIMRING & R. FRASE, THE CRIMINAL JUSTICE SYSTEM 11 (1980). As Zimring and Frase note, it is difficult to check the accuracy of police data on the number of homicides, since homicides are so uncommon by comparison to other crimes that public surveys of victimization rates, the best alternative to police data, are unreliable. Data on homicide rates, however, can be obtained from another source—homicide mortality statistics compiled from death certificates that designate willful homicide as the cause of death. In Appendix 1, we tabulate the numbers of criminal homicides reported by the police together with the homicide mortality figures compiled by state bureaus of vital statistics. Precise comparisons between these two sets of figures are of limited value for two reasons: the classification of homicide used by the police is somewhat narrower than that used by the bureaus of vital statistics, and, in any event, homicides overlooked by one governmental agency are likely to be overlooked by the other. Nonetheless, this comparison suggests that a high proportion of all homicides are reported to the police. For a useful discussion of the relationship between those two sources of data on homicide rates, see T. SELLIN, *supra* note 5, at 132–37.

10. From 1973 through 1980, no one was sentenced to death in the United States for a homicide committed at an age younger than fifteen. Brief for Petitioner at 35–46, Eddings v. Oklahoma, 455 U.S. 104 (1982). It may be constitutional to impose death sentences on fourteen-year-olds, or even on younger adolescents—the issue is now pending before the Supreme Court in Thompson v. Oklahoma, *cert. granted* 479 U.S. ____, 107 S.Ct. 1564 (1987)—but in practice it has not been done. Accordingly, we have restricted our study, for the most part, to homicides for which the reported age of the suspect at the time of the killing was at least fifteen. We have conducted a parallel analysis using all reported homicides, and the racial patterns that we report here are the same in every case. Unless otherwise indicated, however, all tabulations and analyses of homicides reported in this book include only cases in which the age of the suspect at the time of the killing was reported and was fifteen or over.

11. This problem also dictated, to some extent, our choice of states for this study. We avoided Texas, California, and Arizona because of

their large Hispanic populations: 21.0 percent, 19.2 percent, and 16.2 percent, respectively, according to the 1980 Census. Among the states that we did study, Florida had 8.8 percent Hispanics, Illinois had 5.6 percent, and the remaining states in our study all had less than 2 percent.

12. *See* ch. 4, pp. 59–69. These omissions affected two death row cases in Florida that involved Asian victims, and three in North Carolina, two of which involved American Indian victims and defendants, and one that involved an Indian defendant only. The few homicides with Asian and Indian victims or defendants are listed in tabulations that do not include racial variables.

13. *See* Table 4.12 and p. 57.

4 | Racial Patterns in Capital Sentencing: Georgia, Florida, and Illinois

A. Predictive Variables

From 1976 through 1980, the homicide rates in Georgia, Florida, and Illinois were all above the national average of 9.3 nonnegligent criminal homicides per 100,000 people[1]— 14.2 per 100,000 in Georgia, 11.7 in Florida, and 10.3 in Illinois.[2] Georgia and Florida had roughly similar death-sentencing rates in this period[3]—2.8 percent and 2.4 percent of all reported homicides, respectively—but the death-sentencing rate in Illinois was considerably lower, 1.0 percent. These rates are all somewhat higher if we consider only homicides with known suspects over fourteen years of age: 3.7 percent in Georgia, 3.7 percent in Florida, and 1.4 percent in Illinois.

1. Racial Variables

In each state a large proportion of homicide victims in this period were black: a majority in Georgia and Illinois (63.5 percent and 58.6 percent, respectively) and nearly half in Florida (43.3 percent). This is consistent with the national pattern of homicides; blacks and other racial minorities are far more likely than whites to be the victims of homicides. A recent study by the FBI used current homicide victimization statistics to estimate the lifetime risk of death by homicide, controlling for race and sex.[4] The study found that in the national population as a whole the risk of death by homicide was over five times greater for nonwhites than for whites, and that for nonwhite males the estimated lifetime probability of death by homicide was astoundingly high: One nonwhite male baby out of every twenty-eight born in this country, over all regions and over all social classes, is likely to die in a homicide. At the same time, the risk of a death sentence was far lower for those suspects charged with killing black people in Georgia, Florida, and Illinois than for those charged with killing whites. In Georgia, those who killed whites were almost ten times as likely to be sentenced to death as those who killed blacks; in Florida the ratio was about 8 to 1, and in Illinois about 6 to 1. (See Table 4.1.)

In Georgia and Florida, white homicide suspects were, on the whole, about twice as likely to get death sentences as black homicide suspects: 5.5 percent versus 2.9 percent in Georgia, 5.2 percent versus 2.4 percent in Florida. In Illinois, there was a similar but smaller difference: 1.8 percent of white homicide suspects were sentenced to death compared to 1.3 percent of black homicide suspects. In each state, however, the relationship between the suspect's race and the likelihood of a death sentence appears to be due entirely to the fact that black suspects were more likely to kill black victims and white suspects were more likely

Table 4.1. *Percentage of Death Sentences by Race of Victim*

	GEORGIA	FLORIDA	ILLINOIS
White victim	8.7%	6.3%	2.9%
	(67/773)	(114/1803)	(35/1214)
Black victim	0.9%	0.8%	0.5%
	(12/1345)	(14/1683)	(10/1866)
All cases	3.7%	3.7%	1.4%
	(79/2126)	(130/3501)	(45/3115)

.o kill white victims. Indeed, when we control for the race of the victim, blacks who killed whites were several times more likely to be sentenced to death than whites who killed whites in each state.[5] (See Table 4.2.)

Each of three nonracial factors reported to the FBI had a strong aggregate effect on the likelihood of death sentences in Georgia, Florida, and Illinois: the commission of a homicide in the course of another felony, the killing of a stranger, and the killing of multiple victims. These effects were comparable in magnitude to the effect of the race of the victim, but as we will see, the race-of-victim disparities that we have observed cannot be explained by any of these nonracial effects.

2. Felony Circumstance

Although only a minority of all reported homicides in each state involved other felonies—17.5 percent in Georgia, 18.1 percent in Florida, and 27.1 percent in Illinois—the great majority of death sentences fell in this category— over 80 percent in Georgia and Florida, and about 75 percent in Illinois. Among homicides with suspects over fourteen years old, the commission of a separate felony increased the likelihood of a death sentence by a factor of about 12 in Illinois, 26 in Georgia, and nearly 24 in

Table 4.2. *Percentage of Death Sentences by Race of Suspect and Race of Victim*

	GEORGIA	FLORIDA	ILLINOIS
Black kills white	20.1% (32/159)	13.7% (34/249)	7.5% (16/213)
White kills white	5.7% (35/614)	5.2% (80/1547)	1.9% (19/980)
Black kills black	0.8% (11/1310)	0.7% (11/1612)	0.6% (10/1809)
White kills black	2.9% (1/34)	4.3% (3/69)	0% (0/56)

Florida. (See Table 4.3.) Nevertheless, the disparities in capital sentencing by race of victim persist when we control for the felony circumstance of the homicide. For both felony and nonfelony homicides, white-victim cases were far more likely to result in death sentences in each state. (See Table 4.4.)

Controlling for both the race of the suspect and felony circumstance does not dilute the capital sentencing disparities by race of victim, but it does change the race-of-suspect pattern seen in Table 4.2. When we consider felony and nonfelony homicides separately, there are no substantial differences in capital sentencing rates between blacks who kill whites and whites who kill whites in Florida; in Illinois there is a sizable difference between these two racial groups of suspects among nonfelony homicides, but essentially none among felony homicides; and in Georgia there are disparities between whites who kill whites and blacks who kill whites in both felony and nonfelony homicides, but they are smaller than those reported in Table 4.2. (See Table 4.5.)

3. Relationship of Victim to Suspect

Relatively few homicide victims in these three states were killed by strangers—17 percent in Georgia, 17 percent in Florida, and 22 percent in Illinois—but the majority of death sentences in each state were pronounced in those cases: over half in Florida, nearly two-thirds in Georgia, and about 70 percent in Illinois. Those who killed strangers were far more likely to be sentenced to death than those

Table 4.3. *Percentage of Death Sentences by Felony Circumstance*

	GEORGIA	FLORIDA	ILLINOIS
Felony homicides	23.8% (64/269)	22.0% (105/478)	5.7% (34/595)
Nonfelony homicides	0.9% (15/1693)	0.9% (25/2747)	0.5% (11/2389)

Table 4.4. *Percentage of Death Sentences by Felony Circumstance and Race of Victim*

	GEORGIA		FLORIDA		ILLINOIS	
	Felony	Non-felony	Felony	Non-felony	Felony	Non-felony
White victim	35.0% (57/163)	1.9% (10/520)	27.5% (95/346)	1.5% (19/1272)	9.4% (24/256)	1.2% (11/890)
Black victim	6.6% (7/106)	0.4% (5/1165)	7.0% (9/128)	0.3% (5/1468)	3.0% (10/330)	0% (0/1475)

Table 4.5. *Percentage of Death Sentences by Race of Suspect and Victim and Felony Circumstance*

	GEORGIA		FLORIDA		ILLINOIS	
	Felony	Nonfelony	Felony	Nonfelony	Felony	Nonfelony
Black kills white	38.5% (30/78)	4.2% (2/48)	28.8% (32/111)	2.5% (2/79)	8.8% (10/114)	7.2% (6/83)
White kills white	31.8% (27/85)	1.7% (8/472)	26.9% (63/234)	1.4% (17/1187)	10.2% (14/137)	0.6% (5/791)
Black kills black	6.3% (6/96)	0.4% (5/1146)	6.0% (7/116)	0.3% (4/1414)	3.1% (10/321)	0% (0/1429)
White kills black	11.1% (1/9)	0% (0/19)	18.2% (2/11)	1.9% (1/53)	0% (0/9)	0% (0/45)

who killed family members, friends, or acquaintances: ten times as likely in Georgia, four times as likely in Florida, and over six times as likely in Illinois. (See Table 4.6.)

Controlling for the relationship of the suspect to the victim, however, does little to change the pattern of disparities in capital sentencing by the race of the victim. Those who killed whites were much more likely to be sentenced to death, in each state, regardless of their relationship to the victim. (See Table 4.7.) Controlling further for the race of the suspect does not alter this pattern. In addition, among both stranger and nonstranger homicides, blacks who killed whites were more likely to be sentenced to death in each state than whites who killed whites. (See Table 4.8.)

4. Number of Victims

Multiple homicides are quite rare; they accounted for only about 2 percent of all homicides reported to the FBI from Georgia and Florida, and for about 4 percent from Illinois. Killing more than one victim increased the probability of a death sentence greatly in Georgia and Florida—by a factor of about 6—and even more dramatically in Illinois— by a factor of more than 18. Despite the small proportion of multiple homicides in Illinois, 44 percent of those sentenced to death in Illinois from 1976 through 1980 killed more than one victim. (See Table 4.9.) But the higher death-sentencing rate for multiple homicides does not explain the racial disparities that we have observed. Table

Table 4.6. *Percentage of Death Sentences by Relationship of Victim to Suspect*

	GEORGIA	FLORIDA	ILLINOIS
Stranger homicides	16.6% (51/307)	9.7% (71/733)	3.7% (32/855)
Nonstranger homicides	1.6% (28/1806)	2.3% (59/2572)	0.6% (13/2212)

Table 4.7. *Percentage of Death Sentences by Race of Victim and Relationship of Victim to Suspect*

	GEORGIA		FLORIDA		ILLINOIS	
	Strangers	Non-strangers	Strangers	Non-strangers	Strangers	Non-strangers
White victim	26.6% (47/177)	3.4% (20/591)	14.5% (68/469)	3.7% (46/1227)	5.8% (26/448)	1.2% (9/745)
Black victim	3.1% (4/130)	0.7% (8/1207)	1.2% (3/257)	0.8% (11/1337)	1.5% (6/389)	0.3% (4/1450)

Table 4.8. *Percentage of Death Sentences by Race of Victim and Suspect and Their Relationship*

	GEORGIA		FLORIDA		ILLINOIS	
	Strangers	Non-strangers	Strangers	Non-strangers	Strangers	Non-strangers
Black kills white	28.6% (28/98)	6.6% (4/61)	19.3% (29/150)	6.5% (5/77)	8.4% (13/155)	5.6% (3/54)
White kills white	24.1% (19/79)	3.0% (16/530)	12.3% (39/318)	3.6% (41/1146)	4.6% (13/285)	0.9% (6/678)
Black kills black	2.6% (3/115)	0.7% (8/1189)	1.3% (3/227)	0.6% (8/1302)	1.7% (6/360)	0.3% (4/1425)
White kills black	6.7% (1/15)	0% (0/18)	0% (0/29)	8.8% (3/34)	0% (0/29)	0% (0/24)

Table 4.9. *Percentage of Death Sentences by Number of Victims*

	GEORGIA	FLORIDA	ILLINOIS
Multiple	20.0%	18.3%	15.3%
homicides	(9/45)	(23/126)	(20/131)
Single	3.4%	3.2%	0.8%
homicides	(70/2081)	(107/3375)	(25/2984)

4.10 shows that the disparities by race of victim persist in each state after we control for the number of victims; Table 4.11 shows that among homicides with white victims the race of the suspect had an additional effect: black suspects were more likely to be sentenced to death than white suspects.

5. *Minor Variables*

Of the items reported to the FBI, the factors discussed thus far—the race of the victim and the suspect, the felony circumstance, the relationship of the victim to the suspect, and the number of victims—were the most important predictors of capital sentencing in Georgia, Florida, and Illinois. Two other circumstances of the homicides had less pronounced and less consistent aggregate effects on the likelihood of death penalties: killing a female victim and using a gun.

KILLING A FEMALE VICTIM. Most homicides in each state had male victims only: about 75 percent in both Georgia and Florida and about 80 percent in Illinois. Killing a woman more than doubled the probability of a death sentence in each state. (See Table 4.12.)

USE OF A GUN. The great majority of homicides in each state were accomplished with firearms—nearly two-thirds in Florida and Illinois and almost three-quarters in Georgia. Homicides committed with guns were somewhat less likely

Table 4.10. *Percentage of Death Sentences by Race of Victim and Number of Victims*

	GEORGIA		FLORIDA		ILLINOIS	
	Multiple	Single	Multiple	Single	Multiple	Single
White victim	27.6% (8/29)	7.9% (59/744)	20.4% (20/98)	5.5% (94/1705)	22.5% (16/71)	1.7% (19/1143)
Black victim	6.3% (1/16)	0.8% (11/1329)	11.1% (3/27)	0.7% (11/1656)	6.8% (4/59)	0.3% (6/1807)

Table 4.11. *Percentage of Death Sentences by Race of Victim and Defendant and Number of Victims*

	GEORGIA		FLORIDA		ILLINOIS	
	Multiple	Single	Multiple	Single	Multiple	Single
Black kills white	42.9% (3/7)	19.1% (29/152)	26.7% (4/15)	12.8% (30/234)	41.2% (7/17)	4.6% (9/196)
White kills white	22.7% (5/22)	5.1% (30/592)	19.3% (16/83)	4.4% (64/1464)	16.7% (9/54)	1.1% (10/926)
Black kills black	6.3% (1/16)	0.8% (10/1294)	12.0% (3/25)	0.5% (8/1587)	6.8% (4/59)	0.3% (6/1750)
White kills black	—	2.9% (1/34)	0% (0/2)	4.5% (3/67)	—	0% (0/56)

Table 4.12. *Percentage of Death Sentences by Sex of Victim*

	GEORGIA	FLORIDA	ILLINOIS
Female victim	7.0%	7.2%	2.7%
	(36/512)	(66/922)	(17/623)
Male victim	2.7%	2.5%	1.1%
	(43/1613)	(64/2578)	(28/2492)

to get death sentences in Georgia and Florida; in Illinois the method of killing had no effect on the likelihood of a death sentence. (See Table 4.13.)

As with the stronger nonracial predictive variables, neither the sex of the victim nor the means of death accounts for the racial disparities in capital sentencing. Tables 4.14 and 4.15 show that white-victim homicides were substantially more likely to result in death sentences in each state, controlling for the sex of the victim and the use of a gun, respectively. Controlling for the race of the suspect as well as the race of the victim does not change these patterns; it merely reproduces the relationships that we have already observed for other variables: among white-victim homicides, those with black suspects resulted in death sentences more often than those with white suspects. (See Tables 4.16 and 4.17.)

THE LOCATION OF THE HOMICIDE. One final factor that was reported to the FBI had a sizable impact on the likelihood of death sentences: the location of the homicide. The majority of homicides in each state were in urban counties:

Table 4.13. *Percentage of Death Sentences by Means of Death*

	GEORGIA	FLORIDA	ILLINOIS
Guns	3.0%	3.0%	1.5%
	(45/1525)	(68/2245)	(30/1989)
Other means	5.9%	5.1%	1.4%
	(34/577)	(62/1224)	(15/1094)

Table 4.14. *Percentage of Death Sentences by Sex and Race of Victim*

	GEORGIA		FLORIDA		ILLINOIS	
	Female	Male	Female	Male	Female	Male
White	15.3%	6.4%	10.8%	4.4%	5.5%	2.1%
victim	(30/196)	(37/577)	(58/537)	(56/1266)	(15/275)	(20/939)
Black	1.9%	0.6%	1.6%	0.6%	0.6%	0.5%
victim	(6/314)	(6/1030)	(6/379)	(8/1304)	(2/343)	(8/1523)

69 percent in Georgia, 85 percent in Florida, and 96 percent in Illinois.[6] Rural homicides were somewhat more likely to result in death sentences in Georgia and Florida, but not in Illinois. (See Table 4.18.) The location of the crime, however, had no more effect on the racial disparities in capital sentencing than any of the other variables we examined. In each state, those who killed whites were more likely to be sentenced to death than those who killed blacks in urban and rural areas alike, and among those who killed whites, black suspects were more likely to get death sentences than white suspects. (See Tables 4.19 and 4.20.)

6. Summary

In each of these three states, death penalties were more likely to be imposed on suspects who killed white victims than on those who killed blacks. Moreover, in each state, blacks who killed whites were more likely to receive death sentences than whites who killed whites.

Table 4.15. *Percentage of Death Sentences by Race of Victim and Means of Death*

	GEORGIA		FLORIDA		ILLINOIS	
	Guns	Other	Guns	Other	Guns	Other
White	7.5%	12.5%	5.3%	8.2%	3.0%	2.7%
victim	(42/562)	(25/200)	(59/1117)	(55/669)	(23/756)	(12/440)
Black	0.3%	2.4%	0.7%	1.1%	0.6%	0.5%
victim	(3/960)	(9/372)	(8/1119)	(6/549)	(7/1206)	(3/647)

Table 4.16. *Percentage of Death Sentences by Sex and Race of Victim and Race of Suspect*

	GEORGIA		FLORIDA		ILLINOIS	
	Female	Male	Female	Male	Female	Male
Black kills	27.5%	17.6%	25.8%	9.3%	10.2%	6.7%
white	(11/40)	(21/119)	(17/66)	(17/183)	(5/49)	(11/164)
White kills	12.2%	3.5%	8.7%	3.6%	4.5%	1.2%
white	(19/156)	(16/458)	(41/470)	(39/1077)	(10/222)	(9/758)
Black kills	1.9%	0.5%	1.1%	0.6%	0.6%	0.5%
black	(6/311)	(5/998)	(4/368)	(7/1244)	(2/3431)	(8/1475)
White kills	0%	3.2%	22.2%	1.7%	0%	0%
black	(0/3)	(1/31)	(2/9)	(1/60)	(0/9)	(0/47)

Three nonracial variables also had strong influences on the likelihood of a death sentence in each of these states: the commission of a separate felony in conjunction with a homicide, the killing of a stranger, and the killing of more than one victim. Controlling for these variables one at a time, however, did not explain the race-of-victim disparities in any of these states, but it did reduce the disparities between white suspects and black suspects in white-victim homicides. Three additional variables—the sex of the victim, the use of a gun, and the location of the homicide—had weak effects on capital sentencing. The racial patterns in

Table 4.17. *Percentage of Death Sentences by Race of Victim and Suspect, and Means of Death*

	GEORGIA		FLORIDA		ILLINOIS	
	Guns	Other	Guns	Other	Guns	Other
Black kills	18.7%	25.0%	14.9%	12.4%	9.7%	3.8%
white	(23/123)	(9/36)	(22/148)	(12/97)	(13/134)	(3/78)
White kills	4.3%	9.8%	3.8%	7.6%	1.6%	2.6%
white	(19/439)	(16/164)	(37/965)	(43/569)	(10/613)	(9/350)
Black kills	0.3%	2.2%	0.7%	0.8%	0.6%	0.5%
black	(3/937)	(8/360)	(7/1071)	(4/528)	(7/1168)	(3/630)
White kills	0%	9.1%	2.1%	10.0%	0%	0%
black	(0/23)	(1/11)	(1/47)	(2/20)	(0/37)	(0/17)

Table 4.18. *Percentage of Death Sentences by Location of Homicide*

	GEORGIA	FLORIDA	ILLINOIS
Rural	5.0%	5.1%	1.6%
	(37/735)	(31/611)	(2/129)
Urban	3.0%	3.4%	1.4%
	(42/1391)	(99/2890)	(43/2986)

capital sentencing hardly changed when we controlled for these minor variables.

B. Racial Discrimination

We have seen that racial factors, in particular the race of the victim, have large aggregate effects on capital sentencing in Georgia, Florida, and Illinois. We have also seen that none of the other variables that we examined can account for the observed racial disparities in nonracial terms. It remains possible, however, that these racial patterns in capital sentencing are a by-product of the combined effects of the other variables. In this section we examine that possibility, and estimate the magnitude of these racial effects.

1. Classes of Nonracial Variables

As we have seen, racial discrimination in capital sentencing is unconstitutional on two grounds. It is a violation both of the general Fourteenth Amendment requirement of equal protection of the law, and of a set of special restrictions

Table 4.19. *Percentage of Death Sentences by Race of Victim and Location of Homicide*

	GEORGIA		FLORIDA		ILLINOIS	
	Rural	Urban	Rural	Urban	Rural	Urban
White victim	10.3%	7.7%	8.5%	5.8%	1.8%	3.0%
	(30/292)	(37/481)	(29/343)	(85/1460)	(2/113)	(33/1101)
Black victim	1.6%	0.6%	0.7%	0.8%	0%	0.5%
	(7/437)	(5/908)	(2/268)	(12/1415)	(0/16)	(10/1850)

Table 4.20. *Percentage of Death Sentences by Race of Victim and Suspect and Location of Homicide*

	GEORGIA		FLORIDA		ILLINOIS	
	Rural	Urban	Rural	Urban	Rural	Urban
Black kills	31.8%	15.7%	19.1%	12.4%	11.1%	7.4%
white	(14/44)	(18/115)	(9/47)	(25/202)	(1/9)	(15/204)
White kills	6.5%	5.2%	6.8%	4.8%	1.0%	2.0%
white	(16/248)	(19/366)	(20/295)	(60/1252)	(1/101)	(18/879)
Black kills	1.4%	0.6%	0.4%	0.7%	0%	0.6%
black	(6/426)	(5/884)	(1/259)	(10/1353)	(0/13)	(10/1796)
White kills	9.1%	0%	11.1%	3.3%	0%	0%
black	(1/11)	(0/23)	(1/9)	(2/60)	(0/3)	(0/53)

on the use of the death penalty that has been imposed under the Eighth Amendment prohibition of cruel and unusual punishments.[7] But disproportionate capital sentencing in a particular racial category of homicide is not equivalent to discrimination; it may be a result of the operation of one or more legitimate sentencing considerations. To test this possibility, it is necessary to decide which of the nonracial variables that influence capital sentencing are legitimate sentencing considerations and which are not.

The fact that a homicide was committed in the course of another felony is clearly a legitimate aggravating consideration for the purpose of deciding whether to impose the death penalty; so is the fact that multiple victims were killed. Each of these facts bears directly and obviously on the severity of the criminal conduct at issue, and racial disparities that can be explained by the operation of these two factors cannot be considered discriminatory. For slightly less obvious reasons, we believe that the existence of a previous relationship between the killer and the victim is also a legitimate sentencing consideration. Only a minority of homicides are committed by strangers, but they evoke more fear than the common types of homicides. The killing of a friend or relative is generally the product of a troubled relationship, often a long one, and the motive is frequently rage or some other transitory passion. Such a killing is relatively unlikely to indicate a general predisposition to kill, and it may well eliminate the only possible object of the killer's homicidal impulses. The killing of a stranger, by contrast, may indicate a more enduring and less differentiated propensity for violence, and the motive is more likely to be the realization of some deliberate objective.[8]

Two of the other variables that we examined have more tenuous standing as legitimate aggravating factors. The sex of the victim, in itself, is legally irrelevant, and perhaps even prohibited as a sentencing consideration.[9] But since the vast majority of homicides are committed by men, and since women are generally smaller and physically weaker than men, female victims are more likely to be defenseless and less likely to be physically threatening to the perpetrators of homicides. Therefore, we cannot reject the possibility that homicides with female victims might properly be regarded as more aggravated than those with male victims.[10]

The use of a gun might be considered either an aggravating or a mitigating circumstance. On the one hand, many premeditated killings and felony homicides are committed with guns, and the fact that a homicide defendant was armed with a gun may indicate a predisposition to use deadly force and a disregard for the lives of others. On the other hand, the wide availability of guns and the great ease with which they kill make shooting the most common means of death in those relatively unaggravated homicides that are the products of passing rages or senseless fights. In contrast, the other common methods of killing—stabbing, choking, and beating to death[11]—often require protracted and deliberate action, and are more likely to result in slow and painful deaths. We therefore cannot exclude the possibility that the use of a gun might properly be defined as a legitimate sentencing variable, either aggravating or mitigating.

The final variable that we examined—geography—is different in kind from the others. For the purposes of sentencing, the location of a killing is not a feature of the homicides but a background fact that determines who will judge its disposition. It is difficult to see how geography could be a legitimate capital sentencing consideration—there is no reason why a given homicide should be considered more heinous if it is committed in the countryside rather than in the city—but it is less clear whether geographical considerations are prohibited. In general, geographical discrimination does not violate the equal protection clause of the Fourteenth Amendment,[12] but in the context of capital sentencing it may violate the Eighth Amendment prohibition of cruel and unusual punishments.[13] In any event, we believe that racial disparities cannot be justified as a legitimate by-product of geographical disparities, but we recognize that the effects of geography might be important. In particular, we were interested in determining whether the observed racial disparities in capital sentencing were the products of differential treatment in both urban and rural areas, or only in one type of location, or whether they were incidental products of separate but evenhanded urban and rural systems of justice.

With this classification of the nonracial variables in mind, we used two techniques to estimate racial effects on capital sentencing, controlling for the combined effects of the other variables in our data. First, we classified the homicides by the number of major legitimate aggravating factors reported for each case and examined the racial patterns in capital sentencing separately at each level of aggravation. Second, we conducted a series of multiple regression analyses, estimating the racial effects on capital sentencing while controlling for the effects of various sets of legitimate and potentially legitimate variables.

2. *A Scale of Aggravation*

The three most clearly legitimate sentencing variables in our data—felony circumstances, relation of victim to suspect, and number of victims—are also the three strongest non-racial predictors of capital sentencing. This is a reassuring comment on the capital sentencing systems in Georgia, Florida, and Illinois, and it is consistent with many previous studies that found strong relationships between these variables and capital sentencing.[14] The effects of these variables vary in magnitude from state to state, but each is more strongly associated with capital sentencing in each of the three states than any other nonracial variable is in any of them. It is possible, therefore, to construct a simple measure of the level of aggravation by summing the number of these major aggravating factors reported for each homicide.[15] The result is a scale of aggravation with scores ranging from 0 to 3. This score is a good predictor of the probability of a sentence of death. In each state, the largest category of homicides is the least aggravated, and death sentences in this group are very rare. In each state, the proportion of death sentences rises sharply as the homicides move up this scale of aggravation. (See Table 4.21.)

In Table 4.22, the homicides in each state are tabulated by level of aggravation and by the racial combination of suspect and victim. The table reveals that this aggregate

Table 4.21. *Percentage of Death Sentences by Level of Aggravation*

NUMBER OF MAJOR AGGRAVATING CIRCUMSTANCES

	0	1	2	3
Georgia	0.4%	7.7%	31.6%	57.1%
	(6/1635)	(26/339)	(43/136)	(4/7)
Florida	0.6%	4.7%	21.9%	44.0%
	(14/2295)	(41/874)	(62/283)	(11/25)
Illinois	0.1%	1.0%	7.4%	22.6%
	(2/1924)	(7/711)	(29/392)	(7/31)

Table 4.22. *Percentage of Death Sentences by Level of Aggravation and Race of Suspect and Victim*

NUMBER OF MAJOR AGGRAVATING
CIRCUMSTANCES

	0	1	2	3	
		Georgia			
Black kills	0%	8.9%	42.4%	66.7%	
white	(0/41)	(5/56)	(25/59)	(2/3)	
White kills	0.9%	10.6%	51.6%	100%	
white	(4/458)	(13/123)	(16/31)	(2/2)	
Black kills	0.2%	5.5%	2.4%	0%	
black	(2/1122)	(8/145)	(1/41)	(0/2)	
White kills	0%	0%	20.0%	—	
black	(0/14)	(0/15)	(1/5)		
p	.117	.078	.00006	.2	Overall p = .002
		Florida			
Black kills	1.8%	3.1%	31.8%	25.0%	
white	(1/55)	(3/98)	(28/88)	(2/8)	
White kills	0.9%	8.0%	22.3%	60.0%	
white	(9/989)	(33/413)	(29/130)	(9/15)	
Black kills	0.2%	0.9%	8.3%	0%	
black	(3/1225)	(3/325)	(5/60)	(0/2)	
White kills	3.8%	5.3%	0%	—	
black	(1/26)	(2/38)	(0/5)		
p	.081	.017	.00019	.778	Overall p = .002
		Illinois			
Black kills	2.9%	2.6%	11.8%	22.2%	
white	(1/34)	(2/77)	(11/93)	(2/9)	
White kills	0.2%	1.6%	9.3%	44.4%	
white	(1/612)	(4/252)	(10/107)	(4/9)	
Black kills	0%	0.3%	4.3%	7.7%	
black	(0/1256)	(1/355)	(8/185)	(1/13)	
White kills	0%	0%	0%	—	
black	(0/22)	(0/27)	(0/7)		
p	.012	.029	.0096	.239	Overall p < .001

measure of aggravation does not account for the effect of the victim's race on capital sentencing in any of these states: at each level of aggravation, white-victim cases are substantially more likely to receive death sentences than black-victim cases.[16] Controlling for level of aggravation, however, essentially eliminates any independent race-of-suspect effect. Table 4.22 reveals only small and inconsistent differences in death-sentencing rates between blacks who killed whites and whites who killed whites, at each level of aggravation.[17] It also reveals that there are, in each state, too few cases with aggravation scores of 3 to make a separate analysis of that column informative. Table 4.23 presents a clearer summary of the relationship between the victim's

Table 4.23. *Percentage of Death Sentences by Level of Aggravation and Race of Victim*

	NUMBER OF MAJOR AGGRAVATING CIRCUMSTANCES			
	0	1	2–3	
		Georgia		
White victim	0.8% (4/499)	10.1% (18/179)	47.4% (45/95)	
Black victim	0.2% (2/1136)	5.0% (8/160)	4.2% (2/48)	
p	.074	.060	<.000001	Overall *p* < .001
		Florida		
White victim	1.0% (10/1044)	7.0% (36/511)	28.2% (68/241)	
Black victim	0.3% (4/1251)	1.4% (5/363)	7.5% (5/67)	
p	.046	.000032	.00013	Overall *p* < .001
		Illinois		
White victim	0.3% (2/646)	1.8% (6/329)	12.4% (27/218)	
Black victim	0% (0/1278)	0.3% (1/382)	4.4% (9/205)	
p	.113	.041	.0024	Overall *p* < .001

race and death sentencing, controlling for aggravation score: cases with scores of 2 and 3 are combined and all cases with victims of the same race are considered together.

The pattern of racial disparities displayed in Table 4.23 is consistent and strong.[18] The magnitudes of these disparities can be evaluated, in part, by considering the right-hand column, which includes the most aggravated homicides. The majority of the death penalties in each state were among those cases, almost 60 percent in Georgia and Florida, and almost 80 percent in Illinois. Although death sentences were not the rule for these homicides, they were given in a fair proportion of those cases in which the victims were white: about 1 in 8 in Illinois, over a quarter in Florida, and almost half in Georgia. But even within this highly aggravated set of cases, death sentences for black-victim homicides were quite rare: in Illinois, they occurred about one-third as often as among white-victim homicides; in Georgia and Florida they occurred even less often than that.

Another way to assess the magnitude of the effect of the victim's race on capital sentencing is to consider what the distribution of death sentences would have been if the death-sentencing rates had been equal for black-victim and white-victim homicides. If, at each level of aggravation depicted in Table 4.23, suspects in black-victim homicides had been sentenced to death at the rate at which suspects in white-victim homicides were actually sentenced to death, the number of killers of black victims on death row would have quadrupled in Georgia and in Florida—from 12 to 48 and from 14 to 56, respectively—and nearly quadrupled in Illinois—from 10 to 36. Correspondingly, if suspects in white-victim homicides had been sentenced to death at the rate at which suspects in black-victim homicides were actually sentenced to death, the number of killers of white victims on death row would have been 14 rather than 67 in Georgia, 28 rather than 114 in Florida, and 11 rather than 35 in Illinois. In each case, between two-thirds and four-fifths of the death sentences pronounced for the killing of white people—over half of the *total* number of death sentences in each state—would have been eliminated.

SUMMARY. We constructed a scale of aggravation using the three major legitimate predictor variables that we studied: felony circumstance, relationship of suspect to victim, and number of victims. This scale is a good predictor of the likelihood of death sentences in each of these three states, but the race-of-victim disparities that we found remain consistent and large in each state after controlling for the level of aggravation of the homicides as measured by the scale. On the other hand, this control does eliminate the additional capital sentencing disparities that were previously observed between black suspects and white suspects in white-victim cases.

3. Regression Analysis

The second multivariate technique that we used to analyze our data is multiple regression analysis. Multiple regression is a statistical technique for sorting out the simultaneous effects of several causal or "independent" variables on an outcome or "dependent" variable.[19] Multiple regression analysis produces a mathematical model of the data that includes estimates of the effects of each independent variable on the dependent variable, controlling for the effects of the other independent variables. This technique can be used to test for racial discrimination in a set of sentencing decisions by designating the sentencing choice as the outcome variable in a model that includes the racial characteristic of interest as a causal variable along with the legitimate variables that might explain these decisions.[20] If the racial variable has a statistically significant effect on the outcome variable in this model (that is, an effect that would be unlikely to occur by mere chance), that demonstrates that the racial characteristic is associated with these outcomes in a way that cannot be explained by the legitimate variables that are included in the model.

In this study, we are interested in estimating the effects of several racial and legitimate variables on the probability of a dichotomous sentencing outcome: whether or not a death sentence was pronounced. We used a regression technique that is specially designed for this purpose, multiple logistic (or "logit") regression.[21] This technique produces a regression model that can be described by three sets of statistics:

1. THE OVERALL "FIT" OF THE MODEL. "Fit" refers to the degree of congruence between the outcomes predicted by the model and the actual outcomes observed in the data. The closer a model comes to predicting the actual outcomes accurately, the better the fit, and the better the model is as a mathematical description of the process that produced these outcomes. Statistical models never predict all outcomes in a data set with precision; the critical question in evaluating the fit of a model is whether the discrepancies between the predicted outcomes and the actual outcomes appear to be due to chance or to some systematic difference between the model and the data. A logit model is said to have good fit if the differences between the observed and predicted outcomes appear to be due to chance.[22]

Fit is also useful as a tool for examining the effect of a single causal variable. If the fit of a given model is significantly reduced when a particular variable is removed from the regression equation, or significantly increased when the variable is added, that indicates that the variable in question has an effect on the outcome that cannot be accounted for by the effects of the other variables in the model.

2. THE SIZE OF THE COEFFICIENTS OF THE INDEPENDENT VARIABLES (B's). In multiple regression, the coefficients of the

independent variables are estimates of the size of the effects of these variables on the outcome variable. In logistic regression these coefficients, in raw form, have a somewhat obscure technical meaning: they measure the effects of the independent variables on the natural log of the odds of the outcome. Fortunately, these coefficients can be reexpressed in a more accessible form—as multipliers of the odds of the outcome.[23] Thus, for example, a logit coefficient of 1.5 means that the effect in question increases the odds of the outcome by a factor of 4.48, and a logit coefficient of .75 means that the odds are increased by a factor of 2.12.

3. THE STANDARD ERRORS (S.E.'S) OF THE COEFFICIENTS OF THE INDEPENDENT VARIABLES. These statistics are measures of the precision of the estimates of the coefficients of the independent variables: the smaller the size of the standard error relative to the size of the coefficient, the more precise the estimate. The ratio of a coefficient to its standard error can be used as a measure of the statistical significance of the effect of the variable in question. For example, if the ratio is equal to or greater than 2, then the effect described by the coefficient meets or exceeds the conventional .05 level of statistical significance.[24]

To test for discrimination by race of victim, we first developed a model for each state that provided the best possible fit to the data without considering the effect of the race of the victim.[25] We then compared this model to an otherwise identical model that included the race of the victim. Table 4.24 reports the coefficients for the race-of-victim variable that we obtained by this procedure.

In each state, the race of the victim had a sizable and statistically significant effect on the odds of a defendant receiving a death sentence. In Florida the overall odds of an offender receiving the death penalty for killing a white victim were 4.8 times greater than for killing a black victim.[26]

Table 4.24. *Best Logistic Regression Models, Summary Statistics*

	GEORGIA	FLORIDA	ILLINOIS
Victim's race: logit coefficient	1.97*	1.56*	1.38*
Victim's race: multiplier of odds of death sentence	7.2	4.8	4.0

*Effect significant at or beyond the .001 level.

In Illinois the overall odds of an offender receiving the death penalty for killing a white were 4.0 times greater than for killing a black.[27] In Georgia the situation is a bit more complex. When the victim's race is added to the best-fitting model that includes no racial variables, it significantly improves the fit of the model, and its coefficient indicates that the odds of receiving the death penalty for killing a white are approximately 7.2 times greater than the odds of receiving the death penalty for killing a black.[28] To construct a model for Georgia with adequate fit, however, it is necessary to include variables representing interactions between the race of the victim and some of the legitimate sentencing variables.[29] Adding these interactions hardly changes the magnitude or the significance of the coefficient of the race of the victim variable,[30] but the presence of these interaction variables makes it difficult to translate the magnitude of the race-of-the-victim effect into non-technical terms.[31]

The magnitude of the racial effects estimated in these models can also be described by comparing the predicted probabilities of receiving the death penalty generated by these models for hypothetical homicide cases that differ only in the race of the victim. In Table 4.25 these predicted probabilities are compared for hypothetical "high-aggravation" and "low-aggravation" homicides.

Table 4.25 shows that in Georgia, for example, the predicted probability of an offender receiving the death penalty

Table 4.25. *Best Logistic Regression Models: Predicted Probability of a Death Sentence in Hypothetical High- and Low-Aggravation Cases, by Race of Victim*

	GEORGIA	FLORIDA	ILLINOIS
High-Aggravation Case[a]			
White victim	.653	.362	.352
Black victim	.025	.107	.120
Low-Aggravation Case[b]			
White victim	.0048	.010	.0020
Black victim	.0006	.002	.0006

[a]Multiple homicide of at least one female during the course of a felony in which a gun was used; all victims were strangers to the offender.

[b]Single-victim homicide of a male relative, friend, or acquaintance not committed with a gun; no other felonies involved.

for a hypothetical highly aggravated homicide involving a white victim (a multiple homicide in which at least one victim was a woman, in which all of the victims were strangers to the defendant, and which was accompanied by another felonious act) was .653, while the predicted probability of an offender receiving the death penalty for a homicide identical in all respects except that only blacks were killed was only .025. As the table demonstrates, these regression analyses indicate substantial racial disparities in each of these three states at both ends of the continuum of aggravation.

We also examined the effect of the race of the suspect in our regression analyses for two purposes: (1) to determine whether the effect of the victim's race on capital sentencing could be explained by the suspect's race, and (2) to determine whether the race of the suspect had any independent effect on capital sentencing beyond the effects of the victim's race and the legitimate and potentially legitimate sentencing variables already considered. Our major procedure was to add the suspect's race as a variable to the "best-fitting" logistic regression model for each state, and then to compare the resulting model to an otherwise identical model that also included the victim's race. In each state the coefficient for the effect of victim's race that was obtained by this procedure was statistically significant and comparable in magnitude to that reported in Table 4.24,[32] indicating that the observed disparities in capital sentencing by the victim's race are not attributable to the race of the suspect. We did not, however, find a separate race-of-suspect effect in any of these states. In Florida and Illinois the effect of the race of the suspect on capital sentencing was not statistically significant. In Georgia, we were unable to construct an adequate regression model that included the race of the suspect as a variable. This means that while our data are sufficient for the task of determining the effect of the race of the *victim* on capital sentencing in Georgia, the effect of the race of the *suspect* cannot be determined, one way or the other, without additional data that were unavailable to us.[33]

A second technique that we used to disentangle the effects of the suspect's race from the effects of the victim's race was to examine two subsets of our data separately: cases with white victims and cases with black suspects. When homicides with white victims are examined by themselves, the only racial effect that is possible is the effect of the suspect's race. Similarly, when only cases with black suspects are examined, the only possible racial effect is that attributable to the race of the victim.[34] (Since very few cases involved white suspects and black victims, we did not examine the complementary divisions—black victims only, and white suspects only.) Among the black-suspect cases, we found that the race of the victim had effects on capital sentencing in each state that were larger than those reported above for models including all homicides.[35] Among the white-victim cases, however, we did not find statistically significant effects for the race of the suspect in Georgia or in Florida,[36] but the race of the suspect together with its interactions with other variables did have a significant effect on capital sentencing in Illinois.[37] In sum, the race of the suspect does not explain the disparities by race of victim in any state, and there is some evidence of independent discrimination by race of suspect in Illinois but not in the other two states.

We also used logistic regression to examine the effect of the urban or rural location of the homicide on capital sentencing. For each of these states, we modified the "best-fitting" model including victim's race to include a variable indicating the location of the homicide. In Georgia and Florida the odds of receiving the death penalty were substantially higher in rural counties;[38] in Illinois, no difference was observed.[39] The addition of geographic location to the other variables did not substantially alter either the size or the statistical significance of the effect of the victim's race in any of the states.[40]

We performed numerous other regression analyses using different combinations of variables and different subsets of the data, and the results of these analyses, in every case, confirm the conclusions we reached on the basis of the results reported earlier.[41]

SUMMARY. Multiple logistic regression (or "logit") analysis reveals large and statistically significant race-of-victim effects on capital sentencing in Georgia, Florida, and Illinois. After controlling for the effects of all of the other variables in our data set, we found that the killing of a white victim increased the odds of a death sentence by an estimated factor of 4 in Illinois, about 5 in Florida, and about 7 in Georgia. This method of analysis reveals some evidence that the race of the suspect had an independent effect on capital sentencing in Illinois, but no evidence of independent race-of-suspect effects in Georgia or Florida.

4. Appellate Review: Georgia and Florida

So far, the racial disparities that we have found describe the operation of the criminal justice system up to the point of judgment in the trial court. Needless to say, that is not the entire process; a judgment of death does not translate into a quick and certain execution. Thirty years ago and more, when executions were relatively common, many capital defendants were killed without a single appellate proceeding to review their sentences,[42] but that is no longer so. Since *Furman* all death sentences are reviewed by the highest court in the sentencing state, with the rare exception of cases in which the defendants will not allow it; with the same rare exceptions, all cases that are affirmed on appeal are litigated beyond that first review in state and federal habeas corpus proceedings.[43] In addition, all states that provide for capital punishment vest the power of clemency in an executive officer or agency, usually the governor.[44] Relatively few cases—as of this writing, about ninety[45]— have completed this entire review process and ended in executions. Many more will have to run that course before we will be able to judge whether our new death-sentencing schemes discriminate in putting people to death, or whether the review and clemency proceedings counteract the racial disparities that pervade the sentencing process. In some states, however, enough cases have passed through the first step in the review process to enable us to judge the effects of that stage. This is important because that first step is a proceeding with special constitutional status under the Supreme Court's 1976 death penalty decisions, the direct review of capital sentences by an appellate court with statewide jurisdiction.

The Supreme Court approved Georgia's capital sentencing statutes in *Gregg v. Georgia*[46] because it found that they contained adequate safeguards against the arbitrariness that the Court had condemned in *Furman*. One important safeguard in the Georgia scheme was the requirement of "proportionality review," a statutory mandate that the Georgia Supreme Court review the punishment in every capital case and determine "[w]hether the sentence of death was imposed under the influence of passion, prejudice, or any other arbitrary factor," and "[w]hether the sentence of death is excessive or disproportionate to the penalty imposed in similar cases. . . ."[47] In contrast, the Florida statute that was reviewed in *Proffitt v. Florida*[48] provided for automatic review of all death sentences by the state supreme court but did not specify the mode of that review. The U.S. Supreme Court found, however, that the Florida Supreme Court had interpreted its task as including a form of proportionality review substantially similar to that required by statute in Georgia.[49] The Court seemed to place great store in these review procedures; both the plurality and the concurring opinions in *Gregg* and *Proffitt* referred to them repeatedly as important aspects of the statutory cures for the problem of arbitrariness.[50]

Despite these Supreme Court endorsements, proportionality review is not a constitutional requirement for capital sentencing. The 1976 death penalty cases were ambiguous on this point, to say the least. The Texas statute that was considered at the same time as the Georgia and Florida statutes contained no provision for such review, and the Texas Court of Criminal Appeals, unlike the Florida Supreme Court, had expressed no interest in it. Nonetheless, the Texas statute was upheld in *Jurek v. Texas*.[51] On the other hand, a plurality of the Court relied in part on the absence of proportionality review in striking down death penalty statutes in Louisiana and in North Carolina,[52] and, in 1983, a majority of the Court reaffirmed the constitutional importance of this procedure for capital sentencing schemes in Georgia and in Florida.[53] The issue was partially resolved in *Pulley v. Harris*,[54] in which the Court held that the Eighth Amendment does not require "a state appellate court, before it affirms a death sentence, to compare the sentence in the case before it with the penalties imposed in similar cases. . . ."[55] But the Court did not say that a state could execute a death sentence without affording the defendant *some* form of appellate review of the sentence, and its reliance on *Jurek v. Texas*[56] suggests that the form of review that is provided by the Texas statute—and by the California statute at issue in *Pulley v. Harris*—may set the constitutional minimum: "prompt judicial review of the jury's decision [to sentence to death] in a court with statewide jurisdiction . . . to promote the evenhanded, rational and consistent imposition of death sentences under law."[57]

We examined the effects of direct review by statewide courts by comparing the racial patterns of death sentences that were affirmed by that process to the racial patterns of all reported homicides. Two states in our sample of eight—Georgia and Florida—had sufficient numbers of affirmed death sentences to permit meaningful comparisons. Although both states have formal proportionality review procedures, there is strong evidence that these procedures are of limited value.[58] Only two death sentences have been reversed under Georgia's post-*Furman* death penalty law on the ground that they were disproportionate,[59] and these two reversals are revealing. In one, a death sentence was held to be disproportionate to a life sentence previously imposed on the same defendant for the same killing, and then reversed.[60] In the other, an accomplice's death sentence was held to be disproportionate to the life sentence given to the actual killer.[61] Both cases involved comparisons to other sentences imposed for the same killings; the Georgia Supreme Court has never found a death sentence disproportionate to sentences given for unrelated killings. The Florida Supreme Court, on the other hand, has reduced death sentences relatively often, but it is not always clear whether these reversals were based on proportionality review.[62] With a few exceptions, however, all these reversals have occurred in one special category of cases. In Florida the trial judge determines the sentence in capital cases after receiving a recommendation from an advisory jury;[63] all but five of these reversals were in cases in which the trial judge imposed the death penalty despite a jury recommendation for life.[64]

It is apparent that proportionality review as such could have only a negligible effect on racial patterns in capital sentencing in Georgia, and that if any substantial effect were to exist in Florida it would be restricted to death penalty cases in which trial judges overrule juries. But the impact of the Georgia and Florida supreme courts on capital sentencing is not limited to reversals that are explicitly based on considerations of proportionality, and an assessment that focuses solely on such reversals may understate the importance of these reviewing courts and may miss the constitutional point. An appellate court that has doubts about the propriety of a death sentence may reverse it on other grounds, or reverse the underlying conviction, rather than decide the case on the issue of proportionality.[65] Moreover, proportionality review is a means to avoid an undesirable end; arbitrariness and discrimination are the ends to be avoided. The fundamental constitutional question is whether state capital sentencing schemes do in fact avoid these problems. In this study we address that question at two stages of the legal process: at the trial court level, by observing the patterns of outcomes of all cases regardless of their disposition on appeal;[66] and—in Georgia and Florida—at the appellate level, by examining the death sentences that have been affirmed on direct review by "a court with statewide jurisdiction."[67]

GEORGIA. Of the seventy-nine death sentences pronounced in Georgia in the period of our study, sixty-one were affirmed by the Georgia Supreme Court on direct appeal.[68] These cases represent about 2.1 percent of the total number of homicides reported to the FBI, or 2.9 percent of those reported homicides with known suspects over fourteen years old. The racial patterns that we found in capital sentencing in Georgia persist when we restrict our attention to affirmed death sentences. About 0.7 percent of the black-victim cases had death sentences affirmed (10/1345) compared to 6.6 percent of the white-victim cases (51/773), a ratio of about 9 to 1. This pattern of disproportionate capital sentencing can no more be explained by the legitimate sentencing variables that we considered than the parallel pattern that we found for all death sentences, regardless of their dispositions on appeal. We have rerun all our previous analyses of Georgia data using affirmed death sentences only, and in each instance the racial disparities remain substantially unchanged.[69] We will report only a few examples.

Controlling for felony circumstance, relationship of victim to suspect, and number of victims does not explain the disproportionate capital sentencing for white-victim homicides. (See Table 4.26.) Controlling for the race of the suspect in addition to these legitimate sentencing variables did not alter this pattern; similarly, controlling separately for the sex of the victim, the use of a gun, and the location of the homicide did not explain the racial disparities in the proportions of affirmed death sentences.

Our earlier findings are reproduced again when we look at the proportions of affirmed death sentences at each level of our scale of aggravation. (See Table 4.27.) As before, white-victim homicides are more likely to receive death sentences at each step of the scale and, as before, the

Table 4.26. *Georgia: Percentage of Death Sentences by Race of Victim, Affirmed Death Sentences Only*

	FELONY CIRCUMSTANCE		RELATIONSHIP OF SUSPECT TO VICTIM		NUMBER OF VICTIMS	
	Felony	Nonfelony	Stranger	Non-stranger	Multiple Victims	Single Victim
White victim	26.4% (43/163)	1.5% (8/520)	20.3% (36/177)	2.5% (15/591)	24.1% (7/29)	5.9% (44/744)
Black victim	5.7% (6/106)	0.3% (4/1165)	2.3% (3/130)	0.6% (7/1207)	6.3% (1/16)	0.7% (9/1329)

Table 4.27. *Georgia: Percentage of Death Sentences by Level of Aggravation and Race of Victim, Affirmed Death Sentences Only*

NUMBER OF MAJOR AGGRAVATING
CIRCUMSTANCES

	0	1	2–3
White victim	0.6% (3/499)	7.3% (13/179)	36.8% (35/95)
Black victim	0.2% (2/1136)	3.8% (6/160)	4.2% (2/48)
p	.170	.121	.000006

Overall $p < .001$

difference is greatest at the highest level of aggravation. Also as before, the magnitude of this racial disparity is large.[70] A comparison between Table 4.27 and the Georgia portion of Table 4.23 demonstrates that the process of direct review did very little to change the racial patterns in capital sentencing in Georgia. The actual percentages of death sentences are somewhat lower in Table 4.27, as they must be after review, but the relative sizes of these percentages are remarkably unchanged.[71]

FLORIDA.   In Florida, a much lower proportion of the death sentences in our study were affirmed than in Georgia, 35 percent (45/128) compared to 77 percent.[72] The difference is due in part to a higher rate of reversals in Florida (49 percent of the appeals that were decided) than in Georgia (21 percent), and in part to the far greater proportion of pending appeals in Florida (30 percent) than in Georgia (1 percent). The high proportion of pending appeals means that for Florida, unlike Georgia, we do not have a final view of the impact of direct review by the state supreme court on racial disparities in capital sentencing. The dispositions in the appeals that have been decided, however, suggest that this appellate process does little if anything to correct the discrimination that we found at the trial court level. As with Georgia, we will report only a few of the analyses that led us to this conclusion.[73]

About 0.8 percent of all criminal homicides reported to the FBI from Florida resulted in affirmed death sentences, or about 1.3 percent of those with known suspects over fourteen years old. As before, affirmed death sentences were far more likely for white-victim homicides, 2.2 percent (39/1803), than for black-victim homicides, 0.4 percent (6/1683), a ratio of about six to one. This disparity cannot be explained by the felony circumstance of the homicides, the relationship of the victim to the suspect, or the number of victims (see Table 4.28), nor by the race of the suspect, the sex of victim, the use of a gun, or the location of the homicide.

The racial disparities in affirmed death sentences in Florida persist when we divide the cases along the scale of aggravation. (See Table 4.29.) A comparison between Table 4.29 and 4.23 reveals that in Florida affirmances are not evenly distributed across the scale of aggravation, as they were in Georgia. At the lowest level of aggravation (level 0), only 14 percent of the death sentences were affirmed, compared to 41 percent at the next highest level and 36 percent at the most aggravated level. This might mean that proportionality review weeded out death sentences in some non-aggravated cases in Florida;[74] but even if the review process

Table 4.28. *Florida: Percentage of Death Sentences by Race of Victim, Affirmed Death Sentences Only*

	FELONY CIRCUMSTANCE		RELATIONSHIP OF SUSPECT TO VICTIM		NUMBER OF VICTIMS	
	Felony	Nonfelony	Stranger	Non-stranger	Multiple Victims	Single Victim
White victim	10.1% (35/346)	0.3% (4/1272)	4.9% (23/469)	1.3% (16/1227)	7.1% (7/98)	1.9% (32/1705)
Black victim	3.9% (5/128)	0.1% (1/1468)	0% (0/257)	0.4% (6/1337)	7.4% (2/27)	0.2% (4/1656)

Table 4.29. *Florida: Percentage of Death Sentences by Level of Aggravation and Race of Victim, Affirmed Death Sentences Only*

NUMBER OF MAJOR AGGRAVATING
CIRCUMSTANCES

	0	1	2–3	
White victim	0.1% (1/1044)	2.7% (14/511)	10.0% (24/241)	
Black victim	0.1% (1/1251)	0.8% (3/363)	3.0% (2/67)	
p	.703	.034	.049	Overall p = .01

had this salutary effect, it did not eliminate racial disparities. At the lowest level of aggravation, only two death sentences were affirmed, and, not surprisingly, they show no particular racial pattern. At the higher levels, however, where almost all the affirmed death sentences are found, strong disparities by race of victim remain.[75]

In sum, our data indicate that direct review by the state supreme court did not solve the problem of racial discrimination in capital sentencing either in Georgia or in Florida.[76]

Notes

1. FEDERAL BUREAU OF INVESTIGATION, UNIFORM CRIME REPORT, CRIME IN THE UNITED STATES 41 (1980) [hereinafter cited as UCR].
2. *Id.* at 38–42 (1976); *id.* at 38–42 (1977); *id.* at 40–44 (1978); *id.* at 42–46 (1979); *id.* at 42–46 (1980).
3. Georgia and Florida had death penalties in effect for the entire period of the study, January 1, 1976, through December 31, 1980; Illinois had a death penalty in effect from July 1, 1977, through the end of 1980. *See* App. 1 *infra*.
4. UCR, *supra* note 1, at app. V, 339–41 (1981).
5. Table 4.2 also suggests that in Florida and Georgia, but not in Illinois, whites who killed blacks were more likely to be sentenced to death than blacks who killed blacks. These comparisons, however, are considerably less trustworthy than those that concern white-victim homicides, because of the small numbers of suspects of both races who were sentenced to death for killing blacks (12 in Georgia and 14 in Florida over a five-year period), and because of the small total numbers

of white suspects charged with killing black victims. This comparison may be particularly misleading in Georgia, where exactly one white person was sentenced to death for killing a black from 1976 through 1980.

6. We classified homicides as urban if they occurred in counties that are within any Standard Metropolitan Statistical Area (SMSA), as defined by the Census Bureau; all other homicides were classified as rural.

7. *See* ch. 1, pp. 5–9.

8. *See generally* Williams, *The Effects of Victim Characteristics on the Disposition of Violent Crimes,* in CRIMINAL JUSTICE AND THE VICTIM 177 (W. McDonald, ed., 1976) (prosecutions of violent crimes between strangers more likely to be pursued to conviction).

9. *See, e.g.,* Mississippi Univ. for Women v. Hogan, 458 U.S. 718, 724 (1982) (a party seeking to uphold a classification based on sex in the face of a challenge under the equal protection clause "must carry the burden of showing an 'exceedingly persuasive justification' . . . showing at least that the classification serves 'important governmental objectives and that the discriminatory means employed' are 'substantially related to the achievement of those objectives' ") (citations omitted).

10. The equal protection clause might be violated if a state explicitly used sex as a proxy for size or strength. *See, e.g., id.* at 726 (condemning "the simplistic, outdated assumption that gender could be used as a 'proxy for other, more germane bases of classification' ") (citation omitted). Here, of course, there are no such explicit sex-based classifications, and since we have no data on the physical traits of the victims or the suspects in our study, we cannot tell whether any apparent use of sex in capital sentencing is really based on these factors.

11. *See* H. BEDAU, THE DEATH PENALTY IN AMERICA 52 (3d ed. 1982).

12. *See, e.g.,* San Antonio School Dist. v. Rodriguez, 411 U.S. 1, 28 n.66 (1973) ("Appellees . . . have avoided [making a claim based on] discrimination between districts *per se* since this Court has never questioned the State's power to draw reasonable distinctions between political subdivisions within its borders") (citations omitted); *cf.* Jenkins v. Georgia, 418 U.S. 153, 157 (1974) (the "community" for the purpose of determining community standards in a state obscenity prosecution need not be the entire state).

13. The capital punishment statutes that were approved by the Supreme Court in 1976 were praised for containing procedures that were designed to insure evenhanded application of the death penalty throughout the relevant states. Jurek v. Texas, 428 U.S. 262, 276 (1976) (plurality opinion); Proffitt v. Florida, 428 U.S. 242, 259–60 (1976) (plurality opinion); Gregg v. Georgia, 428 U.S. 153, 204–5 (1976) (plurality opinion);

id. at 223 (White, J., concurring); *cf.* Spinkellink v. Wainwright, 578 F.2d 582, 604 (1978). *See generally* pp. 70–72. Nothing in this area is certain, but it seems to follow that the Court considered geography to be an arbitrary factor in capital sentencing, and geographical disparities a species of the arbitrariness that was condemned in *Furman.*

14. *See* Bowers & Pierce, *Arbitrariness and Discrimination under Post-*Furman *Capital Statutes,* 26 CRIME & DELINQ. 598–99 (1980) (felony); Radelet, *Racial Characteristics and the Imposition of the Death Penalty,* 46 AM. SOC. REV. 918 (1981) (relationship); Riedel, *Discrimination in the Imposition of the Death Penalty: A Comparison of the Characteristics of Offenders Sentenced Pre-*Furman *and Post-*Furman, 49 TEMPLE L. Q. 261 (1976) (relationship); *A Study of the California Penalty Jury in First-Degree Murder Cases,* 21 STAN. L. REV. 1297 (1969) (felony, relationship, multiple homicide); Wolf, *Abstract of Analyses of Jury Sentencing in Capital Cases: New Jersey: 1937–1961,* 19 RUTGERS L. REV. 60 (1964) (felony); Wolfgang & Riedel, *Race, Judicial Discretion, and the Death Penalty,* 407 ANNALS 130–131 (1973) (felony); Zimring, Eigen, & O'Malley, *Punishing Homicide in Philadelphia: Perspectives on the Death Penalty,* 43 U. CHI. L. REV. 232–33 (1976) (relationship); Note, *Discrimination and Arbitrariness in Capital Punishment: An Analysis of Post-*Furman *Murder Cases in Dade County, Florida, 1973–1976,* 33 STAN. L. REV. 88–90 (1980) (felony); Kleck, *Racial Discrimination in Criminal Sentencing: A Critical Evaluation of the Evidence with Additional Evidence on the Death Penalty,* 46 AM. SOC. REV. 792–93 (1981) (felony, relationship).

15. Inevitably, some of the cases in our study lacked data on one or another of the items that we used to construct this scale of aggravation. For those cases, we imputed the missing values as follows: if the SHR file did not indicate whether a homicide was accompanied by a separate felony, we assumed it was a nonfelony homicide; if the file did not indicate the relationship between the suspect and the victim, we assumed that they were strangers. (There were no cases in our data in which the number of victims was unknown.) The choice of these imputed values was based on the assumption that a separate additional felony or an existing relationship between the suspect and victim would generally be noticed and recorded if they were present in a case. In the case of felony circumstance, the assigned value is also the modal value for that variable.

We checked the results of this procedure in two ways. (a) We reanalyzed all our scale-of-aggravation tables, assuming in cases that lacked information on the relationship between the suspect and the victim that they were nonstrangers. The results, in every instance, were nearly identical to the results we obtained when we assumed they were strangers. (b) For Georgia, we also reanalyzed these tables using only cases for which we had complete data. The results, again, were substantively indistinguishable from those reported in the text. The percentages of cases with complete data were Georgia, 92 percent (1946/2117); Florida, 88 percent (3073/3477); and Illinois, 95 percent (2895/3058).

16. Table 4.22 reports several calculations of statistical significance. Statistical significance—commonly denoted by "p-values"—is a measure of the probability that a deviation from an expected pattern of events as extreme as that observed, or more extreme, would have occurred if the process that produced the observed pattern were mere chance. Thus a p-value of .01 signifies the observed deviation from the expected pattern, or a more extreme one, would have occurred by chance no more often than one time in 100. (By a venerable but arbitrary scientific convention, findings are said to be "statistically significant" if they could have occurred by chance one time in twenty or less often, that is, if they have a p-value of .05 or smaller.) Note that the *smaller* the p-value the *greater* the certainty that the results do not reflect mere chance fluctuations.

Two types of measures of statistical significance are reported for Table 4.22 and for other tables that employ this scale of aggravation. The p-value at the foot of each column for each state reflects the probability that racial disparities as large as those reported, or larger, could have occurred by chance among the homicides at that level of aggravation if capital sentencing in that set of homicides were not affected by the tabulated racial characteristics. The overall p-value reported for each state reflects the probability that the observed pattern of race-of-victim disparities, or a more disproportionate pattern, could have occurred by chance if capital sentencing for all homicides in the state were unaffected by the victim's race. App. 3 *infra* includes a description of the statistical methods used to calculate these two sets of p-values.

17. As we have mentioned, there were too few cases in which white suspects killed black victims to permit meaningful comparisons between that group of homicides and those in which black suspects killed black victims. *See* note 5 *supra*.

18. When urban and rural homicides are tabulated separately, the same pattern of disparities by race of victim is found in both types of locations in each state. In Illinois, however, there were too few rural homicide cases, and in particular too few rural homicides with black victims, to permit statistically useful comparisons. *See* Table 4.19.

19. For a useful nontechnical discussion of the use of multiple regression in legal contexts, see Fisher, *Multiple Regression in Legal Proceedings,* 80 COLUM. L. REV. 702 (1980).

20. *See id.* at 721–25 (application to wage discrimination against women).

21. A brief discussion of logistic regression is included in App. 3. More detailed treatments of the technique are available in many statistics texts, including Y. BISHOP, S. FEINBERG, & P. HOLLAND, DISCRETE MULTIVARIATE ANALYSIS: THEORY AND PRACTICE (1975); D. R. COX, THE ANALYSIS OF BINARY DATA (1970).

22. This type of fit is measured by a "goodness-of-fit" chi-square statistic (χ^2) and its associated probability value (p): the greater the probability that differences between the predicted outcomes and the observed outcomes are merely due to chance, the smaller the chi-square and the better the fit. In general, models will be rejected for poor fit if the chi-squares are so large that there is a probability of less than .05 that the differences between the predicted and observed values are due to chance. Note that the use of p-values here appears to be the opposite of their common use as measures of statistical significance. *See* note 16 *supra.* Thus while *findings* with *high* p-values may be rejected because they lack statistical significance, *models* with *low* p-values may be rejected because of poor fit.

23. "Odds" is defined as $O = (p/1 - p)$ where O is the odds of an event and p is the probability of the same event. This definition corresponds to the common use of the term "odds" that is often associated with betting. Thus, for example, a probability of .5 translates into odds of 1 (or "1 to 1", or "even money"); a probability of .4 translates into odds of .67 (or 2/3, or "2 to 3"); and so on.

24. *See* note 16 *supra.* Technically, the ratio of a regression coefficient to its standard error can be compared to the t distribution to obtain a rough estimate of the significance of the estimated effect, and the standard error can be used to develop rough confidence intervals around the regression coefficients. However, a more appropriate measure of the statistical significance of an effect can be obtained by testing the significance of the change in the chi-square value of a model that occurs when the variable in question is added to or removed from the model.

25. We constructed each model to include all the legitimate and potentially legitimate sentencing variables discussed above: felony circumstances, the relationship of the offender to the victim, the number of victims, the sex of the victim, and the weapon used. In addition, we entered various "interaction variables" to the extent that they significantly improved the fit of the model, up to the point where no additional interaction variables would significantly improve the fit further, singly or in combination. (An "interaction variable" makes it possible to determine whether the effect of a given main variable depends in part on the presence or absence of another variable. For example, the variable

"felony" might have a greater influence on the likelihood of a death sentence when the homicide involves multiple victims than when the homicide involves a single victim. An interaction variable makes it possible to capture this effect. See App. 3 *infra* for a discussion of some issues of interpretation that are raised by the presence of interaction variables.) For cases with missing data on felony circumstances, number of victims, and the relationship of the offender to the victim of the homicide, we followed the procedure described in note 15 *supra;* for cases with missing data on the means of death, we assumed that it was not by means of a firearm. No cases were missing data on the location of the homicide; a single case in Georgia with missing data on the sex of the victim was omitted.

26. Change in $\chi^2(1)$ due to the victim's race = 28.579, $p < .001$; $B = 1.56$, s.e. = .331; model $\chi^2(32) = 43.167$, n.s.

27. Change in $\chi^2(1)$ due to the victim's race = 12.625, $p < .001$; $B = 1.38$, s.e. = .418; model $\chi^2(47) = 33.728$, n.s.

28. Change in $\chi^2(1)$ due to the victim's race = 37.445, $p < .001$; $B = 1.97$, s.e. = .366; model $\chi^2(33) = 59.477$, $p = .003$.

29. *See* note 25 *supra.* The need for these interaction variables in Georgia reflects the fact that the killing of a white increases the odds that the defendant will receive the death penalty by a larger factor in the presence of some legitimate sentencing variables. This pattern can be seen in Table 4.23, which shows that the difference in capital sentencing rates between white-victim and black-victim cases increases dramatically as the cases become more aggravated. A variable representing an interaction with an illegitimate variable is, of course, itself illegitimate. For example, a coefficient that represents the increase in the probability of a death sentence for homicides that involve both a white victim *and* a separate felony indicates discrimination by the race of the victim among homicides that include the commission of another felony.

30. Change in $\chi^2(4) = 55.369$, $p < .001$, B (victim's race) = 2.01, s.e. = .804, model $\chi^2(30) = 41.553$, n.s.

31. See App. 3 *infra* for an explanation of the problems of interpretation caused by the presence of interaction variables.

32. Georgia: change in $\chi^2(1)$ due to victim's race = 27.216, $p < .001$, $B = 1.93$, s.e. = .406, model $\chi^2(62) = 106.76$, $p < .001$, change in $\chi^2(2)$ due to victim's race and interactions with victim's race = 31.024, $p < .001$, model $\chi^2(61) = 102.95$, $p = .001$; Florida: change in $\chi^2(1)$ due to victim's race = 19.404, $p < .001$, $B = 1.56$, s.e. = .379, model $\chi^2(70) = 79.705$, n.s.; Illinois: change in $\chi^2(1)$ due to victim's race = 13.856, $p < .001$, $B = 1.72$, s.e. = .481, model $\chi^2(78) = 80.192$, n.s.

33. To obtain a model that included race of suspect and that adequately fit the Georgia data, we had to include as variables numerous interactions between the suspect's race and legally relevant and irrelevant sentencing factors. See App. 3 *infra* for a discussion of the meaning and interpretation of interaction variables. However, reliable estimates of the effects of these interaction variables on capital sentencing could not be obtained because of problems of multicollinearity between these interaction variables and the suspect's race; black suspects were much more likely than white suspects to commit certain types of aggravated homicides, and vice versa. Hence, in Georgia, the effect of the suspect's race on capital sentencing cannot be disentangled from the effects of interactions among the legally relevant and irrelevant variables without access to more information on the individual cases than was available to us.

34. This procedure avoids any possible statistical problem of multicollinearity that could be caused by the correlation between the victim's race and the suspect's race.

35. Georgia: change in $\chi^2(1) = 29.325$, $p < .001$, $B = 2.43$, s.e. = .512, model $\chi^2(29) = 54.893$, $p = .003$. (Using a model modified by adding interactions between the race of the victim and legitimate variables: change in $\chi^2(1)$ due to victim's race $= 32.098$, $p < .001$, $B = 2.72$, s.e. $= .573$, model $\chi^2(28) = 40.052$, n.s.); Florida: change in $\chi^2(1) = 17.667$, $p < .001$, $B = 1.99$, s.e. $= .515$, model $\chi^2(33) = 24.939$, n.s.; Illinois: change in $\chi^2(1) = 11.389$, $p = .001$, $B = 1.80$, s.e. $= .568$, model $\chi^2(12) = 29.095$, n.s.

36. Georgia: change in $\chi^2(1) = .990$, model $\chi^2(27) = 52.52$, $p = .002$; Florida: change in $\chi^2(1) = .07$, model $\chi^2(33) = 39.663$, n.s.

37. Illinois: change in $\chi^2(3)$ due to suspect's race and interactions with suspect's race $= 20.002$, $p < .001$, model $\chi^2(36) = 38.789$, n.s.

38. Georgia: B (urban) $= 1.17$, s.e. $= .324$; Florida: B (urban) $= .886$, s.e. $= .272$.

39. B (urban) $= .502$, s.e. $= .790$.

40. Georgia: change in $\chi^2(1) = 33.837$, $p < .001$, $B = 1.92$, s.e. = .372, model $\chi^2(64) = 81.424$, n.s. (change in $\chi^2(4)$ due to victim's race and victim's race interactions $= 52.04$, $p < .001$, model $\chi^2(61) = 63.221$, n.s.); Florida: change in $\chi^2(1) = 27.906$, $p < .001$, $B = 1.55$, s.e. $= .333$, model $\chi^2(70) = 101.424$, $p = .016$; Illinois: change in $\chi^2(1) = 13.059$, $p < .001$, $B = 1.42$, s.e. $= .421$, model $\chi^2(70) = 51.102$, n.s.

41. The most conservative test of the effect of the victim's race on the odds of the offender receiving the death penalty would entail comparing a model that includes all possible interactions between all legitimate and potentially legitimate sentencing variables to an identical model

with the race of the victim added as a predictor variable. Given the large number of interaction variables needed for this analysis, these models have limited value: The assumptions of logistic regression are strained, and it may not be possible to obtain unique estimates for the coefficients of all these variables in such a model. Nonetheless, such analyses can provide further confirmation of a conclusion reached by other means. We have performed these analyses, and the results in each state indicate discrimination by race of victim.

42. Greenberg, *Capital Punishment as a System,* 91 YALE L.J. 909–10 (1982).

43. *Id.* at 910–13.

44. Note, *A Matter of Life and Death: Due Process Protection in Capital Clemency Proceedings,* 90 YALE L.J. 889, 892 n.10, 899 n.52 (1981).

45. NAACP Legal Defense and Educational Fund, Death Row U.S.A. (December 20, 1987) (unpublished document).

46. 428 U.S. 153 (1976).

47. *Id.* at 166–67 (plurality opinion), 211–12 (White, J., concurring).

48. 428 U.S. 242 (1976).

49. *Id.* at 250–51 (plurality opinion).

50. *Gregg,* 428 U.S. at 166–67, 198, 204–6, 207 (plurality opinion), 211–12, 223–24 (White, J., concurring); Proffitt v. Florida, 428 U.S. at 250–51, 253 (plurality opinion).

51. 428 U.S. 262 (1976).

52. Roberts v. Louisiana, 428 U.S. 325, 335–36 (1976); Woodson v. North Carolina, 428 U.S. 280, 302–3 (1976).

53. Zant v. Stephens, 462 U.S. 862 (1983); Barclay v. Florida, 463 U.S. 939 (1983); *see* ch. 1, note 30.

54. 465 U.S. 37 (1984); *see* ch. 1, note 30.

55. *Id.* at 44.

56. 428 U.S. 262 (1976).

57. *Id.* at 276.

58. Baldus, Pulaski, & Woodworth, *Comparative Review of Death Sentences: An Empirical Study of the Georgia Experience,* 74 J. CRIM. L. & CRIMINOLOGY 661 (1983); Dix, *Appellate Review of the Decision to Impose Death,* 68 GEO. L.J. 97 (1979) (a study of appellate review of death sentences under post-*Furman* statutes in Georgia, Florida, and Texas); *see also* Blake v. Zant, 513 F.Supp. 772, 803–18 (S.D. Ga. 1981) (commenting on the failure of the Georgia Supreme Court to conduct meaningful proportionality review in a specific case); *id.* at 822–27 (commenting on the difficulties inherent in such review in general).

59. As of July 1983. Only one of these two reversals, Hall v. State, 241 Ga. 252, 244 S.E.2d 833 (1978), involves a case in our sample.

60. Ward v. State, 239 Ga. 205, 236 S.E.2d 365 (1977); see Dix, *supra* note 58, at 117.

61. Hall v. State, 241 Ga. 252, 244 S.E.2d 833 (1978); see Dix, *supra* note 58, at 117.

62. Between the beginning of 1973 and the end of 1981, the Florida Supreme Court reversed a death sentence about thirty times in 145 reported death penalty appeals. *See* Radelet & Vandiver, *The Florida Supreme Court and Death Penalty Appeals*, 74 J. CRIM. L. & CRIMINOLOGY 913, 919, 923 (1983). The basis for many of these reversals is ambiguous, however, since in Florida, unlike Georgia, proportionality review is not statutorily mandated. *See* Dix, *supra* note 58, at 124.

63. Dix, *supra* note 58, at 125–26; see FLA. STAT. ANN. § 921.141(3) (West 1973).

64. Radelet & Vandiver, *supra* note 62, at 923; see also Dix, *supra* note 58, at 125–26, 134–35.

65. See, e.g., Whittington v. State, 252 Ga.168, 313 S.E.2d 73 (1984) (Georgia Supreme Court reversed a death sentence without engaging in formal proportionality review because the record did not support the jury's finding of aggravating circumstances); see Dix, *supra* note 58, at 159.

66. Our comparative analysis at this level focuses on the same issue that the state supreme courts themselves address in proportionality review—the patterns of actions by trial judges and juries in the entire state. The Georgia Supreme Court has said explicitly that the universe of cases that it uses for this purpose is the same as ours, and that in exercising its statutory function of comparative review it will consider all murder convictions whether or not they were subsequently reversed on appeal. Ward v. State, 239 Ga. 205, 208–9, 236 S.E.2d 365, 368 (1977).

67. Jurek v. Texas, 428 U.S. 262, 276 (1976).

68. In this section we compare affirmed death sentences to all other cases. We classified a death sentence as "affirmed" if it was affirmed in the most recent direct appeal to the Georgia Supreme Court, and that designation was not changed if the sentence, or the underlying conviction, was later vacated or reversed on collateral review by a state or a federal court. This classification reflects the subject of our inquiry, the effect of direct appellate review. If a case was retried after a reversal by any court, it would retain its original classification unless the Georgia Supreme Court reached a different result in a direct review of a death sentence pronounced at that second trial. Thus, for example, a death

sentence that was reversed by the Georgia Supreme Court would remain classified as a reversal unless and until that court affirmed a death sentence that resulted from a subsequent retrial of the same case. On the other hand, a death sentence that was affirmed by the Georgia Supreme Court but vacated on collateral review would be classified as an affirmance, unless the Georgia Supreme Court reversed a second death sentence in a direct appeal from a retrial of the same case. We completed our review of the appellate status of the death sentences in our sample at the end of March 1983. At that time the eighteen Georgia cases in which the death sentences were not affirmed on direct appeal were distributed as follows: three cases in which the convictions were reversed; thirteen cases in which the convictions were affirmed but the death penalties were reversed; one pending appeal; and one case in which the defendant committed suicide.

69. *See* pp. 43–55 and 59–69 and notes 2–6, 14–41 *supra*.

70. The magnitude of the racial disparity can be assessed by considering what the distribution of affirmed death sentences would have been but for this pattern of disproportionate sentencing. *See* p. 62. If, at each level of aggravation in Table 4.27, black-victim homicides in Georgia had resulted in the same proportion of affirmed death sentences that white-victim homicides actually produced, their number would have nearly quadrupled, from 10 to 36. Conversely, if, controlling for level of aggravation, white-victim homicides had been treated as black-victim homicides, the number of affirmed white-victim death sentences would have been reduced from 51 to 12, and the total number of affirmed death sentences in this period in Georgia would have been reduced from 61 to 22.

71. The reason for this lack of change is that the reversals by the Georgia Supreme Court were evenly distributed both with respect to race of victim and with respect to level of aggravation. The overall reversal rate for this sample was about 23 percent. Two of the six cells of reported Georgia homicides in Table 4.23 included only two death sentences each, and in each of these cells there were no reversals. In each of the other four cells the reversal rate was very close to the overall average of 23 percent, ranging from 22 percent to 28 percent.

72. *See* note 68 *supra* for a description of the methodology used in this section, and for the definition of "affirmed" cases. The eighty-three Florida death sentences in our study that were not affirmed were distributed as follows: thirteen cases in which the convictions were reversed; thirty in which the convictions were affirmed but the death penalties vacated; thirty-eight pending appeals; and two cases in which the defendants committed suicide.

73. *See* p. 74 and note 69 *supra.*

74. We can neither confirm nor disconfirm the possibility that proportionality review produced this effect. This possibility, however, has an interesting consequence. Recall that proportionality review in Florida is essentially restricted in practice to cases in which judges imposed death sentences despite jury recommendations for life, *see* pp. 72–73 and notes 62–64 *supra;* if proportionality review is responsible for the low proportion of affirmances in the lowest category of aggravation, that would imply that judges in Florida were more willing than juries to impose death sentences for relatively unaggravated homicides.

75. The magnitude of this disparity can be quantified, as we did in Georgia, by comparing the actual distribution of affirmed death sentences to two hypothetical distributions. *See* note 71 *supra.* If, at each reported level of aggravation, black-victim homicides in Florida had resulted in the same proportions of affirmed death sentences as white-victim homicides actually did, there would have been 18 such cases in our study rather than 6. If white-victim homicides at each level of aggravation had been treated as black-victim homicides were actually treated, the number of affirmed white-victim death sentences would have been reduced from 39 to 12, eliminating 60 percent of the total number of affirmed sentences of death.

76. In addition to the analyses reported in the text, we used these data to estimate logistic regression models following the procedures outlined earlier. *See* pp. 63–69 and notes 19–41 *supra;* App. 3 *infra.* In Georgia the race of the victim had a significant effect on capital sentencing beyond that attributable to the action of legitimate and potentially legitimate sentencing factors, both alone (change in $\chi^2(1) = 24.170$, $p < .001$) and in interaction with other variables (change in $\chi^2(2) = 31.221$, $p < .001$, model $\chi^2(31) = 42.420$, n.s., $p < .001$). In Florida the effect of the race of the victim on capital sentencing was in the predicted direction and nearly statistically significant (change in $\chi^2(1) = 3.101$, $p = .078$, model $\chi^2(42) = 34.499$, n.s.). Adding the location of the homicide (urban or rural) to these models did not substantially alter these racial effects in either state (Georgia: change in $\chi^2(2) = 28.466$, $p < .001$, model $\chi^2(62) = 66.376$, n.s.; Florida: change in $\chi^2(1) = 2.978$, $p = .084$, model $\chi^2(80) = 63.330$, n.s.). After controlling for the legitimate and potentially legitimate sentencing variables, the overall odds of receiving a death sentence that was later affirmed were 5.4 times greater for the killing of a white victim than for the killing of a black victim in Georgia, and 2.2 times greater in Florida.

5 | Racial Patterns in Capital Sentencing: Oklahoma, North Carolina, Mississippi, Virginia, and Arkansas

Thus far we have discussed only Georgia, Florida, and Illinois. In this section we will briefly present the major racial pattern that we found in the other five states in our study—Oklahoma, North Carolina, Mississippi, Virginia, and Arkansas.[1]

A word of caution is in order. As we go down the list of states from Oklahoma to Arkansas, our data become increasingly attenuated. Our study includes 43 death sentences in Oklahoma, 27 in North Carolina,[2] 22 in Mississippi, 19 in Virginia, and 15 in Arkansas. Considered in isolation, such small numbers make any sentencing patterns hard to discern: only very strong effects can be seen clearly with so few observations.[3] Some of the racial disparities that we report would not, on their own, constitute convincing proof of racial discrimination; this is particularly true for Arkansas and Virginia, in each of which we had fewer than 20 death sentences. If we were examining the data from one of the states separately, we would conclude that there is good reason to suspect racial discrimination in capital sentencing—indeed, that it is more likely than not—but that it is too early to tell for sure. But we are not considering these states in isolation, and we are not primarily interested in determining the existence of racial discrimination in any particular state.

Viewed collectively, the data from these five states show a remarkably consistent pattern of racial disparities. Table 5.1 illustrates this pattern: considering felony and nonfelony homicides separately, black-victim homicides in each state were substantially less likely to result in death sentences than white-victim homicides.

In Table 5.2 white-victim and black-victim homicides are tabulated by level of aggravation. Again, as in Georgia, Florida, and Illinois,[4] we find disproportionate capital sentencing for white-victim cases in each state at each level of aggravation.

We also constructed logistic regression models for these five states, following the procedures described earlier.[5] The race-of-victim coefficients for the "best-fitting" models for

Table 5.1. *Percentage of Death Sentences by Felony Circumstance and Race of Victim*

	FELONY	NONFELONY
Oklahoma		
White victim	30.6% (22/72)	3.7% (18/482)
Black victim	0% (0/17)	1.4% (3/221)
North Carolina		
White victim	13.6% (14/103)	1.0% (7/678)
Black victim	4.3% (2/46)	0.2% (2/869)
Mississippi		
White victim	32.5% (13/40)	2.6% (4/151)
Black victim	9.5% (4/42)	0.2% (1/564)
Virginia		
White victim	14.3% (13/91)	0.4% (2/497)
Black victim	6.9% (4/58)	0% (0/649)
Arkansas		
White victim	9.2% (8/87)	1.5% (5/332)
Black victim	4.5% (2/44)	0% (0/406)

Table 5.2. *Percentage of Death Sentences by Level of Aggravation and Race of Victim*

NUMBER OF MAJOR AGGRAVATING
CIRCUMSTANCES

	0	1	2–3	
		Oklahoma		
White victim	1.5%	12.8%	38.8%	
	(6/389)	(15/117)	(19/49)	
Black victim	0.5%	6.3%	0%	
	(1/210)	(2/32)	(0/8)	
p	.231	.243	.030	Overall p = .05
		North Carolina		
White victim	0.9%	1.7%	17.6%	
	(5/588)	(3/176)	(13/74)	
Black victim	0.1%	0%	8.0%	
	(1/803)	(0/133)	(2/25)	
p	.052	.183	.207	Overall p = .018
		Mississippi		
White victim	1.5%	15.9%	27.6%	
	(2/134)	(7/44)	(8/29)	
Black victim	0%	1.1%	21.1%	
	(0/525)	(1/95)	(4/19)	
p	.041	.001	.437	Overall p = .006
		Virginia		
White victim	0%	4.5%	13.2%	
	(0/454)	(5/112)	(10/76)	
Black victim	0%	2.0%	7.1%	
	(0/615)	(2/99)	(2/28)	
p	—	.227	.319	Overall p = .14
		Arkansas		
White victim	0%	8.9%	12.2%	
	(0/265)	(8/90)	(5/41)	
Black victim	0%	2.2%	6.7%	
	(0/338)	(1/45)	(1/15)	
p	—	.134	.485	Overall p = .14

each of these states are reported in Table 5.3. As the table shows, the race of the victim had sizable and statistically significant effects on the likelihood that a defendant would receive the death penalty in Oklahoma, North Carolina, and Mississippi, while in Virginia and Arkansas the race of the victim had less pronounced and statistically non-significant effects.

In each state, the overall odds that an offender would receive the death penalty were much greater for killing a white victim than for killing a black victim.[6] When we added race of the victim to models that included race of the suspect, the general picture remained essentially unchanged.[7] In North Carolina the race-of-victim effect became smaller and statistically nonsignificant; in the remaining four states—Oklahoma, Mississippi, Virginia, and Arkansas—the effect became larger.[8] (In Arkansas a previously non-significant effect became statistically significant when we controlled for the race of suspect.[9])

Table 5.4 displays the predicted probabilities of a death sentence generated by the "best-fitting" regression models for these five states, comparing hypothetical high-aggravation and low-aggravation cases with black victims to otherwise identical cases with white victims. In each state the predicted probability of a death sentence was much higher for ho-

Table 5.3. *Best Logistic Regression Models, Effect of Victim's Race*

	OKLAHOMA	NORTH CAROLINA	MISSISSIPPI	VIRGINIA	ARKANSAS
Victim's race logit coefficient	1.46*	1.47*	1.70**	0.88	1.27†
Victim's race multiplier of odds of a death sentence	4.31	4.35	5.47	2.41	3.56

**Effect significant at the .01 level.
*Effect significant at the .05 level.
†Effect significant at the .10 level.

Table 5.4. *Best Logistic Regression Models: Predicted Probability of a Death Sentence in Hypothetical High- and Low-Aggravation Cases, by Race of Victim*

	OKLAHOMA	NORTH CAROLINA	MISSISSIPPI	VIRGINIA	ARKANSAS
High-aggravation case[a]					
White victim	.658	.944	.372	.215	.446
Black victim	.309	.796	.098	.102	.184
Low-aggravation case[b]					
White victim	.047	.014	.016	.0006	.0003
Black victim	.011	.003	.003	.0002	.0001

[a]Multiple homicide of at least one female during the course of a felony in which a gun was used; all victims were strangers to the offender.
[b]Single-victim homicide of a male relative, friend, or acquaintance; no other felonies involved.

micides with white victims than for homicides with black victims, among high-aggravation and low-aggravation cases alike.[10]

SUMMARY. In each of the five states considered in this section, white-victim homicides were more likely to result in death sentences than black-victim homicides. These racial effects cannot be explained by the other variables in our data: in each state we found large race-of-victim effects after controlling for the nonracial variables in our data. In the two states with the smallest numbers of death sentences (Virginia and Arkansas), the effects of race-of-victim on death sentencing, controlling for nonracial factors, do not meet conventional standards of statistical significance; in the other three states (Oklahoma, North Carolina, and Mississippi) these effects are statistically significant.

Notes

1. See App. 2 infra for a more complete presentation of our findings from these five states.

2. Two of these cases involved Indian victims and defendants, and one involved an Indian defendant and a black victim. See ch. 3, p. 37 and note 12.

3. The problem of small numbers is considerably less pronounced in Oklahoma, where we had only two fewer death sentences than in Illinois, than it is in the remaining four states. But in Oklahoma there is an additional problem: because the proportion of black-victim homicides is relatively small—less than a third of the total—the expected numbers of black-victim death sentences in some categories (that is, the numbers that would be found in the absence of racial disparities) are low. This statistical fact makes it more difficult to detect disparities that further reduce the numbers of black-victim death sentences.

4. See Table 4-23 supra.

5. See ch. 4, pp. 63-69 and notes 19-41.

6. In Mississippi the odds that an offender would receive the death penalty for killing a white victim were 5.47 times greater than the odds that an offender would receive the death penalty for killing a black victim (change in $\chi^2(1)$ = 9.49, p = .002, B = 1.70, s.e. = .580, model $\chi^2(31)$ = 30.258, n.s.). In North Carolina the overall odds that an offender would receive the death penalty for killing a white were 4.35 times greater than for killing a black (change in $\chi^2(1)$ = 5.767, p = .016, B = 1.47, s.e. = .683, model $\chi^2(30)$ = 23.399, n.s.). In Oklahoma the odds of receiving the death penalty for killing a white were 4.31 times greater than the odds of receiving the death penalty for killing a black (change in $\chi^2(1)$ = 6.468, p = .011, B = 1.46, s.e. = .660, model $\chi^2(25)$ = 22.001, n.s.). In Arkansas the odds of receiving the death penalty for killing a white were 3.56 times greater than the odds of receiving the death penalty for killing a black (change in $\chi^2(1)$ = 2.84, p = .092, B = 1.27, s.e. = .838, model $\chi^2(32)$ = 18.753, n.s.). And in Virginia the odds of receiving the death penalty for killing a white were 2.41 times greater than the odds of receiving the death penalty for killing a black (change in $\chi^2(1)$ = 2.136, p < .20, B = .88, s.e. = .636, model $\chi^2(38)$ = 25.546, n.s.).

7. See ch. 4, pp. 67–68.

8. North Carolina: change in $\chi^2(1)$ due to victim's race = 1.96, n.s., B = 1.13, s.e. = .826, model $\chi^2(51)$ = 32.312, n.s.; Oklahoma: change in $\chi^2(1)$ due to victim's race = 5.29, p = .021, model $\chi^2(46)$ = 43.936, n.s.; Mississippi: change in $\chi^2(1)$ due to victim's race = 9.88, p .002, B = 1.94, s.e. = .655, model $\chi^2(50)$ = 56.031, n.s.; Virginia: change

in $\chi^2(1)$ due to victim's race = 2.41, n.s., model $\chi^2(60)$ = 43.509, n.s.; Arkansas: change in $\chi^2(1)$ due to victim's race = 8.00, p = .005, B = 2.49, s.e. = 1.02, model $\chi^2(51)$ = 35.897, n.s.

9. The race-of-suspect coefficient itself was statistically significant in Arkansas (B = 1.79, s.e. = .719) but not elsewhere. We also controlled for race of the suspect by looking separately at the subsets of cases with black suspects. See ch. 4, p. 68 and notes 34–37. We found significant race-of-victim effects within these subsets in Oklahoma, Mississippi, Virginia, and Arkansas, but not in North Carolina. When we examined white-victim cases separately, we found significant race-of-suspect effects in Mississippi and Arkansas but not in the other three states. (Mississippi: change in $\chi^2(1)$ due to suspect's race = 6.53, p = .011, B = 1.83, s.e. = .735, model $\chi^2(27)$ = 34.832, n.s.; Arkansas: change in $\chi^2(1)$ due to suspect's race = 8.70, p = .003, B = 2.34, s.e. = .875, model $\chi^2(28)$ = 24.026, n.s.).

10. The location of the homicide—urban or rural—did not have a statistically significant effect on capital sentencing in any of these states. Furthermore, controlling for geographic location as well as for the other variables included in the reported models did not substantially alter the effect of the race of the victim on capital sentencing in any of these states.

6 | Alternative Explanations

A. Missing Data and Omitted Variables

Although the nonracial factors in our data cannot explain the disproportionate imposition of death sentences on defendants charged with killing white victims, it remains possible that information that is not included in our data could explain these racial disparities on nonracial grounds. Such an explanation could derive, in principle, from two sources: missing data and omitted variables.

1. Missing Data

The problem of missing data is one of degree. In any large data set, some cases will lack particular items of information and some cases will be missed altogether. As official criminal justice data go, the FBI's homicide statistics are uncommonly complete, but they are not exhaustive.[1] As we have indicated, however, much of the missing data concern cases that are properly excluded from our analysis:[2] unreported homicides, or homicides for which insufficient information is reported to form the basis for official action. Since we are not concerned with the histories of homicides in the abstract but with the treatment of known homicides by the criminal justice system, these cases are not part of the relevant

95

universe. There are, of course, some cases and items that ought to have been in our data but that are missing—homicides that were known to local police agencies but never reported to the FBI or ones that were reported imperfectly—but the problem is smaller than it would be if we were concerned with patterns in the commission of homicides or with rates of victimization, rather than with the imposition of official sanctions.

For missing data to change the observed racial relationships, they would have to fall into a pattern that substantially counteracts the patterns in the available data. While this is possible, it seems unlikely. The observed data show a disproportionately high ratio of death sentences among white-victim homicides; since the number and characteristics of the death sentences are reflected in the data with a very high degree of accuracy, unreported data could change this racial pattern only if there were a strong pattern of underreporting of white-victim homicides as compared to black-victim homicides, or if such a pattern were to exist among the more aggravated homicides. We know of no empirical or theoretical basis for supposing that this is so; if anything, we would suspect the opposite.

2. Omitted Variables

The problem of omitted variables is more severe than the problem of missing data. The FBI's data on homicides are reasonably complete in their coverage, but they include a relatively small number of items. The missing items include some important judicial processing and sentencing variables; one could argue that the observed racial disparities might have been produced by the operation of one or more of these omitted variables. In particular, the FBI's data lack information on the strength of the evidence of the suspects' guilt and on their criminal records, and while these data include several items that permit us to assess the relative gravity of the homicides, they lack many others.[3]

To say that it is possible that omitted variables might explain the observed racial pattern is to say very little. Most things are possible. Moreover, it is almost inevitable, in any study of this nature, that information on some variables that have not been examined would change the estimates of the size of the effects of the variables that were examined, to some extent. The important question is whether the observed pattern of discrimination by race of victim might be substantially explained by the legally permissible operation of omitted variables. That possibility seems remote.

For a legally permissible sentencing variable that is absent from our data to substantially change the estimated size of the effect of the victim's race on capital sentencing, the variable would have to satisfy three conditions: (1) it must be correlated with the victim's race; (2) it must be correlated with capital sentencing; and (3) its correlation with capital sentencing must not be explainable by the effects of the variables that are already included in our analysis. For example, let us assume that it is appropriate to consider homicides that are committed at night as more aggravated than those committed during the day. For this variable to explain the victim-based racial disparity, the data would have to show that white-victim homicides are more likely to have occurred at night than black-victim homicides, that nighttime homicides are in fact more likely to result in the death penalty than daytime homicides, and that the effect of the time of the homicide on capital sentencing persists after controlling for the felony circumstance of the homicide, the number of victims, the relationship of the victim to the killer, and the other variables that we have already considered. Moreover, the magnitude of the effect of the time of the killing on capital sentencing would have to be quite large—comparable to the magnitude of the racial effect it is offered to explain.

Given these requirements, it is reasonable to accept the

observed patterns as valid descriptions of the systems of capital sentencing that we studied unless some plausible alternative hypothesis can be stated that explains how some legitimate sentencing variable that we did not consider, or some combination of such variables, could account for these patterns. No such hypothesis is apparent. It is true that white-victim homicides in each state were generally more aggravated than black-victim homicides during the period we studied, but we have considerable data on the level of aggravation, and the racial pattern that we observed is apparent in each state after controlling for the several aggravating factors in our data. Data on omitted aggravating factors could explain the observed racial disparities only if they were to show that black-victim cases were systematically less heinous than white-victim cases *within the categories defined by the included variables,* for example, among felony killings of strangers, using guns. This does not seem likely. Similarly, it is almost certain that homicides with weak evidence of the suspect's guilt are less likely to result in death sentences than those with strong evidence.[4] But for data on the strength of the evidence to undercut our findings, they would have to show that, within the levels of aggravation identified by our analysis, black-victim cases had systematically weaker evidence than white-victim cases. In the absence of any empirical evidence of such a pattern, and there is none, it must be considered improbable—especially considering the magnitudes of the racial effects that we found.[5]

Finally, the criminal record of the suspect undoubtedly has an effect on the chances of a death sentence.[6] Moreover, we know that black defendants in general are more likely to have serious criminal records than white defendants,[7] and we can safely assume that this general relationship applies to the homicide suspects in our study. This association, however, explains very little. After controlling for level of aggravation, the race of the suspect is not a significant predictive variable, and the principal racial pattern that we did find—discrimination by race of victim— persisted when we controlled for the race of the suspect. Indeed, we were careful to make sure that the effect of the race of the victim could be determined separately from any possible race-of-suspect effect.[8] To assert that the criminal records of the *suspects* might account for discrimination by the race of the *victim,* one would have to suppose that, controlling for the nature of the homicide and for their relationship to the victims, the killers of whites, regardless of their own race, were more likely to have serious criminal records than the killers of blacks. We know of no empirical or logical basis for such a supposition, and it seems unlikely that any unforeseen effect of this type could be large enough and consistent enough to have the power to explain the racial patterns that we have reported.

In sum, we are aware of no plausible alternative hypothesis that might explain the observed racial patterns in capital sentencing in legitimate nondiscriminatory terms.

B. Relationship to Other Research

There is a further and important reason to trust our findings of racial discrimination in capital sentencing: they are consistent with the findings of other researchers who have studied capital sentencing under post-*Furman* statutes in some of the same states.

As we mentioned earlier, Bowers and Pierce examined capital sentencing in Georgia and Florida from 1973 through 1977 using data from the same sources that we used— SHR data from the FBI's Uniform Crime Reports Division and death row data from the NAACP Legal Defense and Educational Fund.[9] Their findings closely parallel some of ours. Controlling for felony circumstance they found, as we did, that white-victim homicides were more likely to result in death sentences than black-victim homicides in each state, and that blacks who killed whites were more likely to be sentenced to death than whites who killed whites.[10] Bowers and Pierce also found, as we did, that direct review by the Florida and Georgia supreme courts had negligible effects on these racial patterns.[11]

The data Bowers and Pierce used were no more detailed than our own. Indeed, they were not able to control for several of the nonracial items that we controlled for, and they were forced, for a portion of the period that they studied, to rely on FBI data that did not include the race of the suspect.[12] But while the Bowers and Pierce study does not speak to the issue of omitted variables, it does show that the racial patterns in capital sentencing that we have observed from 1976 through 1980 have been stable phenomena in Georgia and Florida since immediately after the *Furman* decision.

Our Florida findings are also supported by the comparable results of the studies by Zeisel,[13] Radelet,[14] and Radelet and Pierce,[15] all noted earlier. Similarly, our finding of race-of-victim discrimination in Illinois is reinforced by a study of capital sentencing in Cook County, Illinois, from 1977 through 1980, by Elizabeth Murphy, which found the same thing.[16] Like Bowers and Pierce's study, none of these studies includes information on items we lacked—on the contrary, they all lacked information on one or several of the items that we included—but they do broaden the base of observations and provide independent confirmation of our analyses. A much more detailed study by Barry Nakell and Kenneth Hardy examined a wealth of data on all homicide prosecutions in North Carolina in the year beginning June 1, 1977.[17] After controlling for the many variables at their disposal, Nakell and Hardy found that among the capital murder trials in their sample, the odds of a first-degree murder conviction were six times greater for defendants charged with killing whites than for those charged with killing nonwhites. Unfortunately, Nakell and Hardy's

data included too few death penalties to justify any conclusions about discrimination at the sentencing stage.
Our study has also been replicated in Louisiana, a state
we did not examine, by M. Dwayne Smith.[18] In addition,
two Texas journalists have reported that they conducted
a survey comparing homicide arrests and death row populations in all death penalty states, and found a nationwide
pattern of capital sentencing discrimination by race of victim.[19] Unfortunately, the methodology of that survey is, at
a minimum, very poorly described. (For example, "16,173
murders that would qualify for capital punishment in states
that employ it" were identified by "[a] computer program
developed by [a] Times Herald systems analyst."[20]) As a
result, no firm conclusions can be based on this report.

The well-known study by Baldus, Woodworth, and Pulaski
provides stronger confirmation of our findings.[21] Baldus
and his colleagues conducted a massive, detailed study of
capital sentencing in Georgia, both before and after *Furman*.
For our purposes, the relevant data are based on 1066
cases of defendants who were arrested for homicides committed between March 28, 1973, and the end of 1979, and
subsequently convicted of murder or voluntary manslaughter. The study considers numerous sentencing and legal
processing variables that are absent from our data, over
400 in all, including detailed information on the backgrounds
of the defendants, their criminal records, the circumstances
of the killings, and the strength of the evidence of the
defendants' guilt. One of the major conclusions of the researchers is the same as ours. In post-*Furman* Georgia,
controlling for all the aggravating and mitigating factors
that they examined, the race of the defendant was a weak
predictor of capital sentencing on a statewide basis, but
the race of the victim had a strong effect: white-victim
cases were much more likely to result in death sentences
than black-victim cases.

The fact that Baldus, Pulaski, and Woodworth reached

the same general conclusion that we reached is significant, but a detailed consideration of their data confirms the accuracy of our conclusions in two more telling respects.

First, the Baldus study establishes that data on the defendants' criminal records have little or no impact on the pattern of discrimination by race of victim in capital sentencing in Georgia.[22] Second, it demonstrates that the magnitude of the race-of-victim effect that we found in Georgia would not be reduced if we were able to control for additional variables concerning the level of aggravation of the homicides and the strength of the evidence against the defendants. The study reports a logistic regression model on the odds of a death sentence, which is comparable to several of our own,[23] as well as many larger regression analyses that include numerous additional control variables. Comparisons between these larger models and the smaller one reveals two important facts: (1) the race-of-victim coefficient remains statistically significant regardless of the other variables included in the equations, and (2) after controlling for the variables in our study, the introduction of any number of additional control variables either has little impact on the magnitude of the race-of-victim effect or else increases the size of the race-of-victim disparities.[24]

Finally, Richard Berk and Joseph Lowery conducted a study of capital sentencing in Mississippi from November 1976 through April 1982, which is comparable in scope and detail to the Baldus, Pulaski, and Woodworth study in Georgia.[25] Some aspects of the data analysis for this study are not yet complete, but one major conclusion is already available: white-victim homicides were much more likely to result in death sentences than black-victim homicides, controlling for any plausible combination of the hundreds of legitimate sentencing variables that were included in the data.

In sum, our findings receive some support from those of Bowers and Pierce, Radelet, and others and, obviously, the results of the Baldus and Berk studies provide strong confirmation of the accuracy of our conclusions about racial patterns in capital sentencing in Georgia and Mississippi, respectively. But the consistency between the Baldus and Berk findings and our own also has another and more general implication: it validates our methodology, and, to some extent, theirs as well. The major potential problem with our study is the impact of omitted variables; the Baldus study indicates that given the variables that are reported in our data and analyzed in this book, it is unnecessary to our conclusion to control for other variables that are missing. The Baldus and Berk studies, on the other hand, include as much information on as many variables as one could ever hope to collect in a study of sentencing practices, but they are susceptible to sample selection bias[26] while our study is not. The fact that their studies and ours all show discrimination in capital sentencing by the race of the victim demonstrates that this is a real and robust phenomenon. It indicates that the potential problems of sample selection bias and of omitted variables are only potential and not actual, and that one can obtain an accurate picture of this racial pattern using either methodology.

Notes

1. *See* ch. 3, p. 36 and notes 6–8; App. 1 *infra*.
2. *See* ch. 3, pp. 36–37 and notes 9–10.
3. The data that we analyzed also lack information on the actual disposition of the homicide cases that did not result in death sentences; consequently, our inquiry is restricted to the effects of the criminal justice system as a whole, from initial investigation through sentencing. Given this focus, the intermediate steps in the processing of homicide cases are relevant in themselves only to the extent that they are reflected in the dependent variable: the division of cases into those that resulted in death sentences and those that did not.
4. *See, e.g.,* Lockhart v. McCree, 106 S.Ct. 1758, 1768–69 (1986), and Smith v. Balkcom, 660 F.2d 573, 580–82 (5th Cir. 1981) (jury may consider doubts about defendant's guilt in penalty deliberations, despite defendant's conviction of a capital offense).
5. Indeed one study, in a noncapital context, found precisely the

opposite: that discrimination by race of victim in the decision to prosecute becomes *more* apparent when the strength of the evidence is held constant. Myers & Hagan, *Private and Public Trouble: Prosecutors and the Allocation of Court Resources,* 26 Soc. PROBS. 439, 447–48 (1979).

6. See *A Study of the California Penalty Jury in First-Degree Murder Cases,* 21 STAN. L. REV. 1326–36 (1969).

7. *See* Kleck, *Racial Discrimination in Criminal Sentencing: A Critical Evaluation of the Evidence with Additional Evidence on the Death Penalty,* 46 AM. SOC. REV. 786–88 (1981).

8. *See* ch. 4, p. 68 and notes 32–37.

9. Bowers & Pierce, *Arbitrariness and Discrimination under Post-Furman Capital Statutes,* 26 CRIME & DELINQ. 590–93 (1980); *see* ch. 2, p. 20 and note 24.

10. *Compare* Bowers & Pierce, *supra* note 9, at 599, table 3, *with* Table 4.5, *supra.*

11. *Id.* at 620–23.

12. *Id.* at 633–34.

13. Zeisel, *Race Bias in the Administration of the Death Penalty: The Florida Experience,* 95 HARV. L. REV. 456, (1981).

14. Radelet, *Racial Characteristics and the Imposition of the Death Penalty,* 46 AM. SOC. REV. 918 (1981).

15. Radelet & Pierce, *Race and Prosecutorial Discretion in Homicide Cases,* 19 LAW & SOC. REV. 587 (1985).

16. Murphy, *Application of the Death Penalty in Cook County,* 73 ILL. B.J. 90 (1984).

17. B. NAKELL & K. HARDY, THE ARBITRARINESS OF THE DEATH PENALTY (1987).

18. Smith, *Patterns of Discrimination in the Assessment of the Death Penalty: The Case of Louisiana,* 15 J. CRIM. JUST. (1987).

19. Henderson & Taylor, *Killers of Dallas Blacks Escape the Death Penalty,* Dallas Times Herald, Nov. 17, 1985, at 1A.

20. *Id.,* at 19A.

21. Baldus, Pulaski, & Woodworth, forthcoming (*see* ch. 1, note 46). Extensive evidence based on this study was presented at an evidentiary hearing in McCleskey v. Zant, 580 F.Supp. 338, 352–79 (N.D. Ga. 1984), *aff'd sub nom.* McCleskey v. Kemp, 753 F.2d 877 (11th Cir. 1985) (en banc), *aff'd,* 107 S.Ct. 1756 (1987).

22. For example, the study reports a logistic regression analysis on the odds of a death sentence in which the independent (or causal) variables are the race of the victim, the race of the defendant, and the felony circumstance of the homicide. The coefficient for the race-of-victim variable in that equation is 1.38, and it is highly statistically significant ($p < .0001$). Baldus study, table 10. The other coefficients in the equation are race of defendant, $B = .25$ ($p = .29$) and felony

circumstance, $B = 2.2$ ($p = .0001$). When a variable for "serious criminal record" is added to the regression analysis, the race-of-victim coefficient remains nearly identical in magnitude (1.35) and highly statistically significant ($p < .0001$). *Id.* at table 21. The other coefficients in that equation are race of defendant, $B = .16$ ($p = .51$); felony circumstance, $B = 2.14$ ($p < .0001$); and serious criminal record, $B = .72$ ($p < .001$).

23. *Id.* at table 22. The independent variables in that model are the race of the victim and of the defendant, the three major aggravating variables that we included (felony circumstance, relationship of defendant to victim, and multiple homicide), a "serious criminal record" variable, and a variable that describes whether the homicide was occasioned by a "family, lover, liquor or barroom quarrel." (This last variable appears to be redundant, to a great extent, with the variable for the relationship between the defendant and the victim.) The race-of-victim coefficient in this equation is .97 ($p = .003$). This coefficient means that, controlling for the other variables in the equation, defendants who were convicted of killing white victims faced twice the odds of receiving a death sentence as those convicted of killing black victims. The magnitude of this effect is smaller than the one we found—*see id.* at table 24; ch. 4, p. 66 and notes 28–31—but that is to be expected: the Baldus study is restricted to cases that resulted in convictions for homicide; as a result it could not detect discrimination in early stages of the processing of homicide cases, and it is subject to the potential problem of sample selection bias. *See* ch. 2, pp. 24–26 and notes 36–44. (The other coefficients in that equation are race of defendant, $B = .09$ ($p = .72$); felony circumstance, $B = 1.7$ ($p = .0001$); serious criminal record, $B = .68$ ($p = .003$); family, lover, liquor, or barroom quarrel, $B = 1.3$ ($p < .0005$); multiple homicide, $B = 1.8$ ($p < .0001$); and victim a stranger, $B = .45$ ($p = .07$).)

24. For example, in a logistic regression model that includes 19 legitimate variables that were found to be strong predictors of death sentencing, the coefficient of the race-of-victim variable increases from .97 in the small model to 1.45, and remains highly statistically significant ($p = .003$). Baldus study, *supra* note 21, at 67–70, table 31B. In another model with 39 legitimate variables, race-of-victim has a coefficient of 1.19 ($p = .01$). *Id.* at 70 n.1. Baldus and his colleagues used other statistical techniques to control for the simultaneous effects of up to 250 separate variables, and all the results support the same conclusion.

25. Berk & Lowery, Sentencing Determinants in Mississippi: A Study of Factors Affecting Penalties for Murder and Manslaughter (September 1984) (unpublished manuscript, Dep't of Sociology, Univ. of California at Santa Barbara) (cited with permission of the authors).

26. *See* ch. 2, pp. 24–26 and notes 36–44.

PART THREE

7 | The Causes of Discrimination in Capital Sentencing

A. Factual Findings

The major factual finding of this study is simple: there has been racial discrimination in the imposition of the death penalty under post-*Furman* statutes in the eight states that we examined. The discrimination is based on the race of the victim, and it is a remarkably stable and consistent phenomenon. Capital sentencing disparities by race of victim were found in each of the eight states, despite their diversity. The legitimate sentencing variables that we considered could not explain these disparities, whether we controlled for these variables one at a time, organized them into a scale of aggravation, or used multiple regression analysis. In two states—Georgia and Florida—we examined the effects of direct review on appeal, and in both cases that process did little or nothing to correct these racial disparities. Our findings are consistent with a large body of previous research, and in two states—Georgia and Mississippi—they parallel the findings of studies that include more detailed information than was available to us. Our conclusion rests on several different sets of data, from different states, analyzed in different forms; this provides "convergent validation" of our hypothesis and makes it particularly unlikely that a fortuitous association or a peculiarity of the research design could have misled us.[1] The data show "a clear pattern, unexplainable on grounds other than race,"[2] or at least unexplainable short of some improbable inanimate conspiracy of numbers.

But while the existence of racial discrimination in capital sentencing is clear, the same cannot be said of its causes. We will discuss this issue briefly.

B. The Psychology of Race-of-Victim Discrimination[3]

The racial disparities that we found could be the result of conscious choices by police, prosecutors, judges, and jurors to discriminate against killers of whites or in favor of killers of blacks. The prevalence of racial prejudice has probably declined over the past three decades, but racism has certainly not disappeared from the United States. Recent surveys indicate that many whites still believe that blacks are lazy (13 percent), ignorant (10 percent), and aggressive (19 percent).[4] Yet it seems unlikely that the observed racial disparities are due entirely to deliberate acts of discrimination by the individual jurors or public officials involved in these cases. The disparities are too great and too widespread to be blamed entirely on racial bigots.

While relatively few people may hold overtly racist attitudes, many show the effects of subtler prejudices. For example, in 1978, 54 percent of the whites questioned in one survey disapproved of marriage between blacks and whites, and in a 1981 survey, 31 percent of white respondents preferred not to have blacks as neighbors.[5] This type of prejudice could have subtle but serious effects on individuals' interpretations of the facts of a legal case, and on their emotional and moral responses to the defendant, the victim, and the crime.

Numerous psychological experiments have established that individuals' attitudes and stereotypes affect their perceptions of others and their interpretations of events.[6] Stereotypes have been found to influence the way in which people allocate their attention,[7] how they interpret what they perceive,[8] whether they remember what they saw,[9] and how they recall the information that they remember.[10] These biases translate into actions. For example, people have been found to be more willing to help strangers who are members of their own race than those who are not,[11] and they are more likely to help people who appear similar to them in other ways.[12] Birt Duncan has demonstrated that whites interpret ambiguous actions performed by blacks to be more violent than identical actions performed by whites.[13] Duncan also found that whites view these supposedly violent actions as indicative of an aggressive disposition when they are performed by blacks, but as mere reflections of situational exigencies when they are performed by whites. Other experimental research suggests that black victims may be seen as stronger and more threatening than equally passive white victims.[14]

These findings suggest that the effects of racial biases ought to be readily apparent throughout the criminal justice system, both in the determination of guilt and in the setting of sentences. One would expect to find two clear patterns: that black defendants are the objects of discrimination, since they are seen as more violent and more aggressive than white defendants, and that those who victimize whites are punished disproportionately harshly, since white victims are viewed as less threatening and less likely to provoke attacks than black victims. But this is not so.

Many experimental and archival studies have indeed found evidence of racial discrimination in the administration of justice.[15] For example, experimental studies of jury decision making have demonstrated that individuals are more lenient toward defendants of the same race, and that the race of the victim can affect the perceived culpability of the defendant[16] and the recommended sentence[17] in noncapital rape cases. However, outside the sphere of capital punishment these findings are inconsistent and uncertain, since there are also many well-controlled studies that have found little or no evidence of racial discrimination in the criminal justice system.[18] This stands in stark contrast to the strong and consistent racial disparities found in our research and in every other major study of the death penalty. Something about capital cases makes them particularly susceptible to racial prejudice, at least with respect to the race of the victim.

Capital cases are not like other criminal proceedings. A human life has been taken and another hangs in the balance. The gravity of the situation weighs heavily on all the participants but particularly on the jurors. The choice confronting a juror in the penalty phase of a capital trial has no parallel in most people's experience. The jurors must decide, probably for the first and last time in their lives, whether another person should live or die. For many jurors this decision will be a source of considerable torment. They cannot rely on experience, and the instructions they receive are inevitably vague. For once, they must answer a question of life or death.

A few jurors would apparently sentence to death any person who is convicted of murder,[19] but for most that judgment requires considerably more. To condemn a man to death, they must be particularly horrified by the crime and perhaps frightened by the defendant. As the jurors review the circumstances of the crime, they will inevitably consider the personal characteristics of the defendant, and the defendant's race might carry some weight; but the jurors may be able to counteract the effect of that characteristic. They know that discrimination against blacks is a major issue in our society, and most jurors (though not all) will probably try to exclude racial considerations from their evaluation of the defendant. They may or may not succeed, but at least they are likely to be aware of the

problem. Furthermore, the defendant—white or black—
is not like them. He belongs to a very different class of
person; he is a murderer. Regardless of his race, the jurors
will probably not see him as similar to themselves, and he
is unlikely to benefit from the favoritism that people show
to similar others.

The race of the victim is a different matter. The victim
is not before the jury, and is not to be judged by them.
In most cases the jurors undoubtedly feel unqualified sympathy for the dead victims and for their survivors, whatever
their race. But that is true in all types of homicides; it
takes more than sympathy for the victim to induce jurors
to condemn a murderer to death. They must feel personally
threatened by the defendant or what he represents, or they
must be horrified by the defendant's acts.

There is, undoubtedly, wide variation among jurors both
in the degree and in the type of horror or fear that will
tip the balance toward death. Particular gruesome facts
will be more terrifying to some than to others. But one
influential process cuts across this uneven range: we are
more readily horrified by a death if we empathize or identify
with the victim, or if we see the victim as similar to ourselves
or to a friend or relative, than if the victim appears to us
as a stranger.[20] In a society that remains segregated socially
if not legally, and in which the great majority of jurors are
white, jurors are not likely to identify with black victims
or to see them as family or friends. Thus jurors are more
likely to be horrified by the killing of a white than of a
black, and more likely to act against the killer of a white
than the killer of a black. This reaction is not an expression
of racial hostility but a natural product of the patterns of
interracial relations in our society. It is simply an emotional
fact.

Jurors who are influenced by the race of the victim are
not likely to be aware of it because the cognitive and
affective processes involved operate, on the whole, outside

consciousness.[21] Moreover, the jurors are not judging the victim, the person whose race is at issue, and they have no way of knowing whether they would have acted differently if this unprecedented decision had come to them with a different racial complexion.

There is also a hint of statistical evidence to support these speculations. In his study of the characteristics of post-*Furman* capital offenders, Riedel compared those who had been sentenced to death under mandatory death penalty statutes with those sentenced under guided discretion statutes.[22] The only difference that merited attention involved the race of the victim: while black-victim homicides were underrepresented on death rows under both types of statutes, they were considerably more rare in states with jury discretion in capital sentencing—5 percent as compared to 16 percent.[23] This difference might be explained by the explicit provision for jury discretion, which gave greater scope for the operation of unconscious biases.

Jurors, of course, are not the only actors in the legal system who determine whether a capital defendant will be sentenced to death. More often than not jurors play no direct role in those decisions because potentially capital cases are weeded out before they come to trial, primarily at the hands of prosecutors. There is no reason to believe that judges and attorneys are immune to the effects of the psychological processes that we have discussed. But even if these professional decision makers are able to counteract some of their own biases, their decisions in a capital case will be influenced by their predictions of the jury's reaction to it. This process is particularly important for prosecutors, since it is part of their official function. Death penalty cases require large allocations of scarce prosecutorial resources, so prosecutors must choose a small number of cases to receive this expensive treatment. In making these choices, prosecutors will try to avoid wasting resources and losing expensive battles that they can sidestep. They may also favor homicides that are visible and disturbing to the majority of the community, and these will tend to be white-victim homicides.[24] This means, as Justice White observed in his concurring opinion in *Gregg v. Georgia,* that "prosecutors will be motivated in their charging decision by . . . the likelihood that a jury would impose the death penalty if it convicts."[25] The operating force in this process is prediction, and its effects are not restricted to legitimate jury behavior. If jurors rely on racial criteria (either consciously or unconsciously), or if prosecutors believe that they do so, the inexorable logic of the adversarial system of adjudicating death sentences will ensure that the criteria "by which [prosecutors] decide whether to charge a capital felony will be the same."[26]

Notes

1. See T. COOK & D. CAMPBELL, QUASI-EXPERIMENTATION: DESIGN AND ANALYSIS FOR FIELD SETTINGS (1979).

2. Village of Arlington Heights v. Metropolitan Hous. Dev. Corp., 429 U.S. 252, 266 (1977).

3. A variety of sociological mechanisms have been offered to explain discrimination in capital sentencing. It has been argued that crimes that cross important social boundaries, in this case racial boundaries, are particularly threatening to the social order and are punished with unusual harshness. Zeisel, *Race Bias in the Administration of the Death Penalty: The Florida Experience,* 95 HARV. L. REV. 456, 467–68 (1981); *cf.* Farrell & Swigert, *Legal Disposition of Inter-group and Intra-group Homicides,* 19 SOC. Q. 565, 571–74 (1978) (discussing the association between social boundary crossing and severity of punishment for homicide). *See generally* E. DURKHEIM, THE DIVISION OF LABOR IN SOCIETY (1933). While this could explain discrimination against blacks who kill whites it does not explain discrimination by the race of victim in general. It has also been argued that our society tends to view blacks as "devalued crime victims," that we simply care less. Kleck, *Racial Discrimination in Capital Sentencing: A Critical Evaluation of the Evidence with Additional Evidence on the Death Penalty,* 46 AM. SOC. REV. 783, 800 (1981); *see also* Bowers & Pierce, *Arbitrariness and Discrimination under Post-Furman Capital Statutes,* 26 CRIME & DELINQ. 563, 573–74 (1980); Zeisel, *supra,* at 467–68. (Myers & Hagan, *Private and Public*

Trouble: Prosecutors and the Allocation of Court Resources, 26 SOC. PROBS. 447 (1979), found a similar bias in the processing of noncapital felonies.) The psychological processes discussed here suggest a reason for black victims being "devalued."

4. Dovidio & Gaertner, *Prejudice, Discrimination, and Racism: Historical Trends and Contemporary Approaches*, in PREJUDICE, DISCRIMINATION, AND RACISM (J. Dovidio & S. Gaertner, eds., 1986).

5. *Id.* at 10.

6. For recent reviews, see Hamilton, *A Cognitive-Attributional Analysis of Stereotyping*, in ADVANCES IN EXPERIMENTAL SOCIAL PSYCHOLOGY 53–85 (L. Berkowitz, ed., 1979); Jones, *Perceiving Other People: Stereotyping as a Process of Social Cognition*, in IN THE EYE OF THE BEHOLDER: CONTEMPORARY ISSUES IN STEREOTYPING 41–91 (A. G. Miller, ed., 1982); Tajfel, *Social Psychology of Intergroup Relations*, 33 ANNUAL REV. PSYCHOLOGY 1–39 (1982).

7. *See, e.g.,* Zadny & Gerard, *Attributed Intentions and Information Selectivity*, 10 J. EXPERIMENTAL SOC. PSYCHOLOGY 34 (1974).

8. *See, e.g.,* Srull & Wyer, *Category Accessibility and Social Perception: Some Implications for the Study of Person Memory and Interpersonal Judgment*, 38 J. PERSONALITY & SOC. PSYCHOLOGY 841 (1980).

9. *See, e.g.,* Rothbart, Evans, & Fulero, *Recall for Confirming Events: Memory Processes and the Maintenance of Social Stereotypes*, 15 J. EXPERIMENTAL SOC. PSYCHOLOGY 343 (1979).

10. *See, e.g.,* Hastie & Kumar, *Person Memory: Personality Traits as Organizing Principles in Memory for Behaviors*, 37 J. PERSONALITY & SOC. PSYCHOLOGY 25 (1979); Rothbart et al., *supra* note 9.

11. Gaertner & Bickman, *Effects of Race on the Elicitation of Helping Behavior: The Wrong Number Technique*, 20 J. PERSONALITY & SOC. PSYCHOLOGY 218 (1971); Gaertner & Dovidio, *The Subtlety of White Racism, Arousal, and Helping Behavior*, 35 J. PERSONALITY & SOC. PSYCHOLOGY 691 (1977); Gaertner, Dovidio, & Johnson, *Race of Victim, Non-Responsive Bystanders, and Helping Behavior*, 117 J. SOC. PSYCHOLOGY 69 (1977).

12. *See, e.g.,* Emswiller, Deaux, & Willits, *Similarity, Sex, and Requests for Small Favors*, 1 J. APPLIED SOC. PSYCHOLOGY 284 (1971).

13. Duncan, *Differential Social Perception and Attribution of Intergroup Violence: Testing the Lower Limits of Stereotyping of Blacks*, 34 J. PERSONALITY & SOC. PSYCHOLOGY 590 (1976).

14. Sagar & Schofield, *Racial and Behavioral Cues in Black and White Children's Perceptions of Ambiguously Aggressive Acts*, 39 J. PERSONALITY & SOC. PSYCHOLOGY 590 (1980).

15. *See, e.g.,* J. PETERSILIA, RACIAL DISPARITIES IN THE CRIMINAL JUSTICE SYSTEM (1983).

16. Ugwuegbu, *Racial and Evidential Factors in Juror Attribution of Legal Responsibility*, 15 J. EXPERIMENTAL SOC. PSYCHOLOGY 133 (1979).

17. Field, *Rape Trials and Jurors' Decisions*, 3 LAW & HUM. BEHAV. 261 (1979).

18. For reviews, see A. BLUMSTEIN, J. COHEN, S. MARTIN, & M. TONRY, eds., RESEARCH ON SENTENCING: THE SEARCH FOR REFORM (1983); Nickerson, Mayo, & Smith, *Racism in the Courtroom*, in Dovidio & Gaertner, eds., *supra* note 4.

19. See Kadane, *Juries Hearing Death Penalty Cases: Statistical Analysis of a Legal Procedure*, 78 J. AM. STAT. A. 544, 549–50 (1983).

20. A familiar example of this phenomenon is reflected regularly in the newspapers. American headlines describing disasters commonly have the following form: "Two Hundred Die in Japanese Air Crash; 10 Americans Among the Dead." The reason for this wording, of course, is that the readers are expected to identify more strongly with the dead Americans than with the remaining majority of the victims.

21. Cf. Wilder, *Social Categorization: Implications for Creation and Reduction of Intergroup Bias*, in Berkowitz, ed., *supra* note 6, at 293–356. See generally R. NISBETT & L. ROSS, HUMAN INFERENCE: STRATEGIES AND SHORTCOMINGS OF SOCIAL JUDGMENT (1980) (discussing the unconscious nature of many of the processes involved in human decision making).

22. Riedel, *Discrimination in the Imposition of the Death Penalty: A Comparison of the Characteristics of Offenders Sentenced Pre-Furman and Post-Furman*, 49 TEMP. L.Q. 282, 284–87 (1976).

23. *Id.* at 282, 285 table 7. Riedel notes that in the period he studied a majority of all homicides in America involved black victims. *Id.* at 282.

24. Radelet & Pierce, *Race and Prosecutorial Discretion in Homicide Cases*, 19 LAW & SOC. REV. 587, 615–19 (1985). Moreover, as Zeisel has pointed out, *supra* note 3, at 467, the black community is not only less numerous and less powerful but also less disposed to favor capital punishment than the white community, and this might reduce the pressure on prosecutors to seek death sentences for black-victim homicides. See Smith, *A Trend Analysis of Attitudes Toward Capital Punishment, 1936–74*, in STUDIES OF SOCIAL CHANGE SINCE 1948, at 2: 255, 266–71 (J. Davis, ed., 1976).

25. 428 U.S. 153, 225 (1976) (White, J., concurring).

26. *Id.* This process of anticipatory discrimination by prosecutors could mask the appearance of racial discrimination in the juries' subsequent penalty decisions. See ch. 2, pp. 24–26 and notes 36–44 (discussing the problem of "sample selection bias").

8 | The Legal Context

The constitutional status of racial discrimination in capital punishment is now governed by the Supreme Court's opinion in *McCleskey v. Kemp*.[1] But *McCleskey* has not ended the political and moral debate on this issue, and it has certainly not solved the problem. It does not even provide a satisfactory legal analysis. Therefore, before discussing the *McCleskey* case, it is useful to review the legal context in which it was decided.

A. The Constitutional Claims

At the beginning of this book we said that racial discrimination in the use of the death penalty is constitutionally prohibited, and, as a general statement, that is beyond dispute. General statements, however, rarely answer all questions, and there are at least three here that are not fully resolved: What types of racial discrimination does this prohibition encompass? What sort of evidence is required to prove such discrimination? And what is the remedy for a proven pattern of discrimination? As we have seen, the answers to these questions turn on the interpretation of two constitutional rules: the Fourteenth Amendment prohibition of intentional racial discrimination, and the

Eighth Amendment prohibition of arbitrary capital sentencing.

A long line of cases holds that the equal protection clause prohibits discrimination in criminal sentencing by the race of the defendant,[2] but prior to *McCleskey* no cases discussed the implications of this rule for discrimination by the race of the victim.[3] The language of the Fourteenth Amendment itself, prohibiting the denial of "equal protection of the law," speaks, if anything, more clearly of victims than of defendants. The sponsors of the Fourteenth Amendment unquestionably intended this language to prohibit unequal punishments for defendants of different races—indeed, one of their major aims was to "constitutionalize" the provisions of the Civil Rights Act of 1866,[4] including the requirement that in every state "inhabitants of every race and color, without regard to any previous condition of slavery or involuntary servitude . . . shall be subject to like punishment, pains and penalties, and no other"[5]—but they were concerned about protecting black victims as well.

A primary purpose of the equal protection clause was to undo the Black Codes. These codes were enacted in southern states after the Civil War in an effort to preserve white supremacy,[6] and they provided not only different punishments for black and white defendants, but also, in some instances, more drastic punishments for crimes when the victims were white.[7] The Joint Committee on Reconstruction, which drafted both the Fourteenth Amendment and the Civil Rights Act of 1866, heard a great deal of testimony that in the period immediately following the Civil War southern state authorities frequently declined to prosecute crimes committed against blacks, or punished those who committed such crimes with undue leniency.[8] In the congressional debates on the Fourteenth Amendment several speakers described this problem as one of the evils that the amendment would cure.[9] Five years later, in the congressional debates over the proposed "Ku Klux Klan

Act" of 1871,[10] senators and representatives alike stated repeatedly that state authorities were violating the Fourteenth Amendment guarantee of equal protection when they refused to enforce their criminal laws to protect black citizens and their white allies.[11] As the Supreme Court recently observed, "[i]t is clear from the legislative debates that, in view of the [1871] Act's sponsors, the victims of Klan outrages were deprived of 'equal protection of the laws' if the perpetrators systematically went unpunished."[12]

It is clear, then, that the type of discrimination at issue here—disproportionately lenient treatment of criminals who victimize blacks—is not a new phenomenon. The Congress that passed the Fourteenth Amendment was aware of this type of discrimination, condemned it, and attempted to prevent this and other forms of racial discrimination by enacting the amendment and by passing statutes to enforce its provisions.[13] But the equal protection clause is now thought to bear—lightly or heavily—on almost any distinction made by a state government, whether or not it was discussed by the 39th Congress in 1866. The real question was never *whether* a claim of discrimination by race of victim would be considered under the equal protection clause, but rather *how* the courts would evaluate it. History suggested that this type of distinction should be carefully scrutinized, but since (prior to *McCleskey*) the courts had not actually discussed this question, the answer was not apparent.

The major difficulty in applying the equal protection clause to discrimination in the imposition of death sentences is not the scope of the prohibition of racial discrimination but the problem of proof of intent. As we have noted, a litigant who alleges discrimination in violation of the Fourteenth Amendment must prove that the discrimination was "intentional" or "purposeful."[14] When a racial classification is explicit, the task is easy. If a state enacted a statute that explicitly permitted juries to consider the race of the victim in sentencing murderers, or if a prosecutor had a stated policy of seeking life sentences only for the rape of white women, no court would hesitate to find that the guarantee of equal protection was violated;[15] indeed, the result would be the same, and equally automatic, if the court faced a statute that made it a capital crime to murder people who are right-handed but not those who are left-handed.[16] But the task here is not so simple. Since racial discrimination in the imposition of capital punishment is not now an explicit or stated policy in any state, intent must be inferred from patterns of actions. If the special constitutional sensitivity to racial discrimination were to make any difference, it would be through its effect on the standard that the courts use to judge the question of intent.

The meaning of "intent" in this context is problematic. Most likely, the discrimination that we found is, on the whole, unconsciously motivated. Unconscious discrimination can be "intentional" for Fourteenth Amendment purposes; the legal concept of "intent" is not synonymous with "design" or "purpose," at least not as these terms are commonly used.[17] Nor are the decisions at issue immune from a finding of discriminatory intent because they are produced by the joint actions of numerous individuals, many of whom never made more than a single choice. But the concept of intent does become increasingly abstract and rarefied under these circumstances, and that enables the courts to mold the requirements of proof of intent to fit policies that are based on other considerations.

But why should litigants have to face this problem at all? In *Furman*, as we know, the Supreme Court held that the cruel and unusual punishment clause of the Eighth Amendment prohibits arbitrariness in capital sentencing.[18] At first glance, one might have supposed that the availability of this rule would have eliminated the need for equal protection claims in this context, for several reasons: the rule in *Furman* is much more specific than the Fourteenth

Amendment; any racial effects on capital sentencing are necessarily "arbitrary"; and the "arbitrary" effects of race on sentencing ought to be easier to prove than a pattern of intentional discrimination. But *Furman* has not preempted the Fourteenth Amendment. It has long been apparent that the prohibition against arbitrariness in capital sentencing is uncommonly subject to the vagaries of judicial reinterpretation. Precisely because this rule is so specific and has so few implications for any context other than capital sentencing, it can be said to mean anything, or nothing at all. The equal protection clause, by contrast, is one of the central provisions of the Constitution. It must be applied to discrimination in capital sentencing in a manner that is at least reasonably consistent with its application in analogous contexts (or so one would have thought).

B. Litigation on Pre-*Furman* Discrimination

The earliest attacks on racial discrimination in the use of the death penalty focused on rape cases. This is not surprising, since capital punishment for rape—when it was still available[19]—was one of the most visible examples of racism in the American system of criminal justice. From the 1880s on, almost all executions for rape in this country took place in the South, and the overwhelming majority of those executed—85 percent—were black.[20] The most important of these early legal challenges was a federal habeas corpus petition by William Maxwell, a black man sentenced to death for the rape of a white woman in Arkansas, who claimed that his sentence violated the equal protection clause of the Fourteenth Amendment.[21] Maxwell based his claim on a major study by Marvin Wolfgang, a noted criminologist, who collected detailed information on 3000 rape convictions in selected counties of eleven southern states from 1945 through 1965.[22] Wolfgang found that black men who were convicted of rape were seven times more likely to be sentenced to death than white men, and that black men who were convicted of raping white women were eighteen times more likely to be sentenced to death than men convicted of rape in any other racial combination.[23] Wolfgang also examined a host of other variables that might bear on sentencing, and found that the only one that was strongly related to capital sentencing—the commission of a contemporaneous felony—did not explain or mitigate these racial patterns. In short, the *Maxwell* case included uncommonly persuasive evidence of a systematic pattern of racial discrimination.

Despite this evidence, Maxwell's claim was rejected both by the district court that heard it and by the Eighth Circuit on appeal. The reasons given for this rejection have set the pattern for similar rejections in many cases since: First, the data are too broad, since few of the rape cases examined came from the county in which Maxwell was convicted.[24] Second, the data are too shallow, since "[t]hey admittedly do not take every variable into account."[25] Third, the social scientific evidence is faulty because it does not demonstrate that Maxwell's own sentence was the product of any specific acts of discrimination by the jury that imposed it.[26] The Supreme Court declined to review the claim of discrimination in *Maxwell,* although it did grant certiorari and vacate the judgment on other grounds.[27] Several years later, in *Coker v. Georgia,*[28] the Court held that the use of the death penalty for rape violates the Eighth Amendment because it is "excessive"; one of the more conspicuous things about the *Coker* opinion is the absence of any reference to race.

The most important case that examines racial discrimination in capital sentencing prior to *Furman* is *Furman* itself. The issue in *Furman,* of course, was the meaning of the Eighth Amendment prohibition of cruel and unusual punishments, but the claim of racial discrimination was a central part of the argument that capital punishment violated the Eighth Amendment, and it is discussed in three of the opinions of the *Furman* majority: Justice Douglas cites evidence that poor people and blacks are more likely than others to be sentenced to death, and concludes that the capital sentencing statutes before the Court are unconstitutional because "[t]hey are pregnant with discrimination."[29] Justice Marshall discusses similar evidence to support his contention that this punishment is unconstitutional because it is abhorrent to the values of the American public.[30] And Justice Stewart, while stating that "racial discrimination has not been proved," agrees that Douglas and Marshall "have demonstrated that, if any basis can be discerned for the selection of these few to be sentenced to die, it is the constitutionally impermissible basis of race."[31] Equally important, in view of later developments, two of the dissenters mention the issue of racial discrimination. Chief Justice Burger and Justice Powell, in separate opinions for the four dissenting justices, both acknowledge the historical evidence of discrimination against blacks, especially for intraracial rapes in the South, and both argue that this issue ought to be presented as an equal protection claim rather than as an Eighth Amendment claim.[32] Indeed, both Burger and Powell point to *Maxwell* as a model for equal protection litigation on the issue—an ambiguous citation, since both also approve the lower courts' rejection of the evidence of discrimination in that case.

C. Early Post-*Furman* Cases

The earliest post-*Furman* case on discrimination in capital sentencing was *Spinkellink v. Wainwright*.[33] In *Spinkellink*, the petitioner raised both an Eighth Amendment and an equal protection claim on the basis of evidence that murderers convicted of killing white victims in Florida were more likely to be sentenced to death than those convicted of killing blacks.[34] The former Fifth Circuit dealt with these two claims separately. First, it refused even to consider the cruel and unusual punishment claim, despite its recognition that the Eighth Amendment concept of arbitrariness that was developed in *Furman* includes racial discrimination as an element,[35] and that *Furman* prohibited discrimination by the race of the victim as well as discrimination by the race of the defendant.[36] The court justified its refusal by interpreting the Supreme Court's 1976 death penalty decisions as not merely affirming the facial validity of the statutes before the Court, but also "as holding that if a state follows a properly drawn statute in imposing the death penalty, then the arbitrariness and capriciousness—and therefore the racial discrimination—condemned in *Furman* have been conclusively removed."[37] The Supreme Court itself has not treated the state death penalty statutes that it upheld in 1976 with that degree of respect.[38]

On the other hand, the circuit court did entertain Spinkellink's equal protection claim, but rejected it on the merits because the evidence "could not prove discriminatory intent or purpose."[39] The *Spinkellink* opinion emphasizes the lack of any direct evidence that a discriminatory motive or purpose resulted in the petitioner's sentence, but it does not clarify whether, and how, Spinkellink might have proved his case in the absence of such direct evidence.[40] Later Eleventh Circuit cases clarify the point somewhat: apparently, under *Spinkellink* discriminatory intent can sometimes be inferred from statistical evidence of racial disparities, but "[o]nly if the evidence of disparate impact is so strong that the only permissible inference is one of intentional discrimination."[41] Evidence of the type offered by Spinkellink is insufficient for that purpose—indeed, insufficient to require a hearing or even a response[42]— because it "leaves untouched countless racially neutral variables."[43]

In sum, *Spinkellink* and the Eleventh Circuit cases following it revived two of the three themes that originated in *Maxwell:* evidence of discrimination in capital sentencing can be ignored if it does not (1) directly demonstrate racial animus in a particular case, or (2) include information on every possible variable. Two other federal courts took an even dimmer view of the possibility of proving discrimination in capital sentencing, resurrecting the third negative theme from *Maxwell:* Evidence of discrimination can be disregarded if it is derived from cases that differ from the one at issue in their location or their facts. In *Shaw v. Martin*[44] in 1984 the petitioner argued, on the basis of Dr. Paternoster's findings,[45] that South Carolina prosecutors violated the equal protection clause by seeking the death penalty more often for white-victim homicides than for black-victim homicides. The Fourth Circuit held that this evidence was insufficient to warrant an evidentiary hearing because, among other reasons, "it did not adequately compare murders of similar atrocity . . . incidents where, for example, black and white young women of tender years have been kidnapped, raped, murdered, and mutilated and the prosecutor has prosecuted only the murderer of the white girl."[46] Needless to say, it is unlikely that any evidence could ever satisfy this requirement. In the same year, in *Prejean v. Blackburn*[47] the Fifth Circuit held that to prove discrimination the petitioner would have to tailor his or her evidence precisely to the facts of the case, and show "that for murders of peace officers engaged in their lawful duties, juries in these two districts of Louisiana recommend death sentences only, or more often, against blacks, young or old, whose victims were white than for non-white victims."[48] This requirement, by no coincidence, made the task impossible. At the time of the *Prejean* decision there had been only three other first-degree murder convictions in those two districts under Louisiana's current death penalty statute; all three involved killings by family members, none of the victims was a police officer, and none of the three resulted in a death sentence.[49]

Notes

1. 107 S.Ct. 1756 (1987).
2. *See* ch. 1, note 40.
3. One reported case, Britton v. Rogers, 631 F.2d 572 (8th Cir. 1980), *cert. denied,* 451 U.S. 939 (1981), discussed a related issue. In *Britton* a prisoner argued that his life sentence for raping a white woman in Arkansas violated the equal protection clause because rapes of black women were less harshly punished. The Eighth Circuit avoided the issue by holding that the aggrieved defendant had no "standing" to raise the issue and that only the black women of Arkansas could do so, if anyone. *Id.* at 577 n.3. Since under present constitutional doctrine the victims of crimes that go unprosecuted do not generally have standing to complain about the lack of prosecution, Linda R.S. v. Richard D., 410 U.S. 614, 619 (1973), the Eighth Circuit holding effectively immunizes discrimination by race of victim from constitutional attack. This is an unsatisfactory answer to the claim in *Britton,* if it is an answer at all.

"Standing" means different things in different legal contexts. One universal requirement, however, is that the claimant have a serious interest in the claim. *See* Baker v. Carr, 369 U.S. 186, 204 (1962). Since Baker v. Carr the Supreme Court may have increased the quantum of interest that the claimant must have, *see* Warth v. Sellin, 422 U.S. 490, 498–99 (1975); *see* Chayes, *Foreword: Public Law Litigation and the Burger Court,* 96 HARV. L. REV. 4, 8–26 (1982), but under any standard it would be incredible to suggest that a prisoner facing a sentence of life imprisonment or death does not have a sufficient "personal stake" in the outcome of litigation concerning the constitutionality of the sentence.

Interest in the outcome of the proceeding, however, is not always sufficient to confer standing. A defendant who challenges a search and seizure, for example, must also show that he or she was a "victim" of the search at the time it was conducted—that it was directed against the defendant or against property that he or she owned or possessed. *See, e.g.,* Combs v. U.S., 408 U.S. 224, 226–27 (1972); *see also* Amsterdam, *Perspectives on the Fourth Amendment,* 58 MINN. L. REV. 349, 360–61 (1974). Similarly a defendant must be a member of a group that was excluded from a grand jury that indicted him or her to establish a violation of equal protection based on this exclusion. *See, e.g.,* Castaneda v. Partida, 430 U.S. 482, 494 (1977). This is a "prudential" limitation on the raising of constitutional claims: The litigant "must ordinarily assert his own legal interests rather than those of third parties." Chayes, *supra,* at 23 (footnote omitted). But this limitation does not apply here either. Discrimination in the selection of a jury panel has no inevitable connection to a particular defendant who may later try to rely on it for some form of legal relief; neither does police misconduct in a search directed at another person. In contrast, discrimination of any type in capital sentencing affects those who are sentenced to death directly, and at the time that it originally occurs.

One could argue that while a defendant has standing to complain that his sentence was affected by discrimination based on the race of his victim, he cannot rely on the extraordinary restrictions that the equal protection clause imposes on racial classifications, *see* note 15 *infra,* because the classification at issue is based on someone else's race. Thus, in Arlington Heights v. Metropolitan Hous. Corp., 429 U.S. 252, 263 (1977), the Supreme Court found that a plaintiff could not assert a claim of racial discrimination in zoning decisions since "as a corporation, it has no racial identity," but could assert its own constitutional rights with respect to the same conduct, namely, the "right to be free of arbitrary or irrational zoning actions." The same could be said here. While a defendant sentenced for killing a white victim may have no standing to argue the equal protection rights of black victims, he should have standing to argue the right not to be sentenced on the basis of arbitrary or impermissible racial considerations. This restriction, however, affects only the *nature* of the defendant's equal protection claim, it does not eliminate the claim altogether. It requires the court to consider the substantive requirements of equal protection in this context. *See* pp. 120–21 and notes 14–17 *infra.*

In any event, the Eighth Circuit's holding in *Britton* has not fared well in other courts. Prior to *Britton,* the former Fifth Circuit reached the opposite conclusion in Spinkellink v. Wainwright, 578 F.2d 582 (5th Cir. 1978), *see* pp. 124–26, and since then this argument has been rejected in the *McCleskey* case by the district court, 580 F.Supp. at 346–47, by the circuit court, 753 F.2d 877, and by the Supreme Court, 107 S.Ct. at 1776 n.8.

4. Ch. 31, 14 Stat. 27 (1866).

5. *Id.; see* Bickel, *The Original Understanding and the Segregation Decision,* 69 HARV. L. REV. 1, 56–58 (1956).

6. *See* Bickel, *supra* note 5, at 13 n.34; Fairman, *Does the Fourteenth Amendment Incorporate the Bill of Rights? The Original Understanding,* 2 STAN. L. REV. 5, 21–22 (1949).

7. *See, e.g.,* ch. 40, §§ 11–12, 1865–1866 N.C. PUB. LAWS. *See generally* W. FLEMING, A DOCUMENTARY HISTORY OF RECONSTRUCTION (1905).

8. *See, e.g.,* H.R. REP. No. 30, 39th Cong., 1st Sess. 25 (1866) (testimony of George Tucker, commonwealth attorney) (The southern people "have not any idea of prosecuting white men for offenses against colored people; they do not appreciate the idea."); *id.* at 141 (testimony of

Brevet Maj. Gen. Wager Swayne) ("I have not known, after six months' residence at the capital of the State, a single instance of a white man being convicted and hung or sent to the penitentiary for crime against a negro, while many cases of crime warranting such punishment have been reported to me."). For a discussion of the role of the Joint Committee on Reconstruction, see Fairman, *supra* note 6, at 19–21, 24–25, 41–42.

9. *See, e.g.*, CONG. GLOBE, 39th Cong., 1st Sess. 2459 (1866) (remarks of Rep. Stevens).

10. Ch. 22, 17 Stat. 13.

11. *See, e.g.*, CONG. GLOBE, 42d Cong., 1st Sess. 697 (1871) (remarks of Sen. Edmunds, Senate sponsor of the bill); *id.*, app. 116 (remarks of Rep. Shellabarger, House sponsor of the bill). Some members of Congress read the Fourteenth Amendment restrictively to apply only to discrimination by state statutes. *See, e.g., id.*, app. 117–18 (remarks of Sen. Blair), 259 (remarks of Rep. Holman). The majority of Congress, however, rejected this restrictive interpretation and recognized that the Fourteenth Amendment applied to unequal protection of particular classes in the administration of the law. *See, e.g., id.* at 505–6 (remarks of Sen. Pool), app. 153 (remarks of Rep. Garfield), app. 300 (remarks of Rep. Stevenson), app. 315 (remarks of Rep. Burchard).

12. Briscoe v. LaHue, 460 U.S. 325, 338 (1983). Discrimination by the race of the victim was not restricted to the Reconstruction era. It remained a conspicuous part of the American criminal justice system, especially in the South, through at least the first half of this century. G. MYRDAL, AN AMERICAN DILEMMA: THE NEGRO PROBLEM AND MODERN DEMOCRACY 547–57 (1944).

13. *But see* R. BERGER, DEATH PENALTIES: THE SUPREME COURT'S OBSTACLE COURSE (1982). Berger argues that the framers of the Fourteenth Amendment merely sought to insure fair trials for black defendants, and that they could not have meant to prohibit any type of racial discrimination in sentencing. "[T]o assume that they also meant to save an undoubtedly guilty black murderer from the death penalty because a jury had sentenced a white to life imprisonment is to ignore the racism that ran deep in the North in 1866." *Id.* at 57 (footnote omitted). From this Berger concludes that the equal protection clause does not prohibit racial discrimination in capital sentencing.

Berger's reading of history is inexplicable. He recognizes, indeed argues, that the Fourteenth Amendment was seen as incorporating the goals of the Civil Rights Act of 1866, *id.* at 198, but he apparently fails to notice that the 1866 act specifically prohibited racial discrimination in the severity of punishments. *See* p. 119. Moreover, Berger's conclusion does not follow even from this incorrect reading of history. A much stronger argument can be made that the framers of the Fourteenth Amendment did not intend to prohibit segregation; Berger makes the argument himself. *Id.* at 197–200; *see also* Bickel, *supra* note 5. Does this mean that segregation does not violate the equal protection clause? It is not clear exactly how far Berger is willing to pursue this logic. Apparently he does not think that school segregation should be restored, but does believe that Brown v. Board of Educ., 347 U.S. 483 (1954), was wrong when decided. R. BERGER, *supra,* at 82 n.29. In any event, Berger's position does not reflect the major trends in current constitutional wisdom. *See generally* J. ELY, DEMOCRACY AND DISTRUST: A THEORY OF JUDICIAL REVIEW 1–41 (1980).

14. *See* ch. 1, pp. 8–9 and notes 40–42.

15. An explicit racial classification would be subject to "strict scrutiny," that is, it would not be upheld unless it was "shown to be *necessary* to promote a *compelling* governmental interest." Shapiro v. Thompson, 394 U.S. 618, 634 (1969) (emphasis added). In practice, strict scrutiny is almost uniformly fatal to a classification. *See. e.g.,* McLaughlin v. Florida, 379 U.S. 184, 192 (1964) (declaring unconstitutional a statute prohibiting cohabitation between people of different races) ("We deal here with a racial classification in a criminal context. . . . Our inquiry, therefore, is whether there [is] . . . some *overriding* purpose *requiring* the [racial classification]. . . .") (emphasis added); *id.* at 198 (Stewart, J., concurring) (racial classifications in criminal statutes are unconstitutional per se); Loving v. Virginia, 388 U.S. 1 (1967) (criminal anti-miscegenation statute violates equal protection); *id.* at 13 (Stewart J., concurring) (racial classification in criminal statute inevitably unconstitutional). *See* Gunther, *Foreword: In Search of Evolving Doctrine on a Changing Court: A Model for a Newer Equal Protection,* 86 HARV. L. REV. 1, 8 (1972).

16. This nonracial classification would not be subject to "strict scrutiny," *see* note 15 *supra,* but it would still have to bear a *rational relationship* to a *legitimate* state interest. *See, e.g.,* Schweiker v. Wilson, 450 U.S. 221 (1981); Railway Express Agency v. New York, 336 U.S. 106 (1949). The preference for right-handed people would fail even this fairly generous test. From the point of view of a condemned defendant, the problem is much the same under either type of classification; it is not that blacks (or left-handed people) fail to receive the same protection from the criminal system as the rest of the population, but that the defendant has been sentenced to death because of a factor that is (at best) completely arbitrary and irrational.

17. *See, e.g.,* Alexander v. Louisiana, 405 U.S. 625, 632 (1972) ("The result bespeaks discrimination, whether or not it was a conscious decision on the part of any individual jury commissioner") (quoting Hernandez

v. Texas, 347 U.S. 475, 482 (1954)); *see also* Brest, *Foreword: In Defense of the Antidiscrimination Principle,* 90 HARV. L. REV. 1, 7–8, 14 (1976).

18. *See* ch. 1, pp. 5–6.

19. *See* p. 123 and note 28, *infra.*

20. W. BOWERS, LEGAL HOMICIDE: DEATH AS PUNISHMENT IN AMERICA, 1864–1982, at 57–58 (1984).

21. Maxwell v. Bishop, 257 F.Supp. 710 (E.D. Ark. 1966), *aff'd,* 398 F.2d 138 (8th Cir. 1968), *vacated and remanded on other grounds,* 398 U.S. 262 (1970).

22. Wolfgang & Riedel, *Race, Judicial Discretion, and the Death Penalty,* 407 ANNALS 119 (1973) [hereinafter cited as Wolfgang & Riedel, *Race*]; *see also* Wolfgang & Riedel, *Rape, Race, and the Death Penalty in Georgia,* 45 AM. J. ORTHOPSYCHIATRY 658 (1975).

23. *See* Wolfgang & Riedel, *Race, supra* note 22, at 122.

24. *Maxwell,* 398 F.2d at 146.

25. *Id.* at 147.

26. *Id.*

27. 398 U.S. 262 (1970).

28. 433 U.S. 584 (1977).

29. 408 U.S. at 257 (Douglas, J., concurring).

30. *Id.* at 363–66, 369 (Marshall, J., concurring).

31. *Id.* at 310 (Stewart, J., concurring).

32. *Id.* at 389 n.12 (Burger, C.J., dissenting); *id.* at 448–50 (Powell, J., dissenting).

33. 578 F.2d 582 (5th Cir. 1978), *cert. denied,* 440 U.S. 976 (1979).

34. Apparently, this was the same type of data later published by Bowers annd Pierce. Bowers & Pierce, *Arbitrariness and Discrimination under Post-Furman Capital Statutes,* 26 CRIME & DELINQ. 563 (1980).

35. 578 F.2d at 613 n.38.

36. *Id.* at 613, 614 n.40.

37. *Id.* at 613–14 (footnotes omitted). The Florida death penalty law under which Spinkellink was sentenced had been upheld in Proffitt v. Florida, 428 U.S. 242 (1976), and was therefore "a properly drawn statute." The *Spinkellink* court recognized a narrow exception to this rule: it would consider claims of arbitrariness if a defendant could point to "some specific act or acts [of] . . . racial discrimination" directed at him or her individually, 578 F.2d at 614 n.40, or show that the death sentence was "patently unjust and would shock the conscience." *Id.* at 606 n.28; *see also* Mitchell v. Hopper, 538 F.Supp. 77, 90 (S.D. Ga. 1982) (applying *Spinkellink*), *vacated sub nom.* Spencer v. Zant, 715 F.2d 1562 (11th Cir. 1983), *order aff'd in part sub nom.* Mitchell v. Kemp, 762 F.2d 886 (11th Cir. 1985); McCorquodale v. Balkcom, 525

F. Supp. 431, 434–35 (N.D. Ga. 1981), *rev'd on other grounds*, 705 F.2d 1553 (11th Cir. 1983), *opn. vacated and aff'd on rh'g.*, 721 F.2d 1493 (11th Cir. 1983) (*en banc*) (same).

38. *See, e.g.*, Godfrey v. Georgia, 446 U.S. 420 (1980), in which the Supreme Court, contrary to the Fifth Circuit's assumption in *Spinkellink*, showed no reluctance to examine Georgia's actual practice under a facially valid capital sentencing statute and to condemn it for arbitrariness.

39. *Spinkellink*, 578 F.2d at 616.

40. Spinkellink offered evidence that "although the estimated number of black felony murder victims and white felony murder victims for 1973–1976 is the same, 92 percent of the inmates on Florida death row had murdered white victims, while only 8 percent had murdered black victims." *Id.* at 612. The court responded variously that (a) no hearing was required on this allegation, *id.* at 590, 616 n.41; (b) Spinkellink had not presented a prima facie case of discrimination, *id.* at 615; and (c) the state had adequately rebutted the evidence of racial disparities by showing "that murders involving black victims generally have been qualitatively different from murders involving white victims," *id.* at 615. This last point was based, apparently, not on any evidence but on an argument by the state that homicides of black victims tended to fall into the category of "family quarrels, lovers' quarrels, liquor quarrels, [and] barroom quarrels," *id.* at 612 n.37; it overlooks the fact that the comparison at issue—between black-victim and white-victim *felony* homicides—already excluded all killings occasioned by quarrels.

41. Adams v. Wainwright, 709 F.2d 1443, 1449 (11th Cir. 1983), *cert. denied*, 104 S.Ct. 745 (1984).

42. Smith v. Balkcom, 671 F.2d 858, 860 (5th Cir. 1982) (modifying 660 F.2d 573 (1981)), *cert. denied*, 459 U.S. 882 (1982). (*Smith* was decided by Unit B of the former Fifth Circuit, the immediate predecessor of the present Eleventh Circuit.)

43. *Id.* at 859 (footnote omitted).

44. 733 F.2d 304 (4th Cir.), *cert. denied*, 105 S.Ct. 230 (1984).

45. *See* ch. 2, p. 22 and note 33.

46. *Shaw*, 733 F.2d at 312 (footnote omitted).

47. 743 F.2d 1091 (5th Cir. 1984).

48. *Id.* at 1102.

49. *Id.* at 1099 n.9. In 1985, after the Eleventh Circuit decision in *McCleskey*, the Fifth Circuit modified this portion of its opinion in *Prejean* and, citing *McCleskey*, substituted a more abstract reason for affirming the district court's denial of an evidentiary hearing: the petitioner's proffer of evidence did not account for "numerous racially neutral variables," and "did not set forth the specific methodology used and its bottom-line results. . . ." 756 F.2d 482, 486–87 (5th Cir. 1985).

In addition to the cases cited in the text, unpublished drafts of the study reported in this book were presented in court several times in support of petitions for stays of execution by death-sentenced prisoners in Florida in 1983 and 1984. They were not well received. *See, e.g,* Ford v. Wainwright, 734 F.2d 538 (11th Cir.), *application to vacate stay denied,* 104 S.Ct. 3498 (1984); Adams v. Wainwright, 734 F.2d 511 (11th Cir.), *application to vacate stay granted,* 104 S.Ct. 2183 (1984); Sullivan v. Wainwright, 721 F.2d 316 (11th Cir.), *petition for stay of execution denied,* 104 S.Ct. 450 (1983). None of these opinions discusses the merits of the study. In *Sullivan* the court concluded that the statistical evidence before it, including our study, was insufficient to prove discrimination in the imposition of the death penalty in Florida, or to warrant a stay. (There is no direct reference to our study in *Sullivan,* but it is mentioned in *Ford,* 734 F.2d at 541, and *id.* at 543 (Henderson, J., dissenting), which describes the *Sullivan* record.) In *Adams,* on the other hand, a panel of the same court found our study sufficient to warrant a stay pending the disposition of Spencer v. Zant, 715 F.2d 1562 (11th Cir. 1983), *vacated for rehearing en banc,* 729 F.2d 1293 (11th Cir. 1984), in which the issue of the right to an evidentiary hearing on a claim of discrimination in the use of the death penalty was pending before the entire court en banc. The panel distinguished *Sullivan* on the ground that the decision to deny a stay in that case preceded both the Eleventh Circuit's vote to rehear *Spencer* en banc, and the Supreme Court's decision to grant a stay of execution on similar grounds in a Georgia case. *Adams,* 734 F.2d at 513 n.2 (citing Stephens v. Kemp, 104 S.Ct. 562 [1983]). The Supreme Court, however, vacated the stay in *Adams* without comment. 104 S.Ct. 2183 (1984). In *Ford,* a panel of the Eleventh Circuit once again granted a stay to permit consideration of two independent claims: a claim of racial discrimination based on this study, and a claim that Ford could not be executed because he was presently insane. The Supreme Court denied an application to vacate the stay in *Ford,* 104 S.Ct. 3498 (1984), but this denial appears to have been based exclusively on the present-insanity claim. Three justices (Chief Justice Burger and Justices Rehnquist and O'Connor) voted to vacate the stay, while Justice Powell, writing for himself and Justices White and Blackmun, concurred in the denial of the application to vacate but stated that "the statistical evidence relied upon by Ford to support his claim of discrimination [is] not sufficient to raise a substantial ground upon which relief might be granted." *Id.* at 3499. The Eleventh Circuit apparently accepted this as a holding on the merits of the study, at least for the purposes of applications for stays of execution from the state of Florida. Washington v. Wainwright, 737 F.2d 922, 923 (11th Cir. 1984). (For a discussion of the Eleventh Circuit's interpretation of these stay opinions in its *McCleskey* opinion, see ch. 9, pp. 148–49 and notes 74–79.

9 | The McCleskey Case, I: The Lower Courts

A. Background

Proof of discrimination in capital sentencing depends on studies that are far beyond the means of any capital defendant. As a consequence, defendants who have raised this issue have had to rely on whatever research happened to be available at the time they presented their claims. The earliest post-*Furman* cases—*Spinkellink* in 1978 and *Smith* in 1980[1]—were based on the studies that could be most readily completed, in particular the work of Bowers and Pierce.[2] As we have noted, the courts rejected this evidence as insufficient, but in *Smith* the Eleventh Circuit specified what was missing: the studies left "untouched countless racially neutral variables"—namely, variables that describe the charging of the reported homicides, the disposition of those charges at trial, and the presence of aggravating and mitigating factors.[3]

By 1982 Baldus and his colleagues had completed the first portion of their study of capital sentencing in Georgia, the *Procedural Reform Study,*[4] and three death row prisoners in Georgia—Ross, Spencer, and Mitchell—offered it in a federal habeas corpus proceeding in support of their joint claim of discrimination in capital sentencing. The district court demurred, stating:

[The petitioners] would show that sentencing patterns under the new statute still reveal glaring disparities in the imposition of the death penalty based upon race, sex and poverty. This allegation may be true, and, if so, would be sad and distressing, but this allegation does not alone show any infirmity in a statute otherwise found to be acceptable under the Constitution.[5]

In a modification of this opinion (entered in light of the intervening revision of the circuit court opinion in *Smith*), the district court added that the proffered evidence still "leaves untouched countless racially neutral variables."[6]

Judicial decisionmaking is often formulaic; once an appellate court has faulted a particular study of discrimination for leaving countless variables untouched, other courts inevitably will reject other studies using identical terms. In this case, however, the rote description was so conspicuously wide of the mark—Baldus's research is noteworthy for the remarkable number of racially neutral variables that it does touch—that it drew a reversal. In *Spencer v. Zant*,[7] the first of these three cases to reach the Eleventh Circuit, a panel of the court reversed and remanded the case for an evidentiary hearing, noting that the petitioner had alleged that "Dr. Baldus's study addressed the very defects identified in the evidence in . . . *Smith*," and that "[t]he merits of this allegation cannot be assessed without a more detailed consideration of the evidence."[8] By the time *Spencer* was decided on appeal, however, in September 1983, the entire Baldus study—including the more comprehensive *Charging and Sentencing Study*[9] as well as the *Procedural Reform Study*—had been completed and presented in support of Warren McCleskey's federal habeas corpus petition in the Northern District of Georgia. As a result, the two cases became interwoven: in December 1983 the Eleventh Circuit voted to rehear *Spencer* en banc;[10] in February 1984 the district court filed its opinion in *McCleskey*;[11] in March 1984 the trial court decision in

McCleskey was appealed, and the Eleventh Circuit ordered the *McCleskey* appeal to be heard originally en banc and stayed consideration of the *Spencer* rehearing pending the determination of *McCleskey.*[12]

B. The District Court

The district court begins its discussion of the discrimination claim in *McCleskey* with a review of the legal framework. The petitioner, having conceded that any claim under the Eighth Amendment was foreclosed by contrary Eleventh Circuit opinions, had pressed his claim under the equal protection clause.[13] The court agrees with this analysis under the compulsion of the *Spinkellink* opinion, but states its own opinion that the major issue before it—discrimination by race of victim—is better analyzed as a violation of the due process clause.[14] The court then emphasizes that to establish a violation of equal protection the petitioner must prove "intentional discrimination" and that statistical evidence alone will not suffice "unless the evidence of disparate impact is so strong that the only permissible inference is one of intentional discrimination."[15]

Given this legal framework, the district court proceeds to analyze and reject the Baldus study at length. Like other courts that faced this issue, the judge here finds that the empirical research is too faulty to support the claim; unlike them, however, he is unable to do so on the usual basis—the failure to examine a sufficient number of variables. Instead, he launches an attack on several other fronts: (1) the data base is too inaccurate to form a basis for useful conclusions;[16] (2) the statistical models are flawed;[17] (3) the data, if they show anything, demonstrate that the capital sentencing system in Georgia is fair;[18] and (4) the statistical methodology used has no value in this context.[19]

Much could be said about the district court opinion in *McCleskey.* Many of the criticisms of Baldus's research are unfair,[20] and many of the statements about statistics are ill informed and wrong.[21] However, since the Eleventh Circuit and the Supreme Court have sidestepped the district court's analysis, the opinion is of limited interest. As a result, this discussion will be confined to a particularly curious aspect of the district court's analysis: its discussion of the appropriate methodology for proving discrimination.

The court starts with an assertion that "[t]o determine whether or not race was being considered, it is necessary to compare very similar cases."[22] Because of the large number of variables that must be considered, however, direct comparisons using cross-tabulations are impractical, and "[a]ccordingly, the [Baldus] study principally relies upon multivariate analysis."[23] So far, so good: the court believes it is essential to consider many variables, and the researcher has done so using the appropriate technique, multivariate analysis—specifically, multiple regression analysis. But there is a catch. After a series of remarkable and inaccurate statements about the meaning and value of multiple regression analysis,[24] the court concludes that "multivariate analysis is ill suited to provide the court with circumstantial evidence of the presence of discrimination, and it is incapable of providing the court with measures of qualitative difference in treatment which are necessary to find that a prima facie case has been established with statistical evidence."[25] This sequence of statements can be reorganized as a simple syllogism: (1) multivariate analysis is the only statistical method appropriate for dealing with the large number of variables that must be considered to prove discrimination; (2) multivariate analysis is incapable of proving discrimination; therefore, (3) discrimination cannot be proved with statistical evidence. Lest the point be lost, the court drives it home: "To the extent that McCleskey contends that he was denied either due process or equal protection of the law, his methods fail to contribute anything of value to his cause."[26] The court makes no attempt to reconcile this position with the many cases in which litigants successfully relied on statistical evidence in general, and multiple regression in particular, to prove intentional discrimination in other contexts.[27]

C. The Circuit Court

1. The Eleventh Circuit Opinion

The district court based its holding on a detailed critique of the study before it, finding numerous problems and errors. The Eleventh Circuit could have simply affirmed these findings and rejected McCleskey's arguments on methodological grounds, but it did not. Rather, it held that the methods of the Baldus study need not be considered at all because its findings, taken at face value, show too little discrimination to state a constitutional claim.

The circuit court begins its analysis with a rambling discussion of the history of the use of social science evidence in litigation.[28] The court notes various problems with such evidence, but nonetheless "take[s] a position that social science research does play a role in judicial decisionmaking in certain situations."[29] Specifically, in discrimination cases statistics can provide circumstantial evidence of discrimination. "[T]he inferences to be drawn from the statistics are for the factfinder, but the statistics are accepted to show the circumstances."[30]

The Eleventh Circuit then reviews the constitutional standards that govern claims of discrimination in capital sentencing, and takes this occasion to overrule its earlier decision in *Spinkellink* that arbitrariness was "conclusively removed" from the capital sentencing statutes approved by the Supreme Court in 1976.[31] As the court points out, that decision is inconsistent with the later Supreme Court holding in *Godfrey v. Georgia*[32] that a portion of the Georgia capital sentencing scheme was unconstitutional as applied. The circuit court goes on to hold, however, that it makes no difference whether the claim is litigated under the equal protection clause, the cruel and unusual punishments clause of the Eighth Amendment, or the due process clause—the factual issue is the same: intentional discrimination. The court recognizes that "[d]ue process and cruel and unusual punishment cases do not usually focus on the intent of the government actor," but it holds that when the content of the claim is racial discrimination in sentencing decisions, "intent and motive are natural components of the proof."[33] The court does not explain what makes this special requirement so natural; in other contexts, courts are usually particularly sensitive to claims of racial discrimination, not peculiarly exacting.[34] (In *Andrews v. Shulsen*,[35] the most important case on this issue in the interval between the circuit court and the Supreme Court decisions in *McCleskey*, the Tenth Circuit reaches the opposite conclusion: "a pattern of discrimination or otherwise arbitrary sentencing decisions in capital cases can violate the Constitution regardless of intent."[36])

The Eleventh Circuit next holds that to prevail under any of these constitutional provisions a prisoner must present proof of a "disparate impact [that] is so great that it compels a conclusion that the system is unprincipled, irrational, arbitrary and capricious such that purposeful discrimination . . . can be presumed to permeate the system."[37] This is a more extreme requirement than the usual standard for proof of discriminatory intent: "a clear pattern, unexplainable on grounds other than race."[38] As a practical matter, the Eleventh Circuit seems to demand proof of specific racial animus in capital sentencing decisions. Once again, there is no explanation for this unusual requirement.

The court proceeds to fit the type of study at issue—a "generalized statistical study"—into the legal framework it has constructed. The court claims to reaffirm its previous holdings that statistical evidence of racial discrimination "may be so strong that the results permit no other inference,"[39] but in fact it transforms these holdings by equating *strong evidence* of discrimination with evidence of a *strong pattern* of discrimination. The court is explicit on this new rule and on its consequences: "[I]t is a legal question as to *how much [racial] disparity* is required before a federal court will accept it as evidence of the constitutional flaws in the system."[40] No hearings are required on statistical studies of capital sentencing discrimination, regardless of their quality, unless they "reflect a disparity *so great* as to inevitably lead to a conclusion that the disparity results from intent or motivation."[41] (On this point, as well as on the issue of intent, the Tenth Circuit concluded the opposite in *Andrews v. Shulsen,* albeit in dicta. The *Andrews* court specifically cites our research as "an appropriate formal study," and says that if such a study had been presented in that case it would have raised a "reasonable possibility" of a constitutional violation and entitled the petitioner to an evidentiary hearing.[42])

This holding on proof of intent makes it possible for the court to avoid any discussion of the merits of the evidence before it. The Eleventh Circuit notes that "[t]he district court held the [Baldus] study to be invalid" and adds that "[t]he district court is to be commended for its outstanding endeavor in the handling of the detailed aspects of this case, particularly in light of the consistent arguments being made in several cases based on the Baldus study."[43] Nonetheless, the circuit court "pretermit[s] a review of this finding concerning the validity of the study itself"[44] on the ground that such a review is unnecessary, given its finding that "even if the statistical results are accepted as valid, the evidence fails to challenge successfully the constitutionality of the Georgia system."[45]

This is the central holding of the circuit court opinion: that the quantity of discrimination found by the Baldus study is insufficient to raise a constitutional claim. This conclusion is based on three separate findings that address different aspects of this study. First, and most important, the court states that "[t]he result of Baldus's most conclusive model, on which McCleskey primarily relies, showed an effect of .06, signifying that on average a white victim crime is 6% more likely to result in the [death] sentence than a comparable black victim crime."[46] This "6% bottom line" is "not sufficient to overcome the presumption that the statute is operating in a constitutional manner."[47] Second, the court notes that the Supreme Court denied a number of stays in Florida death penalty cases despite evidence from our own study that the odds of a death sentence for killing a white victim in that state were 4.8 times greater than for killing a black. The court finds that the Supreme Court rejected this evidence because the "bottom line" was too small rather than because of the study's methodological limitations and that this disposition compels a rejection of the Baldus study, since it made a comparable finding—that killing a white victim increases the odds of a death sentence in Georgia by a factor of 4.3.[48] Third, Baldus presented evidence that for Georgia homicides in the middle range of aggravation—and McCleskey's case fell in that range—the race-of-victim effect was 20 percent. The court rejects this evidence on two grounds: because it is "unpersuaded that there is a rationally classified, well-defined class" of mid-range cases; and because "[a] valid system challenge cannot be made only against the mid-range of cases," but must encompass "the system as a whole."[49]

The court concludes that the constitutionally required discretion in capital sentencing will necessarily produce some unevenness in results. Therefore, racial disparities that cannot be explained by other considerations still do not constitute prima facie evidence of discrimination.[50] Indeed, the court asserts that despite the unexplained racial disparities (which it characterizes as "marginal"), the evidence presented "confirms rather than condemns the system" of capital sentencing in Georgia.[51]

Three judges, Johnson, Hatchett, and Clark, dissent from the court's holding on McCleskey's discrimination claim.[52] Judge Johnson's dissent is the most wide-ranging. It argues that claims under the Eighth Amendment prohibition of arbitrariness in capital sentencing, unlike Fourteenth Amendment claims, include no element of intent; that Baldus's findings prove both arbitrariness and intentional discrimination; and that the Baldus study is methodologically valid.[53] Judge Hatchett's dissent focuses on the 20 percent disparity that Baldus found in the middle range of cases, and concludes that this difference is "intolerable."[54] Judge Clark's dissent argues that under traditional standards of proof the Baldus findings demonstrate intentional discrimination in violation of the equal protection clause.[55]

2. How Much Is Not Enough?

At first blush, the Eleventh Circuit's analysis in *McCleskey* seems plausible enough. We all have a reasonably clear notion of what 6 percent means from other common contexts: 6 percent might be the rate for a sales tax, and, in happier times, 6 percent was a common annual interest rate on loans. It sounds right when the court describes the "6% disparity" found by Baldus as a "marginal difference." In fact, it is nothing of the sort. Although the court seems to have missed the point entirely, this disparity—like the racial disparities reported here—actually means that defendants in white-victim cases are several times more likely to receive death sentences than defendants in black-victim cases.[56]

Percentage disparities that look similar to this one appear frequently in the case law of discrimination, especially in jury representativeness cases. Not surprisingly, both the majority and the dissenters in *McCleskey* discuss the disparities found by the Baldus study against the background of earlier jury discrimination claims. The comparison is misleading. In *Swain v. Alabama*,[57] the leading jury-representativeness case that seems comparable, the Supreme Court announced a rule that sounds similar to the Eleventh Circuit holding in *McCleskey*: "We cannot say that purposeful discrimination based on race alone is satisfactorily proved by showing that an identifiable group in a community is underrepresented [in the jury pool] by as much as 10%."[58] This is an unfortunate decision and it has been severely criticized on several grounds,[59] but only one is directly relevant here: the measure of underrepresentation used in *Swain* is of questionable value at best.

The 10 percent disparity described in *Swain* is the difference between the absolute proportion of blacks in the population and the absolute proportion of blacks in the jury pool. Specifically, 26 percent of the male county population over twenty-one was black, but only 10 percent to 15 percent of the jury panels—which, by the Court's arithmetic, is a difference of 10 percent. The problem with this measure, as various courts and commentators have pointed out,[60] is that a 10 percent difference in the rate of representation means various things in different contexts. It is one thing to have 60 percent black jurors in a county that is 70 percent black, and quite another to have 2 percent black jurors in a county that is 12 percent black. Indeed, if blacks (or any other group) constitute less than 10 percent of the population of a jurisdiction, then, under *Swain*, even their total exclusion from jury service will not constitute prima facie evidence of discrimination.

These obvious anomalies have led many commentators to suggest measures of disparity other than the absolute difference in representation.[61] In particular, the size of the group at issue can be taken into account if one examines the "comparative underrepresentation" of that group, a measure that answers the following question: by what percentage does the actual number of black jurors fall short of the expected number of black jurors? By this measure, the underrepresentation of blacks in *Swain* ranged from

42 percent to 62 percent. Some lower courts, recognizing the problems with *Swain,* have managed to distinguish it and have adopted other standards for reviewing jury discrimination cases;[62] other courts, unfortunately, have followed *Swain* uncritically,[63] sometimes openly embracing its worst consequences. For example, in one case a defendant presented evidence that Hispanic citizens constituted 5.3 percent of the jury-eligible population in the district, but only 1.1 percent of the jury pool; the court held that "[b]ecause Hispanics comprise a small percentage of the eligible population and because the absolute disparity is under 10 percent, the court, again, finds that the *prima facie* elements of a fair-cross-section violation have not been proved."[64]

Numerical guidelines for determining constitutional violations, however, are not all equally flawed. In *Gaffney v. Cummings*[65] and *White v. Regester*[66] the Supreme Court held, in effect, that disparities of up to 10 percent in the populations of state legislative districts are presumptively constitutional under the "one person, one vote" rule announced in *Baker v. Carr*[67] and *Reynolds v. Sims.*[68] This rule of thumb, unlike the one in *Swain,* creates relatively few problems because the 10 percent disparity at issue is different in kind from the 10 percent disparity in *Swain.* The issue in redistricting cases is the *number* of voters in the districts and the measure used is the disparity in *distribution.* In jury cases the issue is the *proportion* of a particular racial group in the jury pools, and the measure is the disparity in *representation.* In general, our common experiences with percentages correspond much better to disparities in distribution than to disparities in representation: taxes and interest payments are distributional events, and most comparisons we commonly make (for example, comparing ourselves to those who earn 10 percent more than we do) are distributional comparisons. In all these situations—unlike the situation in *Swain*—the percentages at issue are considered against a base of 100 percent.[69]

The problems with the 10 percent guideline in *Swain* illustrate a general rule: It is impossible to evaluate percentages meaningfully without considering the baseline against which they must be compared. If this elementary rule is ignored, absurd results follow—as when courts require a 10 percent absolute disparity in the representation of a group that constitutes 5 percent of the population. The Eleventh Circuit's discussion of "6% disparity" in the Baldus study is a telling example of how courts can be misled in just this way.

The "6% disparity" that Baldus and his colleagues found is not, literally, a 6 percent difference in death-sentencing rates between white-victim and black-victim homicides. The actual overall disparity they found was 10 percent; the 6 percent figure reflects the size of a multiple regression coefficient that represents the average difference between the probability of a death sentence in a white-victim case and the probability of a death sentence in a black-victim case, after taking into account the effects of many other variables.[70] The meaning of the *McCleskey* holding can be described, however, by calculating what the black-victim and white-victim death-sentencing rates would be if this adjusted disparity were the actual difference in the sentencing rates of these two groups. To do so it is necessary to take three numbers into account: (1) the overall death-sentencing rate in the Baldus sample, which was quite low, 5.2 percent; (2) the proportion of white-victim homicides, which was 39 percent; and (3) the proportion of black-victim homicides, which was 61 percent. Given these characteristics of the Baldus sample, there would be about a 6 percent disparity between the death-sentencing rates in white-victim and black-victim cases if the white-victim rate were approximately 9 percent and the black-victim rate were approximately 3 percent.[71]

It is immediately obvious that in comparing these two rates it is crucial to consider the overall rate of capital sentencing. Death sentences are uncommon, and so, inevitably, absolute differences in death-sentencing rates will be small. This is, therefore, a particularly inappropriate context in which to apply a *Swain*-type guideline, every bit as inappropriate as jury-selection cases that concern minorities of 5 percent. This point is missed by both the majority and the dissenters in *McCleskey*.

But there is a more basic problem. Note that the disparity here—6 percent—is *greater* than the overall death-sentencing rate—5.2 percent. How is that possible? The answer is that the difference here is not a difference in levels of *representation* (as in *Swain*) but in rates of *selection*. Focusing on absolute differences in rates of selection without considering the overall selection rate is even less meaningful than focusing on absolute differences in levels of representation without considering the sizes of the groups being compared.

Consider a hypothetical county in which there are 80,000 whites and 20,000 blacks who are eligible for jury service. If the jury pool consists of 900 whites and 100 blacks, the absolute disparity in the representation of blacks (the measure in *Swain*) would be 10 percent—blacks are 20 percent of the population and 10 percent of the jury pool. The disparity in *selection rates,* however, is an entirely different matter. For whites the selection rate is 1.1 percent (900/80,000), and for blacks it is 0.5 percent (100/20,000); the difference in the rates of selection (the measure in *McCleskey*) is 0.6 percent, far lower than the "marginal" 6 percent disparity that Baldus found. In fact, the maximum possible disparity in selection rates—the disparity that would exist if all 1000 potential jurors in the county were white—is 1.3 percent. (Similarly, in our illustration based on the Baldus data the maximum possible disparity in rates of selection—the difference that we would find if *all* death sentences occurred in white-victim cases—is 13 percent.) In other words, while the rule in *Swain* implies that any disparity in *representation* will be tolerated if the group in question is sufficiently small, the rule in *McCleskey* implies that any disparity in *selection* is permissible, regardless of the size of the groups, as long as the overall rate of selection is low.

If one were to apply the *Swain* rule in this context (and we would not recommend it) one would have to compare levels of representation, not selection. The disparity in representation can be estimated reasonably accurately using our illustration: in the absence of discrimination one would expect 61 percent of the death sentences to occur in black-victim cases, but if 9 percent of white-victim cases and only 3 percent of black-victim cases result in death sentences, then only 34 percent of the death sentences would be meted out for the killing of blacks.[72] This means that the absolute underrepresentation of black-victim cases on death row (as these things are calculated in *Swain*) would be 27 percent, and the comparative underrepresentation would be 44 percent.[73]

It is accurate to say that there is a "disparity of 6 percent" when 9 percent of white-victim homicides receive death sentences compared to 3 percent of black-victim homicides, but it is uninformative. A more informative statement would be that white-victim cases are three times as likely to receive death sentences as black-victim cases—hardly a "marginal effect." The Eleventh Circuit does not discuss this ratio of probabilities, most likely because no comparable figures were before it, and, strictly speaking, they are not appropriate in this context. Our 3 percent–versus–9 percent illustration is based on a simplification: we assume that all black-victim and all white-victim cases had the same probabilities of death sentences. In fact, many factors other than race affect those probabilities, and the analyses in the Baldus study control for those factors. Accordingly, the disparity found is the average disparity, across all levels of likelihood of a death sentence. At some such levels a ratio of probabilities of 3 to 1 would be not only incorrect but impossible. No probability can be larger than 1, certainty; if the probability of a death sentence for a black-victim homicide in a particular category is .5 (or 50 percent), the maximum possible increment in this probability for a similar white-victim case is a factor of 2.

The court, however, does discuss an analogous measure: the odds multiplier,[74] a measure we use extensively in this book.[75] Odds, unlike probability, is an open-ended measure— it ranges from zero to infinity—and the multiplier of the odds is an appropriate measure of the overall effect of a racial variable on capital sentencing. Baldus found that killing a white victim increased the odds of a death sentence by a factor of 4.3; the Eleventh Circuit found this insufficient. In fact, the court says that it might be "compelled" to reach this conclusion by cases in which the Supreme Court denied stays to death-sentenced inmates in Florida who presented evidence of our own finding that killing a white in that state increased the odds of a death sentence by a factor of 4.8.[76]

The Eleventh Circuit states that it might be bound by these Supreme Court rulings because the High Court held that evidentiary hearings were not required on the Florida discrimination claims, and, therefore, the Court must have found our "bottom line" to be constitutionally insufficient. "A contrary assumption, that the Supreme Court analyzed the extremely complicated Gross and Mauro study and rejected it on methodological grounds, is much less reasonable."[77] Perhaps. On the other hand, the Eleventh Circuit itself rejected other evidence of discrimination in capital sentencing on methodological grounds, without a hearing, in *Smith v. Balkcom,*[78] and it did so for a simple reason: an insufficient range of control variables. The Supreme Court could have followed that lead. Needless to say, we do not agree with this criticism of our findings, but we suspect—in charity to the Supreme Court—that this is the problem the Court had in mind.[79] In any event, mathematical misstatements are no more correct when they are pronounced by the Supreme Court rather than by some other body—although they may be more misleading. In this case the Eleventh Circuit might have misunderstood the meaning of "death odds multiplier of 4.3 to 1," and may have been led by the Supreme Court to believe that an effect that increases the odds of an event by more than a factor of 4 can be "marginal." An Atlantic City casino that operated on that premise, however, would go bankrupt in a weekend.

The cases that the Eleventh Circuit cites turn on our findings in Florida. But in Georgia—the jurisdiction of the Baldus study and of the *McCleskey* case—we found that killing a white victim increased the odds of a death sentence by a factor of 7.2, more than the factor of 4.8 that we report for Florida and more than the factor of 4.3 that Baldus reports.[80] Given the differences in the samples and the methodologies of these two studies, such discrepancies are to be expected. From a scientific point of view, the consistency between our findings and those of Baldus and his colleagues is more impressive than the differences. The Eleventh Circuit's focus on the size of the estimates of these racial effects is fundamentally misplaced, since the exact figures are less important than the overall pattern. Nonetheless, it is important to realize that at least part of this discrepancy is due to the fact that the Baldus study inevitably *underestimates* the magnitude of race-of-victim discrimination, to some extent. Several factors contribute to this systematic underestimation.

First, the Baldus study does not cover all stages in the process of adjudicating capital cases. Any discrimination in charging defendants with homicide, or in convicting them, would not be reflected in the Baldus findings.

Second, the more extensive of the two samples that Baldus used—the *Charging and Sentencing Study* sample— was restricted to cases that were charged as homicides and that resulted in prison or death sentences for a conviction of homicide. The sample for the *Procedural Reform Study* was even more restricted. That means that these samples were created by discretionary decisions within the criminal justice system—decisions by prosecutors and judges and juries—and these discretionary decisions may have involved elements of discrimination by race of victim; indeed, the findings in the area suggest that is likely. If so, these studies are susceptible to the methodological problem of "sample selection bias," which, in this context, would have the effect of obscuring the magnitude of similar patterns of discrimination at later stages of the process.[81]

Third, Baldus's analyses assume that any apparent racial effect that *might* be explained by a legitimate factor *was* indeed caused by that factor. As a result, some apparently neutral effects may conceal actual discrimination. For example, prior criminal record is a legitimate aggravating factor, but its apparent use in capital sentencing may reflect an actual pattern of discrimination—either because criminal record is given weight as an aggravating factor in part because blacks are more likely to have records, or because the criminal records of black defendants are due in part to prior discrimination against them.[82]

Finally, the Baldus study relies on data from files that were generated by major actors in the criminal justice system: police officers, prosecutors, judges, and probation officers. These actors generally know how they intend to deal with the cases they describe, and they write their descriptions accordingly. If a prosecutor, for example, has decided to reduce a charge from murder to manslaughter, he or she will make sure that the file reflects mitigating factors that justify his or her decision. In part, this is an unconscious process of self-justification. In part, it is simply a response to bureaucratic and legal realities: these decisions are subject to internal and external review, and must be supported. As a result, the data will (to some extent) describe the sentencing system as more consistent and less discriminatory than it actually is.

By contrast, the research reported in this book, while not nearly as comprehensive as the Baldus study, is less susceptible to three of these four problems, and less likely to produce systematic underestimates of racial effects. Specifically:

1. We compared initial reports on homicides to ultimate death sentences, thereby encompassing all stages of the criminal justice system.

2. Our study is based on all reported homicides in each state, effectively eliminating sample selection bias as an issue.

3. Our data are derived from the initial police reports of the homicides, before legal proceedings were undertaken, thus minimizing (if not eliminating) the problem of self-serving reporting bias by state officials.

In sum, to the extent that the exact magnitude of race-of-victim discrimination in Georgia is important, we must recognize that the Baldus study almost certainly presents a low estimate of the actual problem—it paints a picture that is rosier than reality.

It might be useful, before moving on, to put these numbers in perspective. Coronary heart disease, it is well known, is associated with cigarette smoking. But what is the magnitude of the effect? One of the pioneering studies in the field, by Hammond and Horn,[83] studied 187,783 men between the ages of fifty and sixty-nine over a forty-four-month period. Deaths from coronary artery disease during the study period were fairly rare—a total of 5297, or 2.8 percent of the sample—but cigarette smokers came in far more than their share: controlling for age, smokers were 1.7 times more likely to die of coronary artery disease than nonsmokers.[84] Expressing this effect as an odds ratio hardly changes its magnitude at all.[85] This is not an isolated example. Another well-known study, by Joseph T. Doyle and colleagues, reports that the smokers it followed faced two times the risk of death from coronary heart disease as the nonsmokers,[86] and many other medical studies reach the same conclusion: smoking cigarettes increases the risk of death from heart disease greatly, but by a considerably smaller amount than the race-of-victim effect that the Eleventh Circuit dismisses as marginal.[87]

Notes

1. Spinkellink v. Wainwright, 578 F.2d 582 (5th Cir. 1978), *cert. denied,* 440 U.S. 976 (1979); Smith v. Balkcom, 660 F.2d 573 (5th Cir. 1981), *modified,* 671 F.2d 858 (5th Cir.), *cert. denied,* 459 U.S. 882 (1982). The dates in the text refer to the presentation of the discrimination claims in the trial courts.
2. *See* ch. 2, pp. 20–21.
3. *Smith v. Balkcom,* 671 F.2d at 860 n.33.
4. *See* McCleskey v. Zant, 580 F.Supp. 338, 353–55 (N.D. Ga. 1984).
5. Mitchell v. Hopper, 538 F.Supp. 77, 90 (S.D.Ga. 1982), *vacated sub nom.* Spencer v. Zant, 715 F.2d 1562 (11th Cir. 1983), *order aff'd in part sub nom.* Mitchell v. Kemp, 762 F.2d 886 (11th Cir. 1985).
6. Ross v. Hopper, 538 F.Supp. 105, 107 (S.D.Ga. 1982) (quoting Smith v. Balkcom, 671 F.2d at 860 n.33), *aff'd in part, remanded in part sub nom.* Ross v. Kemp, 756 F.2d 1483 (11th Cir. 1985).
7. 715 F.2d 1562 (11th Cir.), *vacated for rehearing en banc,* 715 F.2d 1583 (11th Cir. 1983), *aff'd in part, remanded in part sub nom.* Spencer v. Kemp, 781 F.2d 1458 (1986).
8. *Id.* at 1582. This decision was followed in the appeal of Spencer's copetitioner, Ross v. Hopper, 716 F.2d 1528, 1539 (11th Cir. 1983).
9. *See McCleskey,* 580 F.Supp. at 353–55.
10. 715 F.2d 1583 (11th Cir. 1983).
11. *McCleskey supra* note 4.
12. Spencer v. Zant, 728 F.2d 1293, 1284 (11th Cir. 1984). At the same time, the court also ordered a rehearing en banc in Ross v. Hopper, and consolidated that hearing with *McCleskey. Id.*
13. *McCleskey,* 580 F.Supp. at 346.
14. *Id.* at 347–49. The district court's argument on this point makes a good deal of sense, although the choice of the clause of the Fourteenth Amendment does not appear to make any practical difference in this context.
15. *Id.* at 349.

16. *Id.* at 354–60.

17. *Id.* at 360–64.

18. *Id.* at 364–69, 372–77.

19. *Id.* at 369–72.

20. By contrast, the social scientific community has expressed very high regard for the Baldus study. For example, Dr. Richard Berk, evaluating it in light of a National Academy of Sciences report on sentencing research, described it as "far and away the most complete and thorough analysis of sentencing" ever conducted. *McCleskey*, 753 F.2d at 907 (Johnson, J., concurring and dissenting); *see also* Barnett, *Some Distribution Patterns for The Georgia Death Sentence*, 18 U.C.D. L. REV. 1327, 1334 (describing the importance of the Baldus study); *id.* at 1355 (praising the data collected for the study). In June 1987 the Law and Society Association awarded its annual Kalven award for excellence in empirical research on the law to Professors Baldus, Woodworth, and Pulaski for this study.

21. A few examples will suffice. (a) The district court says that "valid" multiple regression models must be able to "predict . . . the variations in the dependent variable [in this case, sentencing] to some substantial degree," 580 F.Supp. at 351, and that the Baldus regression models are unreliable because the proportion of this variance that they explain, as measured by the R^2 statistic, is under .5. *Id.* at 361. In fact, R^2 is a difficult statistic to interpret and is not generally useful in this context, and a high R^2 is not a requirement for a valid (i.e., well-specified) multiple regression model. *See* R. PINDYCK & D. RUBINFELD, ECONOMETRIC MODELS AND ECONOMIC FORECASTS 78–82 (2d ed. 1981); Fisher, *Multiple Regression in Legal Proceedings*, 80 COLOM. L. REV. 702, 720 (1980). (b) The district court says that "[m]ultiple regression requires complete correct data to be utilized." 580 F.Supp. at 360. It seems that the court is referring to the well-known "errors in variables" problem in multiple regression analysis, *see* Finkelstein, *The Judicial Reception of Multiple Regression Studies in Race and Sex Discrimination Cases*, 80 COLOM. L. REV. 737, 747–49 (1980); if so, it overstates the issue. As with most things, this problem is one of degrees, and useful analyses are regularly and inevitably performed with imperfect data. *See* PINDYCK & RUBINFELD, *supra*, at 176–80. (c) The district court faults the regression models before it because they fail to include many "unique circumstances or uncontrolled-for variables." 580 F.Supp. at 362. As a result, the court says that these models "are insufficiently predictive to support an inference of discrimination. *Id.* In fact, it is neither required nor generally useful that a regression model include all possible variables; what is important is that the model be "well specified," which, in this context, means

(roughly) that the omitted variables be uncorrelated with the key variables of interest. *See* PINDYCK & RUBINFELD, *supra*, at 128–30; Fisher, *supra*, at 713–15. (d) The district court says that "[i]f the variables in an analysis are correlated with one another, this is called multicollinearity." 580 F.Supp. at 363. Multicollinearity occurs, in the court's view, whenever "there is any degree of interrelationship among the variables," and it distorts the regression coefficients. *Id.* This is false. There is nothing in the assumptions of multiple regression analysis that requires uncorrelated regressors; indeed, multiple regression analysis is primarily useful in analyzing data in which there *are* correlations among the predictor variables. Multicollinearity exists when two or more predictor variables are *very highly* correlated, and it is not necessarily a problem. In this context, multicollinearity would only be a problem if one of the highly intercorrelated variables was a racial variable of interest. *See* D. BELSLEY, E. KUH, & R. WELSCH, REGRESSION DIAGNOSTICS 92 (1980); PINDYCK & RUBINFELD, *supra*, at 87–90, 99–103; Fisher, *supra*, at 713. (e) The district court says that the Baldus analyses are unreliable because many variables "are correlated to the race of the victim and to the death sentencing result," 580 F.Supp. at 363, and, therefore, "it is not possible to say with precision what, if any, effect the racial variables have on the dependent [sentencing] variable." *Id.* This is a fundamental misunderstanding. If there were no variables that were correlated both to the racial variables and to death sentencing, multiple regression analysis would be completely unnecessary. In that unlikely situation, no nonracial variables could possibly explain the correlations between race and sentencing, and racial effects could be determined simply and directly by comparing the death-sentencing rates of different racial categories of cases. The purpose of multiple regression analysis is precisely to separate the effects of different causal variables that are partially intertwined. *See generally* BELSLEY, KUH, & WELSCH, *supra*, at 85–191.

22. 580 F.2d at 354 (emphasis omitted).

23. *Id.* (emphasis omitted).

24. *Id.* at 360–72.

25. *Id.* at 372 (emphasis omitted).

26. *Id.* (emphasis omitted).

27. *See generally* D. BALDUS & J. COLE, STATISTICAL PROOF OF DISCRIMINATION (1980); Finkelstein, *supra* note 21.

28. *McCleskey*, 753 F.2d at 887–90.

29. *Id.* at 888.

30. *Id.* at 890.

31. *Spinkellink*, 578 F.2d at 613–14; *see McCleskey*, 753 F.2d at 891.

32. 445 U.S. 420 (1980).
33. *McCleskey*, 753 F.2d at 892.
34. See generally Brest, *Foreword: In Defense of the Antidiscrimination Principle*, 90 HARV. L. REV. 1 (1976). The Eleventh Circuit's holding on this point draws a sharp response from Judge Johnson in dissent: "After today, in this Circuit arbitrariness based on race will be more difficult to eradicate than any other sort of arbitrariness in the sentencing process." *McCleskey*, 753 F.2d at 910–11.
35. 802 F.2d 1256 (10th Cir. 1980).
36. *Id.* at 1267 (dictum).
37. *McCleskey*, 753 F.2d at 892.
38. Village of Arlington Heights v. Metropolitan Hous. Dev. Corp., 429 U.S. 252, 266 (1977).
39. *McCleskey*, 753 F.2d at 892 (quoting *Smith v. Balkcom*, 671 F.2d at 859).
40. *Id.* at 893 (emphasis added).
41. *Id.* at 894 (emphasis added).
42. Andrews v. Shulsen, *supra* note 35, 802 F.2d at 1269.
43. *McCleskey*, 753 F.2d at 894.
44. *Id.* at 895.
45. *Id.* at 894.
46. *Id.* at 896.
47. *Id.* at 897.
48. *Id.*
49. *Id.* at 898.
50. *Id.* at 898–99.
51. *Id.* at 899.
52. There are also three separate opinions concurring in the court's holding on the discrimination claim. Judge Tjoflat argues that aggregate sentencing statistics are entirely inappropriate to show discrimination in capital sentencing. *Id.* at 904–5. Judge Vance expresses doubts about the court's assertion that the equal protection and Eighth Amendment claims require equivalent proof, but adds that a claim of discrimination— such as the one presented by McCleskey—is only appropriate under the equal protection clause. *Id.* at 905–6. Judge R. Lanier Anderson, joined by Judge Kravitch, argues that the requirements for proof of intentional discrimination ought to be less exacting in death cases than in other contexts, but that the distinction has no consequences in this case. *Id.* at 906–7. In addition, Chief Justice Godbold wrote an opinion, in which three other judges joined, dissenting from the court's holding on a separate issue, McCleskey's *Giglio* claim. *Id.* at 906–7; *see also id.* at 882–85 (majority opinion on *Giglio* issue).

53. *Id.* at 907–18. This opinion was also signed by Judges Hatchett and Clark.

54. *Id.* at 918–19.

55. *Id.* at 920–27.

56. We will not specifically discuss the 20 percent disparity in capital sentencing that Baldus found in the middle range of capital cases, but our discussion of the overall 6 percent disparity is, obviously, applicable to that finding as well. Nor will we discuss Baldus's findings on discrimination by race of defendant, which the court, for no apparent reason, ignores entirely. *See* ch. 10, pp. 191–92.

57. 380 U.S. 202 (1965).

58. *Id.* at 208–9.

59. In addition to the problem discussed in the text, this holding in *Swain* has been faulted on the following grounds. First (and least important), the Court's arithmetic is faulty. The figures cited in the opinion itself show racial disparities ranging from 11 percent to 16 percent. *Id.* at 205; *see, e.g.,* Note, *Fair Jury Selection Procedures,* 75 YALE L.J. 322, 326 n.22 (1965). Second, the issue in *Swain* (as in *McCleskey*) was not whether discrimination had been "satisfactorily proved" but whether the state would be required to rebut a showing of apparent discrimination. Third, as John Hart Ely has pointed out, rules such as these create powerful temptations: "to announce that a ten per cent disparity is not sufficient to call for such a rebuttal is practically to guarantee . . . [that] race very likely will be considered, [and] minorities very likely will be underrepresented—by about ten per cent." *See* Ely, *Legislative and Administrative Motivation in Constitutional Law,* 79 YALE L.J. 1205, 1264–65 (1970). A telling example of this problem is cited in Judge Clark's dissent in *McCleskey,* 753 F.2d at 926 n.29: In Bailey v. Vining, No. 76-199 (M.D. Ga. 1978), the court declared the jury-selection system in Putnam County, Georgia, to be unconstitutional because the Office of the Solicitor had sent a memorandum to the jury commissioners instructing them how to underrepresent blacks and women on juries but stay within Supreme Court and Fifth Circuit guidelines. "The result was that a limited number of blacks were handpicked by the jury commissioners for service." 753 F.2d at 926 n.29.

60. *See, e.g.,* United States v. Maskeny, 609 F.2d 183, 191 (5th Cir.), *cert. denied,* 447 U.S. 91 (1980); Quadra v. Superior Court of City & County of San Francisco, 403 F.Supp. 486, 495 n.9 (N.D.Cal. 1975); Finkelstein, *The Application of Statistical Decision Theory to the Jury Discrimination Cases,* 80 HARV. L. REV. 338, 348 (1966); Kairys, Kadane, & Lehoczky, *Jury Representativeness: A Mandate for Multiple Source Lists,* 65 CALIF. L. REV. 776, 793–94 (1977).

61. Kairys, *Juror Selection: The Law, A Mathematical Method of*

Analysis, and a Case Study, 10 Am. Crim. L. Rev. 771, 776–77 (1972); Kairys, Kadane, & Lehoczky, *supra* note 60, at 788–99; Kuhn, *Jury Discrimination: The Next Phase,* 41 S. Cal. L. Rev. 235, 253 (1968); Note, *Fair Jury Selection Procedures,* 75 Yale L.J. 322, 325–26 (1965).

62. *See, e.g.,* Hirst v. Gertzen, 676 F.2d 1252, 1258 n.14 (9th Cir. 1982); Bradley v. Judges of Superior Court for County of Los Angeles, 531 F.2d 413, 416 n.8 (9th Cir. 1976); Blackwell v. Thomas, 476 F.2d 443, 447 (4th Cir. 1973); Witcher v. Peyton, 382 F.2d 707, 710 (4th Cir. 1967); Waller v. Butkovich, 593 F.Supp. 942, 954 (M.D.N.C. 1984); Hillery v. Pulley, 563 F.Supp. 1228, 1240–41 (E.D.Cal. 1983), *aff'd,* 733 F.2d 644 (9th Cir. 1984); Villafane v. Manson, 504 F.Supp. 78, 83–88 (D. Conn. 1980); Quadra v. Superior Court of City & County of San Francisco, 403 F.Supp. 486, 495 n.9 (N.D.Cal. 1975). *See generally* Foster v. Sparks, 506 F.2d 805, 811, 835 (5th Cir. 1975).

63. *See, e.g.,* United States v. Clifford, 640 F.2d 150, 155 (8th Cir. 1981); United States v. Butler, 611 F.2d 1066, 1070 (5th Cir.), *cert. denied,* 449 U.S. 830 (1980); United States v. Maskeny, 609 F.2d 183, 190 (5th Cir.), *cert. denied,* 447 U.S. 921 (1980); United States v. Test, 550 F.2d 577, 587 (10th Cir. 1976); United States v. Newman, 549 F.2d 240, 249 (2d Cir. 1977); United States v. Musto, 540 F.Supp. 346, 356 (D.N.J. 1982), *aff'd sub nom.* United States v. Aimone, 715 F.2d 822 (3d Cir. 1983), *cert. denied,* 104 S.Ct. 3585 (1984); United States v. Haley, 521 F.Supp. 290, 293 (N.D.Ga. 1981); United States v. Facchiano, 500 F.Supp. 896, 899 (S.D.Fla. 1980); United States v. White Lance, 480 F.Supp. 920, 922 (D.S.D. 1979); United States v. Hunt, 265 F.Supp. 178, 194 (W.D. Tex. 1967).

64. United States v. Musto, 540 F.Supp. 346, 356 (D.N.J. 1982), *aff'd sub nom.* United States v. Aimone, 715 F.2d 822 (3rd Cir. 1983), *cert. denied,* 104 S.Ct. 3585 (1984). The court goes on to say that it need not consider the difference between the proportion of Hispanics in the total population (8.6 percent) and in the jury pool (1.1 percent) because "the absolute disparity is only 7.5 percent." *Id.* at 357.

65. 412 U.S. 735 (1973).

66. 412 U.S. 755 (1973).

67. 369 U.S. 186 (1962).

68. 377 U.S. 533 (1964).

69. Even when the issue is equality of distribution, announcing a permissible level of disparity can become a license to generate disparities that are just under the limit. *See supra* note 59. Perhaps for this reason the Court has gone to the opposite extreme in its decisions on congressional districts, and held that *no* level of deviation from absolute equality is permissible. Karcher v. Daggett, 462 U.S. 725 (1983). This rule, however, cannot be taken literally, since some deviations from equality

in population are an inevitable consequence of measurement error. *See id.* at 769–70 (White, J., dissenting).

70. *McCleskey,* 753 F.2d at 896.

71. This illustration is derived from the following equation: .39 × (9%) + .61 × (3%) = 5.3%.

72. The actual, unadjusted proportion of black-victim death sentences in the Baldus data is only 16 percent (20/128). *McCleskey,* 753 F.2d at 920 (Clark, J., dissenting and concurring).

73. *See supra* note 71.

74. *McCleskey,* 753 F.2d at 897.

75. *See supra* ch. 4, p. 65 and note 23, and App. 3.

76. *McCleskey,* 753 F.2d at 897. *See* ch. 4, p. 66, Table 4.24, and ch. 8, note 49.

77. *Id. McCleskey,* 753 F.2d at 897.

78. 660 F.2d 573 (5th Cir. 1981), *modified,* 671 F.2d 858 (5th Cir.), *cert. denied,* 459 U.S. 882 (1982). *Smith,* to be precise, was decided by Unit B of the former Fifth Circuit, which was the immediate predecessor of the present Eleventh Circuit.

79. Moreover, as Judge Hatchett points out in his dissent, "[n]either the Supreme Court nor the Eleventh Circuit has passed on the Florida studies on a fully developed record (as in this case)." *McCleskey,* 753 F.2d at 919 n.2.

80. *See* ch. 4, p. 66, Table 4.24.

81. *See* ch. 2, pp. 24–26 and notes 36–44.

82. *See, e.g.,* Hunter v. Underwood, 105 S.Ct. 1916 (1985) (provision of Alabama Constitution disenfranchising those convicted of certain crimes held unconstitutional because choice of crimes was motivated by intent to discriminate against blacks and had racially disproportionate impact); J. PETERSILIA, RACIAL DISPARITIES IN THE CRIMINAL JUSTICE SYSTEM 30–32 (1983) (citing evidence of sentencing discrimination against blacks).

83. Hammond & Horn, *Smoking and Death Rates—Report on Forty-Four Months of Follow-up of 187,783 Men,* 166 J.A.M.A. 1294 (1958).

84. *Id.* at 1295 table 1.

85. When, as here, *P* (probability) is small, then $(1-P)$ is very close in value to 1 and the odds ratio $(P/(1-P))$ becomes very close in value to *P*.

86. Doyle, Dawber, Kanmel, Kinch, & Kahn, *The Relationship of Cigarette Smoking to Coronary Heart Disease,* 190 J.A.M.A. 886, 889 table 3 (1964).

87. *See* U.S. DEP'T OF HEALTH, EDUCATION & WELFARE, SMOKING AND HEALTH, A REPORT OF THE SURGEON GENERAL, 4-19 to 4-41, 4-65 (1979); U.S. DEP'T OF HEALTH, EDUCATION & WELFARE, THE HEALTH CONSEQUENCES OF SMOKING, A REPORT OF THE SURGEON GENERAL: 1971, at 21–40 (1971).

10 | The McCleskey Case, II: The Supreme Court

On July 7, 1986, when the Supreme Court issued a writ of certiorari in *McCleskey v. Kemp*,[1] it was already apparent that the case was uncommonly troublesome. The petition for certiorari had been filed over a year before, in May of 1985. In the normal course of events it would have been granted or denied soon after the beginning of the October 1985 Term, but in this case the Court took no action on it until the very end of its session. It is fairly common for the Court to hold a certiorari petition for a long period while it considers another pending case that presents a similar issue. In that situation, however, the trailing case is not ultimately heard by the Supreme Court; after the leading case is decided, either certiorari is denied or it is granted and the case is immediately remanded to a lower court for reconsideration in light of the related Supreme Court opinion.[2] It is extremely unusual for the Court to withhold action for so long and then to *grant* a hearing in a major precedential case. The Court's decision in *McCleskey*, in April of 1987,[3] was consistent with this early signal. It is clear from the majority and dissenting opinions that this was a difficult and divisive case; it is also clear that the Court's judgment marked the end of an era in the constitutional regulation of the death penalty in the United States.

This chapter begins with a summary of the Supreme Court's opinion in *McCleskey*, and of the dissents. We then discuss the Court's ambivalent treatment of the empirical record, and its analysis of the two legal claims before it: that the evidence of racial discrimination in capital sentencing established a violation of the equal protection clause, and that this evidence proved "arbitrariness" in violation of the cruel and unusual punishments clause. Finally, we explore the Supreme Court's view of the changes in capital sentencing since the *Furman* decision.

A. The Opinions

The majority opinion in *McCleskey* was written by Justice Powell, who was joined by Chief Justice Rehnquist and by Justices White, O'Connor, and Scalia. Following the example of the Eleventh Circuit, Justice Powell begins his analysis by purporting to remove all factual issues from consideration ("we assume the [Baldus] study is valid statistically without reviewing the factual findings of the District Court"[4]) and ruling against McCleskey on strictly legal grounds. For the equal protection claim, the legal basis is predictable: the statistical evidence is inherently "insufficient to support an inference that any of the decisionmakers in McCleskey's case acted with discriminatory purpose."[5] This holding requires an explanation, since the Court has repeatedly accepted similar (indeed, *weaker*) statistical evidence as proof of intentional discrimination in other contexts. Justice Powell provides three distinctions: (1) Death sentencing decisions involve an exceptionally wide range of relevant variables and are made by a large and dispersed set of decisionmakers.[6] (2) Those who are responsible for sentencing decisions cannot meaningfully rebut a presumptive showing of discrimination by testifying to the true motives for these decisions.[7] (3) Because "discretion is essential to the criminal justice process, . . . exceptionally clear proof [is required] before we would infer that the discretion has been abused."[8]

In theory, the required showing of discriminatory intent could also be satisfied by evidence of purposeful discrimination by the state legislature in constructing the legal system that produced this outcome. The Court dismisses this possibility briefly: "McCleskey would have to prove that the Georgia Legislature enacted or maintained the death penalty statute *because* of an anticipated racially discriminatory effect,"[9] but there is no contemporary evidence to support this accusation, and the historical evidence of purposeful discrimination by the state of Georgia in the past is too remote.[10]

Justice Powell's treatment of McCleskey's Eighth Amendment claim is more complex. He begins with a review of the Court's opinions on the meaning of the cruel and unusual punishments clause and on the constitutionality of the death penalty. From these he extracts two constitutional rules: (1) The death penalty can be imposed only for crimes above a certain level of severity, and the state must establish "rational criteria" that guide the sentencer in deciding whether this minimum is met (unless the offense is of a type—rape or robbery, for example—for which the death penalty is categorically disproportionate). (2) The state "cannot limit the sentencer's consideration of any relevant circumstance that could cause it to decline to impose the penalty."[11] These rules provide no basis for McCleskey's claim that his death sentence is constitutionally disproportionate to the severity of the offense. He was convicted of murder in the course of a robbery, a crime for which the death penalty may be constitutionally imposed; other prisoners on death row were convicted of similar offenses. In any event, he is not constitutionally entitled to challenge his sentence by comparing himself either to defendants who were sentenced to death, or to those who were not.[12]

McCleskey's main Eighth Amendment claim, however, was not that his death sentence was disproportionate but rather that it was "arbitrary" because it was determined in part by racial considerations that permeate capital sentencing in Georgia. The majority finds that McCleskey's evidence does not "*prove* that race enters into any capital sentencing decisions or that race was a factor in McCleskey's particular case";[13] it merely shows a "risk" of racial discrimination. The Court holds that this risk is constitutionally acceptable—indeed, that it is necessary, in order to preserve discretion in the prosecution and sentencing of capital cases.

Discretion, the Court states, is a fundamental aspect of our system of justice, a major benefit to criminal defendants, and a specific constitutional requirement of capital sentencing. In other cases the Court has acted repeatedly to reduce the danger that racial prejudice might infect criminal proceedings in general and capital sentencing in particular, but it has done so without jeopardizing the discretion that prosecutors and juries enjoy in the execution of their duties. The danger that McCleskey points to is a direct product of this discretion, and it would take a much more compelling showing than the one he makes to require that so basic a feature of the system be overhauled—especially in view of the procedural safeguards that already protect the death penalty against racial discrimination.[14] The danger of granting this claim is particularly great since "there is no limiting principle" that would restrict the range of this revolution to claims based on race or to those addressed to capital sentencing procedures.[15]

Finally, the majority adds that this type of argument is properly addressed to legislative bodies, not to courts. Legislatures have the authority to make policy in direct response to the popular will, and they are well qualified to weigh and consider this type of long-term study, while the courts' duty is simply to uphold the law case by case.[16]

There are three dissenting opinions. Justice Brennan, writing for himself and for Justices Marshall, Blackmun, and Stevens, addresses the Eighth Amendment claim.[17]

Justice Brennan starts with a concrete consequence of the system the majority upholds: given the facts that the Court accepts, a careful defense attorney in Georgia must advise a capital defendant in McCleskey's circumstances that the defendant may face a higher risk of a death sentence because of his race and that of the victim.[18] It is this sort of *risk* of arbitrariness and discrimination that was condemned in the Court's previous death penalty cases, starting with *Furman*; the type of evidence that the majority now demands—proof that racial considerations actually affected the outcome of an individual case—has never been required.[19] Here the risk is great and it is exceptionally well documented, both by the Baldus study and by historical evidence of past patterns of extreme overt discrimination in Georgia's criminal justice system.[20] Those old laws and practices are now gone, but their history suggests that other, more "subtle, less consciously held racial attitudes"[21] may have been left behind.

Justice Brennan addresses each of the affirmative justifications that the majority offers for tolerating racial patterns of death sentencing. First, while discretion may be desirable in the criminal justice system, it is a means, not an end. If it leads to racial discrimination, it must be limited, as the Court has done in other contexts.[22]

Second, the fact that the Court has attempted in other cases to safeguard the process of capital sentencing with procedural rules is beside the point. The evidence in this case shows that these reforms have failed, at least in one major aspect.[23]

Third, the fear that entertaining this argument will open the door to a host of others is potentially unprincipled and certainly unfounded. If there are other equally strong claims, they should be granted. However, Brennan argues, that is unlikely since the circumstances of this case can hardly be duplicated. Death is a unique penalty, for which the Court has long demanded an exceptional degree of reliability;

race is a variable of unique importance, historically and constitutionally; and the Baldus study is so unprecedented in scope and detail that acting on it would "establish a remarkably stringent standard of statistical evidence unlikely to be satisfied with any frequency."[24]

Finally, despite the general constitutional preference for legislative policy making, this is an area in which judicial intervention is particularly appropriate, both because of the extreme and irrevocable nature of the state conduct, and because those condemned by it, prisoners convicted of murder, are not likely to be carefully heard in bodies that attend primarily to "the majoritarian chorus."[25]

The same four dissenters join in a second lengthy opinion, by Justice Blackmun, which deals with the equal protection issue.[26] There is an interesting historical symmetry to this opinion, since in 1968 it was Justice Blackmun, then a judge of the Court of Appeals, who wrote the Eighth Circuit opinion in *Maxwell v. Bishop*,[27] rejecting on empirical grounds the first major equal protection challenge to racial discrimination in capital sentencing. Blackmun is explicit on the reasons for his conversion: "McCleskey's evidence . . . is of such a different level of sophistication and detail that it simply cannot be rejected on those grounds," and also "[i]t is this experience [in *Maxwell*], in part, that convinces me of the significance of the Baldus study."[28]

Justice Blackmun begins by criticizing the framework of the majority opinion. First, the majority has reversed the usual presumption and, instead of requiring particularly careful constitutional scrutiny in death cases, has set a lower standard for review.[29] Second, the majority treats the fact of McCleskey's conviction as an answer to his claim of racial discrimination, ignoring a long history of cases that recognize that this is no defense.[30] Third, the majority minimizes the impact of McCleskey's evidence by focusing almost entirely on the actions of the trial jury and the state legislature and largely ignoring the other state officials whose conduct is implicated, in particular the prosecutor.[31]

Blackmun discusses McCleskey's claim in traditional equal protection terms: The defendant must establish a prima facie case of purposeful discrimination;[32] if he succeeds, the burden shifts to the state to justify its conduct, if it can, on the basis of "permissible racially neutral selection criteria."[33] Blackmun finds that McCleskey's evidence— the Baldus study, the depositions of the prosecutors who were in charge of his case, and the historical evidence of past discrimination in the Georgia criminal justice system— easily satisfied his initial burden, and that the state's rebuttal was too general and vague to be sufficient.[34] The majority's justifications for treating discrimination in capital sentencing differently from discrimination in other spheres are unconvincing. These other decisions do not necessarily involve fewer variables and fewer decisionmakers, as the majority asserts, especially not when compared to prosecutorial decisionmaking in capital cases. Similarly, the majority's claim that the state has no practical opportunity to rebut claims of sentencing discrimination ignores the fact that prosecutors can (and do) respond to such allegations.[35]

Blackmun is equally unimpressed with the majority's reliance on the importance of discretion in the criminal justice system. The majority's argument begs the question, since the *issue* in the case is the extent of the constitutional restrictions on the state's sentencing discretion. Finally, Blackmun is disturbed by the majority's fear that this discrimination claim could be a precursor to others. If such claims have merit, they too should be heard.[36]

The third dissent is short.[37] It is written by Justice Stevens, who is joined by Justice Blackmun only, and it addresses only one substantive point: The majority need not fear (as it apparently does) that accepting McCleskey's claim would eliminate capital punishment in Georgia. The Baldus study demonstrates that race was *not* a factor in the prosecution and sentencing of the most aggravated homicides, so it seems that Georgia could (if it wished) restrict its capital prosecutions to that category of cases and continue to use capital punishment without serious risk of racial discrimination.

B. The Law and the Facts

A striking aspect of the succession of opinions in the *McCleskey* case is the progressive evaporation of the factual question with which the case began: Does the Baldus study demonstrate race discrimination in capital sentencing in Georgia? The district court took on the empirical record directly, and held that it is so flawed that it proves nothing. The Eleventh Circuit retreated from that position, but only halfway: *assuming* the evidence is valid, the *quantity* of discrimination it found is insufficient to pose a constitutional problem. In theory, this still left open a factual issue, but a peculiar one. The Supreme Court simply eliminated the empirical issue entirely by deciding that this type of evidence is insufficient in principle to establish a violation of the Constitution.

The traditional method of rejecting a claim of discrimination in capital sentencing is to fault the methodology of the study on which it is based. That is what the district court did in *McCleskey*, at great length, providing an easy basis for similar rejections on appeal. But the higher courts did not follow the usual practice. Instead of denying the existence of racial patterns in capital sentencing, they took the less attractive line of admitting these patterns but denying their constitutional significance. There are several possible explanations for this novel approach.

The first explanation is intellectual honesty. The circuit court and the Supreme Court may have been unwilling to rest their judgments on the ground that the most thorough study of sentencing ever conducted in this country[38] is inadequate to satisfy their methodological requirements. Alternatively—but in a related vein—they may have been reluctant to enter into a methodological debate that was beyond their competence.[39] Initially, the position taken by the Eleventh Circuit probably looked like a plausible solution to this problem. It sidestepped the methodology of the Baldus study and focused on a problem that could, it seemed, be defined as a legal question. But this was a mistaken impression. The issue of the magnitude of the Baldus findings had not been addressed in these terms in the district court or on appeal to the Eleventh Circuit, but it received a great deal of attention *after* the circuit court opinion. By the time the case was argued in the Supreme Court the fundamental error of the circuit court's analysis had been described by the petitioner,[40] by *amici curiae*,[41] and by legal scholars,[42] and it was apparent that this approach simply avoided one statistical debacle by walking into another. The best solution was to step away from the empirical realm entirely.

The second explanation is expediency. It is apparent from their decisions that the Eleventh Circuit and the Supreme Court wanted to put an end to litigation on claims of discrimination in capital sentencing, and, needless to say, they have succeeded. To a great extent, this was already accomplished by the circuit court opinion, since, while methodological flaws can be repaired, nothing can be done to overcome a decision that the *level* of discrimination in a jurisdiction is simply too small to matter. Moreover, since racial discrimination in capital sentencing seems to be at least as pronounced in Georgia as in any other state,[43] the logic of this opinion would probably have foreclosed similar claims elsewhere. This was a sweeping achievement, but it came at a cost. The Eleventh Circuit opinion hinges on the conclusion that the demonstrated effects of the race of the victim on capital sentencing in Georgia are too small to be regarded as "systematic" and "pervasive," and this conclusion, as we have seen, is bizarre.[44] The Supreme Court closed the door more neatly, and with no remaining crack.

The third explanation is power. A district court has great

power to judge the evidence before it, but relatively little authority to interpret or revise the law. A circuit court can do a good deal to modify or extend existing judicial doctrine, as the Eleventh Circuit did here, but it is bound by general rules that it cannot alter. The Supreme Court, however, has extensive power to decide a case on broader terms than either of the courts beneath it. At each step up this ladder the court could hold against McCleskey on broader legal grounds, and it therefore had less need to quarrel with his undeniable factual assertions. This enabled the courts to decide the case in increasingly principled terms: first, a denial of the existence of racial disparities; then, an admission of their existence but a denial of their extent; finally, a tacit admission of the extent of the racial disparities in capital sentencing coupled to a legal judgment that they are constitutionally unobjectionable.

Strictly speaking, of course, the Supreme Court (like the Eleventh Circuit before it) did not actually endorse the Baldus study, it merely "assumed" that it was valid. This suggests a final explanation for this sequence of decisions: intellectual *dis*honesty or laziness. The Court might have "assumed" the validity of the study disingenuously, not because they were convinced by it but as a shortcut, in order to dismiss it without going through the trouble of refuting it. This explanation is persuasive to the extent that it appears that the justices in the majority misunderstood the study or failed to appreciate how thoroughly it proves its claims. As we have seen, the Eleventh Circuit did in fact misunderstand major aspects of the Baldus study,[45] and the Supreme Court follows suit, although more moderately. Nonetheless, we take the Court's "assumption" as something more than a prelude to dismissal. The tone and structure of the Court's opinion seem to concede a good deal more.

A year before *McCleskey*, in *Lockhart v. McCree*,[46] the Court faced an equally compelling social scientific record on a different death penalty issue, the constitutionality of "death-qualified" juries as triers of guilt or innocence in capital cases.[47] But in *Lockhart*, unlike *McCleskey*, the Court did not simply "assume" the studies were valid and then hold that they were legally insufficient. Instead, it argued at length that they had little or no value and *then* held that in any event the validity of the studies did not matter since what they might prove had no constitutional significance. Moreover, in *Lockhart* the Court launched this empirical attack despite the fact that both the district court that tried the case and the circuit court that reviewed it had been persuaded by the studies before them.[48] It would have been at least as easy to repeat this performance in *McCleskey*, where the district court had already found the evidence to be faulty, if the Supreme Court had wanted to do so. But the majority makes no attempt to criticize the Baldus study, or to respond to the strong endorsements of the four dissenters. Instead, it seems at one point to attempt to base its argument on this very study,[49] and it ends its opinion by suggesting that this evidence might be useful to legislatures who will be better equipped to evaluate and act on it.[50]

Still, while the Court may have gone a long way toward admitting the undeniable fact of discrimination, it does so inconsistently, with many backward glances. The Court is explicit in its main reservation:

> Our assumption that the Baldus study is statistically valid does not include the assumption that the study shows that racial considerations actually enter into any sentencing decisions in Georgia. Even a sophisticated multiple regression analysis such as the Baldus study can only demonstrate a *risk* that the factor of race entered into some capital sentencing decisions and a necessarily lesser risk that race entered into any particular sentencing decision.[51]

The meaning of this qualification turns on the interpretation of the phrase "enter into." If the Court means that the study does not prove that race "entered into" sentencing decisions as a conscious, purposeful factor, that is true. It is also true that the study does not prove whether race was a determinative factor in any particular case. But if it means that Baldus and his colleagues have not demonstrated that race, in part, determines the outcomes of the entire set of capital cases, whether or not this effect is conscious or intentional, then the Court has claimed to assume the validity of this study while denying its central finding.

The Eleventh Circuit took a similar position in its opinion:

> The Baldus approach, however, would take the cases with different results on what are contended to be duplicate facts, where the differences could not be otherwise explained, and conclude that the different result was based on race alone. . . . This approach ignores the realities. It not only ignores quantitative differences in cases: looks, age, personality, education, profession, job, clothes, demeanor, and remorse, just to name a few, but it is incapable of measuring qualitative differences of such things as aggravating and mitigating factors. There are, in fact, no exact duplicates in capital crimes and capital defendants.[52]

In other words, disclaimers to the contrary notwithstanding, the circuit court cannot resist coming home to rest on the arguments first framed in *Maxwell*: not enough variables are considered, no two cases are alike. In this case, however, these arguments have a particularly hollow ring—and not only because the court committed itself to assuming the truth of the Baldus findings. Consider the list of factors that the court says might, somehow, explain Baldus's findings: "Looks, age, personality, education, profession, job, clothes, demeanor, and remorse." At least some of these factors were in fact considered by Baldus— age, employment, and expression of remorse—and their effects are already reflected in his findings.[53] But that is not the worst problem with this peculiar list. Can differences in "looks" justify racial disparities in capital sentencing? And what aspects of looks have this power—attractiveness? hairstyle? complexion? Can leniency be legally justified on the ground that the victim of a killing had an unattractive face or wore baggy clothes? Judge Clark in his Eleventh Circuit dissent says that "these differences . . . are often used to mask, either intentionally or unintentionally, racial prejudice."[54] But that is not the only problem. These factors are themselves arbitrary bases for imposing death sentences. In *Furman* the death penalty was condemned in part because it was used primarily against "the poor, the ignorant, and the underprivileged members of society."[55] It is incongruous that the Eleventh Circuit uses similar features to attempt to justify apparent racial discrimination.

The Supreme Court takes a more modest line. It offers no alternative explanations for the racial disparities found by Baldus, but simply insists, in the teeth of the study itself, that these disparities are "unexplained."[56]

At most, the Baldus study indicates a discrepancy that appears to correlate with race.[57]

[W]e decline to assume that what is unexplained is invidious.[58]

In *Smith v. Balkcom* it made sense to say that the sketchy evidence of discrimination could be disregarded because it left "untouched countless racially neutral variables."[59] When that is true, it is plausible that some unexamined variable, or several, might explain the racial pattern. But the Baldus study examined hundreds of nonracial variables, and none of them, separately or in combination, accounted for the effects of race. If this study does not adequately "explain" that these large racial "discrepancies" are in fact caused by race, then the task is meaningless.

Once again, the relationship of smoking to heart disease may serve as a useful comparison. Numerous factors contribute to the development of coronary heart disease; the medical consensus seems to be that cigarette smoking is a major risk factor, but not an essential condition for this pathology.[60] Some of the studies on which this conclusion is based control for a number of important variables that might explain the association between smoking and heart disease—age, blood pressure, diabetes, and obesity, for example—but, inevitably, they do not completely explain the incidence of mortality from coronary heart disease.[61] As with capital sentencing, there are always many other factors that influence the health of each individual. None of these studies has as many control variables as the Baldus study. Moreover, as most people know, the effects of smoking on heart disease are disputed. In particular, some researchers have claimed that the association between smoking and heart disease reflects a genetic makeup that predisposes some people to smoke and simultaneously makes them more susceptible to heart attacks.[62] These objections notwithstanding, few medical authorities seem to doubt the surgeon general's conclusion that "cigarette smoking is a cause of coronary heart disease."[63]

There are, to be sure, many more studies on the relationship between smoking and heart disease than on the effects of race on capital sentencing in Georgia.[64] This is only natural since the issue is much more general: the physiological effects of cigarette smoke on the human heart. Indeed, there is some evidence that the effect of smoking on coronary heart disease may not be universal: a major study in Japan found that smokers there were only 1.16 times as likely to die of cardiovascular disease as non-smokers.[65] By contrast, the question addressed by the Baldus study is quite specific: was there racial discrimination in the administration of the death penalty in Georgia between 1973 and 1978? Baldus and his colleagues examined nearly half of all the homicide convictions in Georgia in that period, collected highly detailed evidence on those cases, and analyzed their data exhaustively.[66] Any causal statement involves some form of inference. But if the question is whether some capital defendants in Georgia received death sentences (and others avoided them) *because* of racial factors, then a strong and consistent finding of discrimination based on this analysis of these data is tantamount to an observation.

C. The Meaning of "Intentional Discrimination"

Doctrinally, the trickiest part of the Court's opinion is the discussion of McCleskey's equal protection claim. The problem is that the Court has made it a policy to rely on statistical evidence as proof of intentional discrimination in other contexts, while here they say such evidence is incompetent for the same purpose. This requires careful reconciliation.

The Court describes three "limited contexts" in which it "has accepted statistics as proof of intent to discriminate":[67] cases where the statistical pattern is "stark"; jury-selection cases; and employment discrimination cases. McCleskey's claim, they say, is different from cases in the first category because the statistical evidence is less compelling; and it is different from cases in the other two categories because death sentencing involves extremely wide discretion, which is exercised by many independent decisionmakers on the basis of numerous possible legitimate considerations.

The first of these distinctions is completely appropriate. The two leading cases in the stark evidence category are *Yick Wo v. Hopkins*,[68] in which each of more than 200 Chinese applicants for permission to operate a laundry in a wooden building was denied a permit, while every white applicant but one was successful; and *Gomillion v. Lightfoot*,[69] in which a state legislature redrew the boundaries of a city, changing it "from a square to an uncouth twenty-eight-sided figure"[70] and excluding 395 of 400 black voters but not a single white voter. In these cases the Supreme Court was persuaded, correctly, that the responsible government agencies implemented deliberate and purposeful policies of racial discrimination.

But *Yick Wo* and *Gomillion* were easy cases. When the conduct of a single government agency produces such extraordinary and conspicuous racial consequences it is easy to conclude that the government must have been aware of these effects and must have intended them. McCleskey never claimed that his death sentence was the product of a similar policy of deliberate racial discrimination in capital sentencing in Georgia, and certainly not that the Baldus study proves this.

The distinctions the Court draws between this case and other types of discrimination cases with less than "stark" evidence are not so compelling. The Court emphasizes two aspects of death sentencing decisions in Georgia that make them intrinsically different from jury-selection and employment decisions: each sentence is passed by a uniquely constituted trial jury, and each jury is permitted—in fact, required—to consider "innumerable factors" that vary from case to case.[71] There is something to this argument—the system for imposing death sentences is extremely complex, and each decision may involve many factors—but these are differences of degree, not of kind. Some employment discrimination cases also implicate decisions based on many variables, and made by numerous individuals on behalf of large organizations.[72] The Court also argues that (at least for jury selection) the factors that may be considered in these other cases are different from those that influence death sentencing, that they are, "to a great degree, objectively verifiable."[73] Unfortunately, the list of "objective" factors that the Court provides belies this claim: sound mind, intelligence, good moral character, and the like.

It is true, of course, that the more complex the decisionmaking process, the harder it is to conclude that a particular pattern of results is necessarily the product of deliberate discrimination. When decisions are made by many different people or agencies it is difficult to say to what extent they reflect anybody's intentions, or just whose intentions are expressed. Intentionality implies self-consciousness, and that is a concept that applies poorly to repetitive conduct by collectivities and bureaucracies. We know quite well what we mean when we say that the general manager intentionally discriminates against women applicants, but it is not so clear what it means to say that General Motors does the same thing. Indeed, in a sufficiently complex organization even a clear and conscious policy of discrimination will be implemented imperfectly, so that unmistakable patterns like those in *Yick Wo* and *Gomillion* will rarely occur.

In practice, however, the Supreme Court has not required proof of deliberate discrimination either in jury selection or in employment cases. The Court has not explicitly abandoned the requirement of discriminatory "intent," but it has, in effect, redefined the term to mean something broader and vaguer than purpose or design. The standard that is most often quoted is from *Village of Arlington Heights v. Metropolitan Housing Corp.*: The plaintiff in a discrimination case may prevail by showing "a clear pattern, unexplainable on grounds other than race."[74] This sounds like deliberate discrimination, but it is not necessarily the same thing.

Consider, for example, a bank that hires only white tellers from a pool of applicants that includes many qualified blacks. This pattern could, of course, be due to purposeful racial discrimination. But it might also be produced by a pervasive but unconscious bias on the part of branch managers and personnel directors that leads them to discount the credentials of blacks without realizing it. This racial disparity might also be caused by social or institutional factors. White bank officials might, for instance, favour applicants whom they have met socially or know through common membership in churches or other largely segregated voluntary organizations. Each of these "unintentional" mechanisms produces a hiring pattern that is "unexplainable" except by reference to race, since the explanations—unconscious bias and social segregation—are themselves racially tainted. In either case, the bank's hiring practices would amount to actionable employment discrimination.

The procedure for proving intentional discrimination in jury selection or employment is even more forgiving. The plaintiff need only present a "prima facie case," evidence of a conduct that, "if otherwise unexplained, [is] more likely than not based on the consideration of impermissible factors."[75] The burden then shifts to the defendant to justify its conduct, if it can, on the basis of some "legitimate, nondiscriminatory reason."[76] In a Fourteenth Amendment jury-selection case a prima facie case is extremely simple: a claimant must present evidence that a jury-selection system that permits discretionary selection has produced a substantial underrepresentation of a protected group to which he or she belongs.[77] In a typical employment case a prima facie case is somewhat more elaborate, but still "not onerous." If the issue is discrimination in hiring, for example, the plaintiff "must prove by a preponderance of the evidence that she applied for an available position for which she was qualified, but was rejected under circumstances which give rise to an inference of unlawful discrimination. . . . [This] eliminates the most common nondiscriminatory reasons for the plaintiff's rejection."[78] In *McCleskey*, of course, the petitioner did more than merely eliminate the "most common" nonracial explanations, and far more than show a simple mathematical disparity in treatment, but the Court refused to consider this a prima facie case.

There might be a certain logic to this apparently inconsistent position, although it is poorly expressed in the *McCleskey* opinion. The Court seems to be saying that a claim of discrimination is measured not by a universal yardstick of "intent" but by reference to the preferred mode of behavior for the particular type of conduct at issue. For jury selection, the standard is simple. More than any other institution in the American legal system, the jury is a tribunal that embodies a broad democratic ideal. "It is part of the established tradition in the use of juries as instruments of public justice that the jury be a body truly representative of the community."[79] Selecting citizens for jury duty can be, and often is, a simple one-step ministerial process. Discretion in choosing jury panels is not constitutionally prohibited, but it is disfavored; the ideal is random selection from the jury-eligible community. Since selection criteria other than the basic requirements for eligibility are disfavored, their "discretionary" use cannot justify racial disparities. Therefore, racial disparities can be evaluated by simple statistical comparisons between the actual jury pool and the one that would have been obtained by random selection.[80]

Employment discrimination is somewhat more complex. There is no general system for hiring or promotion that is as simple and powerful as random selection, but there is an underlying assumption that employment decisions ought to be based on fairly straightforward economic considerations. The terms that are relevant will vary from case to case, but a rational employer will (presumably) always follow nondiscriminatory policies that are designed to maximize the productivity of its workforce. Deviations from this norm are harder to spot than in the case of jury selection, since for employment purposes all eligible candidates are *not* considered equal. But the relevant factors that differentiate them—their qualifications—can be identified (at least reasonably well) in any specific context, and those factors can be controlled, to eliminate "the most common nondiscriminatory" explanations for suspicious disparities.

But while employment practices may be considerably less structured than the elegant simplicity of jury selection, capital punishment is at the extreme unstructured end of the decisionmaking spectrum. There is no positive model whatever for the proper functioning of a death-sentencing system. There is no preferable method for weighing the severity of homicides—for deciding, for example, whether the method of killing counts more or less than the number of victims. There is no general agreement on the set of outcomes that the system should strive to achieve. Is it better to execute most capital murderers, or very few, or is there some optimal medium rate? Even basic value questions are indeterminant. Is retribution a proper basis for executions? If so, is it more important than deterrence or less? Since there is no affirmative standard by which to evaluate capital sentencing decisions, there is no way to specify how they should have been made. Therefore it is exceedingly difficult to find fault with a set of procedurally correct death sentences—to say, for example, that they were influenced by racial discrimination.

This progression of standards, from well defined to loose, can be viewed as the complement of the appropriate role of discretion. In jury selection, discretion is unnecessary and disfavored. In employment decisions discretion is inevitable since predictions of future productivity are always imperfect and often intuitive, but it is best minimized and regularized. In capital sentencing discretion is central and constitutionally required; it is the essence of the decision.

The Supreme Court does not spell out this theory of proof of discrimination, but it is suggested by marginal comments. For example, the Court explains that its uncommon willingness to consider statistical evidence in jury discrimination cases is a reflection of the special "nature of the jury selection task,"[81] which is not otherwise specified. Similarly, the Court argues that "while employment decisions may involve a number of relevant variables, these variables are to a great extent uniform for all employees," while for capital sentencing "[t]here is no common standard by which to evaluate all defendants."[82] But the Court does not state explicitly the two central elements of this scheme: first, that it uses affirmative models of proper conduct—standards of behavior that are not in themselves required—in evaluating claims of jury and employment discrimination; and second, that if a pattern of racial disparities is found to violate these standards, proof of deliberate intent is unnecessary.

This is a consistent and sensible theory. It *is* more difficult to detect misconduct to the extent that correct conduct is poorly defined. As a result, for capital punishment the problem of detection is uncommonly severe. But difficult is not impossible, and it is possible to prove that a complex process is influenced by an illegitimate factor without specifying how the process ought to operate and which legitimate factors it ought to employ. It is a forbidding task, but in this case it has been accomplished.

Where there is no single model for the proper operation of a system, one must prove discrimination by excluding all plausible legitimate schemes that could explain the observed outcomes. This is what we have attempted to do here with the evidence at our disposal, and we believe that we can confidently infer racial discrimination from our findings. This is what Baldus, Woodworth, and Pulaski did with extraordinary thoroughness for capital sentencing in Georgia. They considered hundreds of nonracial variables and analyzed them in countless separate statistical models, and the race of the victim never failed to emerge as a major determinant of death sentences. To be sure, even this exhaustive study does not answer all the questions we might have about the death penalty in Georgia—how it is used or how it should be used. But it does show that the answers to these questions, whatever they may be, cannot undermine this extraordinarily secure finding of race-of-victim discrimination.

The nature of the task of proving discrimination in this

context also eases the burden of rebuttal on the opposing side. The Court justifies its refusal to rely on statistical evidence in part on the ground that the state "has no practical opportunity to rebut" a prima facie case with an authoritative description of the nonracial factors that might explain the decisions to prosecute and to sentence.[83] But with this type of evidence of discrimination, that is unnecessary.

McCleskey maintained that there is *no* plausible justification for the racial disparities in capital sentencing in Georgia. To contradict that sort of claim, all the responding party has to do is point to *some* reasonable and legitimate explanation that could account for the observed outcomes; it is not necessary to establish what actually occurred. In this case, it appears that most if not all of the possible responses of this type were already considered and rejected in the Baldus study itself. In any event, if the state cannot describe even a single possible legitimate explanation for its racially disparate decisions—and that seems to be the case here—no opportunity to rebut, no matter how extensive, could make any difference.

While the Court discusses the difficulty of presenting a rebuttal to McCleskey's equal protection claim, it ignores the possibility of a legally sufficient justification for the practices he challenges. The reason for this omission may be the strictness of the traditional requirement for upholding an official distinction based on race or any other "suspect classification" in the face of an equal protection challenge. Such practices are subject to "strict scrutiny" under the Fourteenth Amendment, and can be justified only if they are "shown to be necessary to promote a compelling governmental interest."[84] This is an impossible standard to satisfy in almost any context. It certainly cannot be met here, since there is no plausible argument that the state has a compelling interest in the death penalty itself, let alone in any particular practices or patterns of imposing it.

But is strict scrutiny the inevitable standard for reviewing a race-of-victim claim? That is not so clear. The state argued that McCleskey lacked standing to complain about discrimination based on someone else's race, and the Court replied that he did have standing because such discrimination would subject him to punishment on the basis of "an irrational exercise of governmental power."[85] In other words, the Court seems to be saying that from McCleskey's point of view, discrimination based on the race of his alleged victim is not a suspect classification that is subject to strict scrutiny, but a form of potentially irrational and arbitrary government conduct. In that case, however, the usual standard for justification is much lower. In general, a non-suspect classification that is challenged under the equal protection clause will be upheld if it merely bears a rational relationship to a legitimate state interest.[86] The Court could have held under this test that the type of race-of-victim discrimination alleged in *McCleskey* is justified by its rational relationship to the state's legitimate interest in preserving prosecutorial and jury discretion in capital sentencing. If the occasion ever occured, the Court could still have held that an *explicit* race-of-victim classification (as opposed to the de facto pattern found here) violates equal protection because it serves no legitimate purpose whatever.

Such a holding seems like a simple solution to the problems raised by McCleskey's equal protection claim. It is internally consistent, it follows reasonably well from existing case law, and it draws a clearer connection than the Court's actual opinion between the rejection of this claim and the Court's repeated endorsement of the importance of discretion. Why then was it not used? The easiest explanation is that it was overlooked. This analysis was not suggested by either party or by any *amicus curiae*, and the majority may simply never have considered it. If it was considered, however, the majority might have rejected this option for either of two very different reasons. On the one hand, the justices might have been troubled by a rule that racial discrimination in capital sentencing can ever be so easily justified, even discrimination by race of victim. On the other hand, they might have been uninterested in this approach because of its limited reach. It would not have touched the separate race-of-defendant claim in McCleskey's case (which would still be subject to strict scrutiny), and, worse, would have done nothing to prevent other such claims in future cases. To truly clear the decks, a less discriminating broom was needed.

There is another way to look at the Supreme Court's inconsistency in dealing with statistical evidence. The Court introduces its discussion of the problem by saying that in the past it "has accepted statistics as proof of intent to discriminate in certain *limited contexts*"[87]—jury-selection and employment cases. This is true, but not because of any demonstrated reluctance to rely on this type of evidence in other types of cases. These are simply the only two contexts in which the Court has had the opportunity to do so. Facing this issue in a new setting, the Court may have been less concerned with applying a general theory of proof of discrimination (however imperfect) than with restricting statistical claims of discrimination to their existing range.

Perhaps the Court meant to say, in effect, something like this: In jury selection and employment cases we have acted on evidence that proves a good deal less than conscious and deliberate discrimination. From these cases one could infer a general rule that by discriminatory "intent" we mean something less than purpose, merely a discriminatory impact that cannot be explained by appropriate decision-making criteria. That is wrong. The rule is really much more specific. In *those two types of cases only* claims may be based on unjustified statistical disparities, but in all other Fourteenth Amendment cases the claimant must prove that the official conduct was the product of a genuine discriminatory purpose.[88]

The history of litigation over racial discrimination in jury selection and employment could justify setting these issues apart from other de facto discrimination claims. In the case of employment, this history is comparatively recent. Although racial discrimination in employment is actionable under a number of provisions of federal law,[89] the main impetus for litigation has been Title VII of the Civil Rights Act of 1964,[90] which made the elimination of employment discrimination a matter of national policy. This statute provided ideological support for a relatively aggressive stance by the Supreme Court: adopting a liberal method for proof of intentional discrimination, and (in some situations) making disparate racial impact a sufficient basis for a claim in itself.[91]

In the case of juries the history is longer. In 1880, in *Strauder v. West Virginia*,[92] jury selection became the first setting in which the Supreme Court used the equal protection clause to prohibit racial discrimination by a state. In dozens of cases following *Strauder*, the Court slowly developed a standardized method of dealing with this issue. The evolution of this system preceded the explicit "discriminatory intent" requirement announced in *Washington v. Davis*,[93] and the standard that was developed did not depend on any showing of "intent," at least not in the usual sense. For example, in *Alexander v. Louisiana*, in 1972, the Court condemned a "result [that] bespeaks discrimination, whether or not it was a conscious decision on the part of any individual jury commissioner."[94] The Court was not about to change this settled practice after *Washington v. Davis* was decided in 1976; indeed, in later jury discrimination cases, it has continued to cite and rely on pre-1976 cases that talk of unintended or unconscious discrimination.[95]

It is also important to notice that the wall the Court builds around jury-selection and employment discrimination cases blocks movement in both directions. The majority is careful not only to limit the spread of statistical evidence to new territory, but also to avoid undermining its use in areas where it is already well established. In other death penalty cases, the Court has sometimes been more hasty. For example, in *Lockhart v. McCree*[96] the Court denied a capital defendant's challenge to the "death qualification," the procedure for choosing juries in capital cases. In the process of doing so, the Court gave the following remarkable reason (among others) for reaching its decision: the petitioner's jury, which was selected by the challenged procedure, *could* have been chosen by chance; if it had been, there would be no cause for complaint. "[I]t is hard for us to understand the logic of the argument that a given jury is unconstitutionally partial when it results from a State-ordained process, yet impartial when exactly the same jury results from mere chance."[97]

The reach of this statement is breathtaking. An all-white jury (or an all-male labor force, or virtually any other outcome) *could* result from "mere chance," and if it did, it would not be objectionable. Therefore it must also be unobjectionable if it is created by a "state-ordained process." So far, this aspect of the *Lockhart* opinion has been ignored, but if it were applied literally it would overturn most if not all of existing anti-discrimination jurisprudence. In *McCleskey*, fortunately, the Court did not leave this sort of unexploded ordnance lying around.

D. The Demise of "Arbitrariness"

In one respect, the Supreme Court opinion in *McCleskey* seems to restore some independent force to the prohibition against arbitrary capital sentencing. The Eleventh Circuit had held that "intent and motive are a natural component"[98] of an arbitrariness claim based on racial discrimination, which made this Eighth Amendment issue redundant with that aspect of equal protection. The Supreme Court devotes the bulk of its opinion to McCleskey's Eighth Amendment claim but never mentions any requirement of intent. In the context of the circuit court decision, and of its own extensive discussion of the intent requirement in Fourteenth Amendment discrimination cases, this silence can only be interpreted as a reversal of the Eleventh Circuit's opinion on that issue. This implicit reversal, however, has no consequences, since the explicit language in the Court's opinion deprives the Eighth Amendment concept of arbitrariness of any vestiges of content it might still have retained prior to the *McCleskey* case.

"Arbitrariness" is simply shorthand for the interpretation one gives to the Supreme Court's decision in *Furman*.[99] The death sentencing statutes in effect in 1972 gave juries unlimited discretion to choose death or to decline to do so. The resulting death sentences were, in the view of the various justices in the majority, arbitrary, rare, capricious, random, and discriminatory. The Supreme Court outlawed these statutes, but four years later, in *Gregg v. Georgia*[100] and its companion cases, it approved new death penalty statutes that were designed to curb arbitrariness by guiding and limiting the discretion of sentencing juries. In the prototypical "guided discretion" statute this was attempted by directing the sentencing jury to consider specific statutory aggravating and mitigating factors, and by appellate "proportionality review." In the years that followed, however, the Court stripped away these procedural restrictions one by one. In 1978, in *Lockett v. Ohio*[101] it held that the state cannot restrict the range of mitigating evidence in capital sentencing proceedings; in 1983, in *Zant v. Stephens*[102] and *Barclay v. Florida*,[103] it permitted sentencing juries to consider nonstatutory aggravating circumstances; and in 1984, in *Pulley v. Harris*,[104] it decided that proportionality review is not required. This left one potential issue unresolved: if a capital sentencing system produced a demonstrably unprincipled pattern of *outcomes*, would that be regarded as "arbitrary" regardless of the procedures that were followed? In *McCleskey* the Court answered: No.

The reasons for this conclusion come in three parts, a core argument and two peripheral ones. The main argument is that these racial disparities must be tolerated because they are simply incidents of the discretionary nature of criminal justice in general, and of capital sentencing in particular.[105] Unevenness is an inevitable consequence of discretion, but it is not necessarily culpable. Considering the value of discretion as an element of this system, and the many procedural safeguards against the intrusion of racial biases into death sentencing and the criminal justice system generally,[106] the Court is unwilling to agree that the evidence in this case shows that race improperly influenced capital sentencing.

On the surface, it sounds as though the Court has reached an empirical decision that this particular record does not satisfy the stringent requirements for proof of systematic arbitrariness in capital sentencing. In fact, it has made such challenges impossible. Without saying it in so many words, the Court has decided that statistical studies are inherently insufficient for this purpose. Even in the extraordinarily unlikely event that some future study could outdo the Baldus study, it still would "at most . . . show only a likelihood that a particular factor entered into some decisions,"[107] and that would still fall short. And yet, there is no alternative. Statistics are the only evidence that can detect system-wide patterns of arbitrariness and discrimination.

The secondary arguments for the holding on arbitrariness are so conspicuously weak that instead of reinforcing the Court's reasoning they taint it with a sense of uneasiness and ambivalence. One of these arguments is a routine bow in the direction of legislative supremacy. Here, as always, policy arguments are "best presented to legislative bodies";[108] federal court interference is always an unfortunate last resort. This general piety says nothing about the merits of any particular case in which action by the courts may be necessary.

The other marginal argument is more specific: "Mc-Cleskey's claim, taken to its logical conclusion, throws into serious question the principles that underlie our entire criminal justice system."[109] Other penalties could be challenged, not just death sentences, and for discrepancies based on factors other than race—membership in a variety of ethnic groups, sex, facial characteristics, attractiveness.

These are not credible fears. The majority cites several empirical studies that are said to find such troublesome nonracial and noncapital disparities, but these studies do little or nothing to support the argument. On the more substantial claim—that racial discrimination may be found in noncapital sentencing—the majority cites two studies "that allegedly demonstrate a racial disparity in the length of prison sentences."[110] These two studies do find that black defendants are somewhat more likely to be sentenced to prison than white defendants, but their findings are equivocal.[111] The majority does not mention that many other studies have failed to find racial disparities in noncapital sentencing, and it does not cite the best summary of research in the area—an authoritative review compiled for the National Academy of Sciences—which concludes that "there is no evidence of a widespread systematic pattern of [racial] discrimination in sentencing."[112] Perhaps capital punishment is different because juries are commonly used to sentence in capital cases but not otherwise; perhaps the emotional stress of capital trials activates latent racial biases; perhaps the infrequency of death sentences gives greater scope to the operation of all types of biases in the process of making these extraordinary choices. Whatever the reasons, capital punishment stands out as the one setting in which racial discrimination in sentencing is consistently found and convincingly proven.

The majority's fear of challenges based on nonracial factors is supported by an even flimsier set of citations. The only listed source that examined the dispositions of actual cases is an unpublished study that found differences by sex in the severity of convictions in murder cases.[113] This finding, however, is uninterpretable since the researchers made no attempt to control for legitimate differences between cases. The other studies cited all rely on the responses of experimental subjects (typically college students) to descriptions of criminal cases, sometimes extremely sketchy descriptions.[114] The findings of these studies are not impressive. They are conflicting, inconsistent, and, as the researchers themselves sometimes acknowledge, impossible to distinguish from alternative explanations for which they did not control. It is puzzling that the majority should purport to rely on a set of studies that are so far inferior both to the Baldus study and to the detailed body of research on death qualification that the same five justices rejected in *Lockhart v. McCree*.[115] Perhaps the most charitable explanation for this apparent inconsistency is a know-nothing attitude toward social scientific research: It all looks the same to us, so if we were to accept one study how could we ever reject any other?

And what if other instances of discrimination could be proven? Would a holding for McCleskey necessarily mean that these future claims would also have to be granted? Justice Brennan in dissent clearly has the better of this debate.[116] The Supreme Court *could* extend a decision in this case to such lengths, but that is hardly a necessary or a "logical" conclusion. The Court has said repeatedly (and no one doubts) that death is a uniquely severe and irreversible penalty, and that there is a correspondingly unique need for "reliability in the determination that death is the appropriate punishment."[117] Similarly, race is not just any factor. "[T]hree constitutional amendments, and numerous statutes"[118] reflect "a moral commitment . . . that this specific characteristic should not be the basis for allotting burdens and benefits,"[119] and race discrimination in capital punishment is "a particularly repugnant prospect."[120] If the Court had wished to do so, it could easily have granted relief in this case but restricted it to exactly this type of claim.

But the Court did not wish to do so. Instead, it brought the constitutional status of the death penalty full circle, back to its pre-*Furman* state in 1971. One of the curiosities of *Furman* is its relationship to *McGautha v. California*,[121] which the Court decided only a year earlier. The *McGautha* Court held that due process was not violated by entrusting capital sentencing to the absolute and unguided discretion of the jury. After *Furman*, it seemed for a while that *McGautha* had simply been bypassed (if not overruled). Technically this is still the governing fiction, since *Furman* reached the opposite conclusion on *Eighth* Amendment rather than *Fourteenth* Amendment grounds, and all the later death penalty cases purport to be faithful applications of *Furman*. In fact, the Court has come, step by step, from *Gregg* through *McCleskey*, to interpret *Furman* to mean no more than what *McGautha* had already said: the Constitution permits open discretion in capital sentencing.

Still, there are differences between the treatment of discretion in *McGautha* and that in *McCleskey*. For one thing, Justice Harlan, writing for the Court in *McGautha*, was explicit about the procedure that was being approved: "committing to the untrammeled discretion of the jury the power to pronounce life or death in capital cases."[122] Justice Powell in *McCleskey* is not nearly so honest. His opinion is laced with references to procedures that "limit," "channel," "direct," and "narrow" the sentencer's discretion. But when all is said and done, what discretion-limiting rules can Powell distill from fifteen years of post-*Furman* jurisprudence? Only the requirement that the state establish a clear threshold below which the death penalty may not be imposed. In *McGautha* itself Justice Harlan had already pointed out that this type of restriction provides no "standards for guiding the sentencing authority's discretion" but is merely "a redefinition of the class of potentially capital murders."[123]

In addition, Justice Harlan described capital sentencing discretion in basically negative terms. For him, it was no more than a necessary evil, a realistic accommodation to the limitations of formal justice:

> To identify before the fact those characteristics of criminal homicides and their perpetrators which call for the death penalty, and to express these characteristics in language which can be fairly understood and applied by the sentencing authority, appear to be tasks which are beyond present human ability.[124]

According to Harlan, any attempt to overcome this problem is doomed to produce "either meaningless 'boiler plate' or a statement of the obvious that no jury would heed."[125] Unregulated discretion is simply the residual category that is left when such unwise experiments are avoided.

By *McCleskey* this same discretion has become a positive virtue. In *Gregg* the Court rejected Harlan's cold logic and embraced the system of guided discretion that he had condemned. At that point the Court emphasized the expected advantages of the *limits* that this method imposed:

> No longer can a jury wantonly and freakishly impose the death sentence; it is always circumscribed by the legislative guidelines.[126]

> No longer should there be "no meaningful basis for distinguishing the few cases in which [the death penalty] is imposed from the many cases in which it is not."[127]

In later cases, culminating in *McCleskey*, the balance has been struck for discretion and against guidance; nonetheless, the Court has maintained its generally cheerful attitude, although the focus has been reversed.[128] Optimism, it seems, is the main requirement of following *Furman*, and not analytic consistency. As a result, discretion has been transformed from an inevitable lesser evil into an essential feature that "offers substantial benefits to the criminal defendant,"[129] and "is fundamental to our criminal process."[130] As the Court now has it, discretion is a virtue of such importance that its preservation justifies vast racial disparities in the imposition of sentences of death.

E. The Present Disparities and the "Major Systemic Defects Identified in *Furman*"

Perhaps the Court is uncomfortable with its decision to make discretion a constitutional counterweight to discrimination. In any event, it does not rest with this justification for Georgia's capital sentencing procedures but adds a factual finding: "The discrepancy indicated by the Baldus study is 'a far cry from the major systemic defects identified in *Furman*.' "[131] In fact, the Baldus study itself "confirms that the Georgia system results in a reasonable level of proportionality among the class of murderers eligible for the death penalty."[132] The Eleventh Circuit reached the same conclusion, and stated it in even stronger terms:

> Viewed broadly, it would seem that the statistical evidence presented here, assuming its validity, confirms rather than condemns the system. In a state where past discrimination is well documented, the study showed no discrimination as to the race of the defendant. The marginal disparity based on the race of the victim tends to support the state's contention that the system is working far differently from the one which *Furman* condemned. In pre-*Furman* days, there was no rhyme or reason as to who got the death penalty and who did not. But now, in the vast majority of cases, the reasons for a difference are well documented. That they are not so clear in a small percentage of the cases is no reason to declare the entire system unconstitutional.[133]

Unfortunately, these claims are not supported by the evidence the courts cite. First, contrary to the circuit court's assertion, Baldus and his colleagues did find discrimination by race of defendant, albeit a lesser amount than by race of victim.[134] Second, the Baldus study does not show "a reasonable level of proportionality" in capital sentencing, and it certainly does not "document" the reasons for death sentences in "the vast majority of cases." This very same study was faulted by the district court because it explains less than 50 percent of the variance in the sentencing outcomes. While this is not a legitimate criticism of statistical evidence of discrimination,[135] it does demonstrate that even with comprehensive evidence—and even when illegitimate factors such as race are considered—it is impossible to predict or explain capital sentencing decisions in Georgia with anything approaching precision. Baldus himself, in an article devoted primarily to the problem of arbitrariness, concludes the opposite. "Our data suggest that Georgia's [post-*Furman*] death-sentencing system has continued to impose the type of inconsistent, arbitrary death sentences that the United States Supreme Court condemned in *Furman v. Georgia*."[136]

The courts' reliance on the Baldus study to justify post-*Furman* sentencing stands in peculiar contrast to their unwillingness to accept it as evidence of discrimination. On this point also, the circuit court is more explicit. After rejecting the Baldus findings on race, the Eleventh Circuit adds an odd observation: "The type of research submitted here tends to show which of the [statutorily] directed factors were effective [in determining death sentences], but is of restricted use in showing what undirected factors control the exercise of constitutionally required discretion."[137] This statement is unexplained and, in fact, inexplicable. Techniques of statistical analysis do not discriminate between variables on the basis of their legal significance. A methodology that is useful to show the effects of statutory aggravating factors on capital sentencing will be equally useful to show the effects of race. The court's assertion amounts, quite simply, to a prejudgment based on faith: evidence of evenhandedness will be believed, evidence of discrimination will not.[138]

In this case, the claim that the system of capital sentencing is now far better than "the one which *Furman* condemned" is based, ostensibly, on the empirical evidence assembled by Professor Baldus and his colleagues. In earlier cases, however, the Supreme Court has made similar pronouncements with no record at all to support them.

This sentiment was first expressed in *Gregg* and its companion cases, when three of the earliest post-*Furman* death penalty statutes were approved: "No longer can a jury wantonly and freakishly impose the death sentence; it is always circumscribed by the legislative guidelines."[139] Etcetera. In *Gregg* these statements, however positive, seem merely to express a prediction. (Nonetheless, some lower courts interpreted them as embodying a rule of law.[140]) Eight years later, in *Pulley v. Harris*, the Court said (in language later quoted in *McCleskey*) that sentencing "aberrations" under California's post-*Furman* death penalty laws "are a far cry from the major systemic defects identified in *Furman*."[141] In *Pulley*, unlike *Gregg*, the statement appears to be a factual observation. But perhaps the most striking expression of this position is contained in Justice Powell's dissenting opinion (written for four members of the Court) in *Stephens v. Kemp*, in which the Court granted a stay of execution pending the outcome of *McCleskey*:

> Surely, no contention can be made that the entire Georgia judicial system, at all levels, operates to discriminate in all cases. Arguments to this effect may have been directed to the type of statutes addressed in *Furman v. Georgia*. . . . As our subsequent cases make clear, such arguments cannot be taken seriously under statutes approved in *Gregg*.[142]

What is the factual basis for this conviction that *Furman* and *Gregg* changed the face of capital sentencing in the United States? To answer that question it is necessary to look first at the evidence of arbitrariness and of discrimination that was before the Court in *Furman*. With the conspicuous exception of the studies of racial discrimination in the use of the death penalty for rape, there was less there than meets the eye.

Much of the evidence of racial discrimination under pre-*Furman* capital sentencing statutes consisted of the opinions of politicians and other prominent people that "[i]t is the poor, the illiterate, the underprivileged, the member of the minority group, who is usually sacrificed by society's lack of concern."[143] The major statistical evidence of racial discrimination was the undeniable fact that a disproportionate number of those executed for murder between 1930 and 1967—1630 out of 3334, or 49 percent—were black.[144] In addition, the petitioners cited a few studies of sentencing patterns that suggested discrimination in capital sentencing[145] (the best of these was Harold Garfinkel's study of capital homicide prosecutions in North Carolina[146]), and a few other studies that found that whites who had been sentenced to death were more likely to receive executive clemency than blacks.[147]

The petitioners in *Furman* made modest claims about this evidence:

> Racial discrimination is strongly suggested by the national execution figures; it has been borne out by a number of discrete and limited but carefully done studies; and it has seemed apparent to responsible commissions and individuals studying the administration of the death penalty in this country. Assuredly, the proof of discrimination is stronger in rape than in murder cases; and, in any case, an irrefutable statistical showing that a particular State has violated the Equal Protection of the Law by consistent racial inequality in the administration of the death penalty is difficult to establish.[148]

This assessment of the evidence reflects in part the existence of nonracial explanations for these data, and of contrary findings. The high proportion of blacks among those executed is consistent with the proportion of blacks among those charged with homicide.[149] Some pre-*Furman* studies found no racial patterns in the commutations of death sentences.[150]

And, as the petitioners themselves pointed out, the most detailed study of capital sentencing then available did "not find racial discrimination . . . at the penalty stage of jury tried cases."[151]

The evidence of "arbitrariness" or "capriciousness" in capital sentencing before *Furman* was even skimpier than the evidence of discrimination. This is inevitable. Arbitrariness in its commonsense meaning is a negative concept, the absence of an explanation for a choice or a pattern of choices; like many negatives, it is difficult to prove. As a rule, proof of arbitrariness depends on indirect evidence, evidence that excludes all plausible explanations other than random caprice. At the time of *Furman*, only one study— the *Stanford Law Review* study[152]—had examined enough factors to be at all useful on this point, and it was cited by the chief justice in his *Furman* dissent as showing the *absence* of arbitrariness because it found that, except for some evidence of discrimination against blue-collar defendants, California "juries do follow rational patterns in imposing the sentence of death."[153] The evidence that was cited in support of the claim of capriciousness, on the other hand, consisted primarily of the opinions of legal scholars and other observers. For example, Professor Herbert Wechsler is quoted to the effect that those who are sentenced to death are "a small and highly random sample of people who commit murder."[154] Of the two justices whose opinions in *Furman* turn on the issue of arbitrariness, one (Stewart) cites a statement by former attorney general Ramsey Clark as the support for his conclusion that the death penalty is imposed on "a capriciously selected random handful" of convicts,[155] and the other (White) relies on his personal experience on the Supreme Court—"10 years of almost daily exposure" to potentially capital cases—to conclude that "there is no meaningful basis for distinguishing the few cases in which [the death penalty] is imposed from the many cases in which it is not."[156]

Our point is not that the evidence of discrimination and

of arbitrariness in *Furman* was deficient. On the contrary, taken as a whole, the evidence was telling. Such large racial disparities in the proportions of those executed over so long a period are hard to explain in the absence of racial discrimination of some sort. The few systematic studies that existed were, on the whole, consistent with that conclusion. And, finally, the extreme infrequency of death sentences made it all but inevitable that those who were executed were selected in part by chance. The Supreme Court knew what it was talking about; it was willing to rely in part on impressionistic evidence, but its factual conclusions were correct. Our point is rather that the evidence is stronger now, and that the comparisons that can be made show little or no change since *Furman*.

The central item of evidence of pre-*Furman* discrimination in capital sentencing was the high proportion of blacks among those executed. Comparisons with post-*Furman* executions are of limited value, since relatively few have occurred, only 98 as of May 1, 1988.[157] (For the same reason, it is too early to assess the racial patterns in post-*Furman* commutations.) Still, for what it is worth, the current pattern seems reasonably comparable to the pre-*Furman* one: 40 percent (39/98) of those executed since 1972 have been black, a decrease from the 49 percent before *Furman* but far more than the proportion of blacks in the population. A more meaningful statistic is the proportion of blacks on post-*Furman* death rows—41 percent (836/2048) as of May 1, 1988.[158] This is a slight decrease from the pre-*Furman* execution figure, but most of the difference is caused by an increase in the proportion of other minorities, from 1.2 percent to 7.8 percent.[159] In short, if there has been any change in the proportions of blacks and whites condemned to death, it has been small.

A different type of evidence on this point is provided by Gary Kleck, who has estimated the risk of a death sentence— the rate of death sentences per 1000 homicide arrests—

for black and white defendants from 1967 through 1978.[160] Kleck found that the risk of a death sentence was higher for a white defendant than for a black defendant throughout this period; this apparently reflects discrimination by race of victim, and the fact that black defendants are charged primarily with killing other blacks, who are "devalued crime victims."[161] For present purposes, Kleck's analysis is useful because it is possible to compare his pre-*Furman* (1967–72) and his post-*Furman* (1973–78) sub-samples. This comparison shows that the ratio of the risk of a death sentence for a black defendant to that of a white defendant changed relatively little after *Furman*, from .58 to .65,[162] but that to the extent that there has been a change, the relative risk of a death sentence for a black defendant has increased.

What about discrimination by race of victim? This issue received little attention prior to *Furman*. A look at the primary type of data used in *Furman* to show discrimination against black defendants—executions and death sentencing rates—reveals pronounced disparities by race of victim in the post-*Furman* period, disparities that approach the size of the race-of-defendant disparities for rape in pre-*Furman* capital sentencing. Eighty-six percent of the post-*Furman* executions through the end of April of 1988 (84/98) were for the killing of white victims;[163] in the same period, nearly 45 percent of all homicide victims in the United States were black.[164] In the eight states that are studied here, fewer than half of the homicides from 1976 through 1980 had white victims, but they received 86 percent of the death sentences.

Only two pre-*Furman* studies of capital sentencing for homicide considered the race of the victim. Garfinkel found discrimination by race of victim as well as race of defendant in North Carolina from 1930 through 1940.[165] The pattern he found is almost identical to the racial patterns found by Bowers and Pierce for the period from *Furman* through

1977,[166] and by our own study of post-*Furman* sentencing.[167] The *Stanford Law Review* study,[168] the only pre-*Furman* study of capital sentencing that is even remotely comparable in scope to the Baldus study, did not find discrimination by race of victim in jury sentencing in California. By contrast, ten or more post-*Furman* studies on this question have been completed; they all show discrimination by race of victim, and they are methodologically superior to the earlier studies. In sum, the evidence of widespread discrimination by race of victim in post-*Furman* capital sentencing is stronger than *any* evidence of racial discrimination in capital sentencing for homicide that was available in 1972.

Finally, there is the issue of post-*Furman* arbitrariness. The strongest evidence of arbitrariness before *Furman* was the infrequency with which the death penalty was imposed and executed; if that has changed since *Furman* the change is truly marginal. In the period from 1976 through 1980, death sentences were given to about one percent of all defendants arrested for homicide;[169] that rate seems to be reasonably stable. Nor is there any evidence that the process by which these defendants are chosen for the death penalty has become more systematic since 1972—indeed, the available research suggests the opposite. The Eleventh Circuit and the Supreme Court point to findings by Baldus that legitimate factors were influential predictors of death sentencing in Georgia, and conclude that the sentencing system is rational and greatly improved since *Furman*. But Chief Justice Burger pointed to similar findings in the *Stanford Law Review* study in his dissent in *Furman*,[170] and the evidence does not support the argument in either case. Those who kill in the course of felonies, for example, may be much more likely to receive death sentences than those who kill in other circumstances—now and before *Furman* alike—but that fact does not negate the possibility of discrimination or of arbitrariness. Indeed, both problems could exist even if felony-murderers were the *only* defendants who were eligible for capital punishment. As long as the death penalty is rarely imposed, there will remain plenty of room for discrimination and for pure chance in the choice of those few among the eligible defendants who will actually receive it.

Rare as post-*Furman* death sentences have been, they are far more common than executions. As noted, there were only 98 executions from *Furman* through May 1, 1988. In the same period, approximately 3500 people were sentenced to death[171] and over 2000 are now on death row.[172] The total number of executions may be somewhat misleading, since reasonably regular executions began again only in late 1983. There were 21 executions in 1984, 18 in 1985, 18 in 1986, and 25 in 1987.[173] But even if this rate were to increase sharply to fifty or seventy executions a year, those executed would remain the exceptions among those sentenced to death and a tiny minority of those convicted of homicide.

And who are these rare defendants who are executed? Victor Streib has compiled detailed descriptions of the cases of the first eleven men executed under post-*Furman* statutes, from Gary Mark Gilmore in January 1977 to John Elden Smith in December 1983. He summarizes his findings:

> While all eleven of the executed men committed homicide, six of the homicides were fairly ordinary killings that occurred during armed robberies. They were not particularly brutal nor did they involve more than one victim. . . . [O]nly one-fourth of these eleven crimes qualified as being particularly heinous.[174]

Comparing these eleven cases with the thousands of other "death sentences not resulting in executions or with the many thousands of similar crimes for which the death sentence was not imposed," Streib concludes: "No particularly distinguishing factors can be identified which would place these eleven cases in a clearly unique category."[175]

To be sure, this is anecdotal evidence on a handful of cases; it is not conclusive proof of arbitrariness, if such a thing is possible. But it is the best evidence that has been assembled on post-*Furman* executions, and it sounds like an echo of the descriptions of arbitrariness by Justices Stewart and White in their concurring opinions in *Furman* itself.[176]

We do not claim that there have been no changes in patterns of capital sentencing since *Furman*. Very likely there have been changes, and it is possible that there has been a decrease in the prevalence of racial discrimination. Indeed, some reduction in capital sentencing discrimination might be expected for reasons unconnected with *Furman* and the cases applying it. The 1960s and early 1970s were a revolutionary period in criminal procedure in general. It is quite possible that the major Supreme Court decisions on right to counsel,[177] police interrogations,[178] and jury representativeness,[179] among others, had more impact on racial discrimination in capital sentencing than all the Court's death penalty cases together. In addition, the 1960s and 1970s were times of profound social change, including a dramatic increase in the political power of the black minority. This transformation must have touched the criminal justice system to some extent.

But these are only hypotheses, however reasonable. They do not prove that any changes in fact took place, or how large they might be, and the existing data are not much help. There may be less discrimination and less arbitrariness now, and, for all the available evidence shows, there may be more. The information on discrimination and on arbitrariness in capital sentencing for homicide was much sketchier in 1972 than it is in 1988, so comparisons are difficult, but to the extent they can be made, they certainly show no marked improvement. The courts' determined assertions that the pre-*Furman* problems have been solved must be seen as statements of faith rather than fact, or perhaps as wishful thinking, since the evidence, if it shows anything, shows remarkable constancy rather than change.

Notes

1. 106 S.Ct. 3331 (1986).
2. Thus, for example, in Griffith v. Kentucky, 107 S.Ct. 708 (1987) the Court held that Batson v. Kentucky, 106 S.Ct. 1712 (1986), which prohibited racial discrimination by prosecutors in the use of peremptory challenges, would be applied retroactively to cases pending on direct review. Following *Griffith*, the Court disposed of over two dozen pending petitions for certiorari that raised this issue by granting certiorari, vacating the judgments, and remanding the cases to the lower courts for further consideration in light of *Griffith*. See 107 S.Ct. 1266–72 (1987). Similarly, after its decision in *McCleskey,* the Court dealt with a comparable list of trailing certiorari, this time by denying them. See 107 S.Ct. 3244–45 (1987).
3. McCleskey v. Kemp, 107 S.Ct. 1756 (1987).
4. *Id.* at 1766 n.7.
5. *Id.* at 1769. The Court also specifically holds that defendants such as McCleskey have standing to complain about discrimination based on the race of homicide victims, because such discrimination subjects them to punishment on the basis of "an irrational exercise of governmental power." *Id.* at 1766 n.8, citation omitted. See ch. 8, note 3.
6. *Id.* at 1767–68.
7. *Id.* at 1768.
8. *Id.* at 1769. Justice Powell also states that without stronger proof no rebuttal should be necessary, because a legitimate justification for McCleskey's death sentence "is apparent from the record: McCleskey committed an act for which the United States Constitution and Georgia laws permit imposition of the death penalty." *Id.* at 1769. In other words, McCleskey was "qualified" for the death penalty. This is a make-weight argument, since it applies to most clearly discriminatory patterns of behavior as well. An employer who hires no women could point to the fact that the company's hiring decisions have a clear "legitimate" explanation—all its (male) employees are qualified. Likewise, a jury commissioner who picks an all-white grand jury panel could argue that no explanation is necessary since each (white) panel member is undeniably qualified to serve. There is no dispute that McCleskey was eligible for the death penalty. The question is why he was among the small proportion of death-eligible defendants that was in fact selected for this extreme and infrequent punishment. This type of issue is common.

As often as not, the central question in a discrimination case is whether the choice among qualified people was made on the basis of legitimate or illegitimate criteria. Justice Powell's approach transforms the existence of minimal qualifications into a strong presumption that the choice in question was not based on illegitimate considerations.

9. *Id.* at 1769, citing Personnel Administrator of Massachusetts v. Feeney, 442 U.S. 256, 279 (1979).

10. 107 S.Ct. at 1770 n.20. *Cf.* Hunter v. Underwood, 471 U.S. 222, 228–33 (1985), in which legislative history was accepted as proof of discriminatory motive in enacting a state statute.

11. 107 S.Ct. at 1774.

12. *Id.* at 1774–75, citing Pulley v. Harris, 465 U.S. 37 (1984), and Gregg v. Georgia, 428 U.S. 153 (1976).

13. *Id.* at 1775, footnote omitted.

14. *Id.* at 1775–78.

15. *Id.* at 1779–81.

16. *Id.* at 1781.

17. *Id.* at 1781–94. Part I of Justice Brennan's dissent, *id.* at 1781–82, restates his long-standing position that the death penalty is an inherently cruel and unusual punishment, forbidden by the Eighth Amendment. Only Justice Marshall joined in that portion of this dissent.

18. *Id.* at 1782. Brennan's choice of an example to illustrate the consequences of the *McCleskey* decision is revealing. Apparently he believed that his readers would more readily identify with lawyers who "must tell their clients that race casts a large shadow" across their cases, *id.*, than with capital defendants whose lives are put in jeopardy by this fact. *See* ch. 7, pp. 113–14.

19. *Id.* at 1782–84.

20. *Id.* at 1784–89.

21. *Id.* at 1789, quoting Turner v. Murray, 476 U.S. 28, 35 (1986).

22. 107 S.Ct. at 1790, citing Batson v. Kentucky, 476 U.S. 79 (1986), in which the Supreme Court held that the equal protection clause prohibits racial discrimination by prosecutors in the exercise of peremptory challenges, a task in which traditionally they enjoyed virtually absolute discretion.

23. 107 S.Ct. at 1791.

24. *Id.* at 1793.

25. *Id.* at 1794.

26. *Id.* at 1794–1805. Justices Brennan and Marshall do not join in the final paragraph of this dissent, Part IV-B, *id.* at 1805. In this section Justice Blackmun expresses his agreement with Justice Stevens's position, *id.* at 1806, *see infra* pp. 165–166, that the problem of racial discrimina-

tion could be cured, and the Georgia death penalty retained, if capital punishment were limited to the most aggravated of the cases now eligible. Justice Blackmun adds that charging guidelines for prosecutors would also help.

27. 398 F.2d 138 (8th Cir. 1968). See ch. 8, pp. 122–23 and notes 21–27.

28. 107 S.Ct. at 1799 n.7.

29. Id. at 1797.

30. Id. at 1797–98.

31. Id.

32. Justice Blackmun spells out the three traditional elements of such a prima facie case. The claimant must show that (1) he is a member of a distinct class that is singled out from the rest of the population, (2) this group is treated differently from others, and (3) the procedure or process in question is susceptible to abuse and discrimination. Id. at 1798–99, citing Castaneda v. Partida, 430 U.S. 482, 494 (1977).

33. 107 S.Ct. at 1798, quoting Alexander v. Louisiana, 405 U.S. 625, 632 (1972).

34. Id. at 1799–1803.

35. Id. at 1803–4. Indeed, in McCleskey itself the prosecutors responsible for the case were deposed and explained their actions. Id. at 1801–2.

36. Id. at 1805.

37. Id. at 1805–6.

38. See McCleskey, 753 F.2d at 907 (Johnson, J., dissenting and concurring in part) (Baldus study characterized in record as "far and away the most complete and thorough analysis of sentencing" ever conducted [quoting Dr. Richard Berk, member of National Academy of Sciences panel on sentencing research]). See ch. 9, note 20.

39. In other cases, the Court has occasionally provoked strong reactions for its poor use of social scientific evidence. For example, in Williams v. Florida, 399 U.S. 78, 101 (1970), the Court said that the existing empirical studies "indicate that there is no discernable difference between the results reached" by twelve-person juries and by smaller panels. In Colgrove v. Battin, 413 U.S. 149, 159 n.15 (1973), the Court added that four post-Williams studies "provided convincing empirical evidence of the correctness of the Williams conclusion." These statements were severely criticized by researchers in the field as inaccurate and uninformed. See, e.g., Lempert, Uncovering "Nondiscernable" Differences: Empirical Research and the Jury Size Cases, 73 MICH. L. REV. 643 (1973); Zeisel & Diamond, "Convincing Empirical Evidence" On the Six Member Jury, 41 U. OF CHI. L. REV. 281 (1974).

40. McCleskey v. Kemp, 107 S.Ct. 1756 (1987), Brief for Petitioner [hereinafter "Petitioner's Brief"], at 77–97.

41. *Id.*, Brief *Amicus Curiae* for Dr. Franklin Fisher *et al.*, at 5, 16–20, 28.

42. Gross, *Race and Death: The Judicial Evaluation of Evidence of Discrimination in Capital Sentencing*, 18 U.C. DAVIS L. REV. 1275, 1298–1308 (1985). *See* ch. 9, pp. 142–51.

43. *See* ch. 4, p. 66, Table 4.24, and ch. 5, p. 91, Table 5.3.

44. *See* ch. 9, pp. 142–52.

45. Ibid.

46. 106 S.Ct. 1758 (1986).

47. Under the form of death qualification that was common when the *Lockhart* case originated, all prospective jurors who said on voir dire that they would not consider voting for the death penalty in any capital case were excluded from the determination of guilt as well as the decision on penalty, even if they could be fair and impartial in deciding guilt or innocence in a capital case. *See Lockhart, supra;* Witherspoon v. Illinois, 391 U.S. 510 (1968). The defendant in *Lockhart* presented fifteen or more separate studies by a variety of researchers, using different methodologies and conducted over a period of nearly three decades. All these studies found that this procedure makes the resulting juries less representative, less diverse, and more prone to convict than ordinary criminal trial juries. On the other side, the state could not point to a single study that failed to find these effects. *See* Grigsby v. Mabry, 569 F.Supp. 1273 (E. D. Ark. 1983), *aff'd* 758 F.2d 226 (8th Cir. 1985) (en banc), *rev'd sub nom* Lockhart v. McCree, 106 S.Ct. 1758 (1986).

48. Under Rule 52(a) of the Federal Rules of Civil Procedure, the factual findings of a lower federal court may be reconsidered by a higher court only if they are "clearly erroneous." In *Lockhart* the Court expressed skepticism about the application of that standard to determinations of "legislative facts"—i.e., facts of general application that are not tied to the individual case before the court—but concluded that it need not reach the issue because its decision did not rest "on the invalidity of the lower courts' 'factual' findings." *See Lockhart,* 106 S.Ct. at 1762 n.3.

49. 107 S.Ct. at 1778 n.36.

50. *Id.* at 1781.

51. *Id.* at 1766 n.7.

52. McCleskey v. Kemp, 753 F.2d at 899.

53. *See* McCleskey v. Zant, 580 F.Supp. at 357–58. The list of factors cited in the district court opinion is not complete, so it is possible that

other factors that were mentioned by the Eleventh Circuit were also considered.

54. *McCleskey*, 753 F.2d. at 925 n.24.

55. 408 U.S. at 365–66 (Marshall, J., concurring) (footnote omitted); *see also id.* at 250, 260 (Douglas, J., concurring).

56. This shift may reflect strong criticism of the Eleventh Circuit's argument in the briefs before the court, Petitioner's Brief, *supra* note 40 at 47–64, and in commentary on the Circuit Court opinion. Gross, *supra* note 42 at 1308–12. In any event, the Supreme Court quotes this portion of the Eleventh Circuit opinion at length, apparently with approval, but omits the most troubling references—"looks, age, personality, education," and so on—and replaces them with ellipses. 107 S.Ct. at 1765, quoting *McCleskey*, 753 F.2d at 898–99.

57. 107 S.Ct. at 1777.

58. *Id.* at 1778.

59. 660 F.2d 573, modified 671 F.2d 858, 859 (5th Cir. 1981). *See* ch. 8, pp. 125–26, and ch. 9, pp. 134–35.

60. U.S. DEP'T OF HEALTH, EDUCATION & WELFARE, SMOKING AND HEALTH, A REPORT OF THE SURGEON GENERAL, at 4—21, 4—65 (1979) (hereinafter cited as SMOKING AND HEALTH).

61. *Id.* at 4—21.

62. U.S. DEP'T OF HEALTH, EDUCATION & WELFARE, THE HEALTH CONSEQUENCES OF SMOKING, A REPORT OF THE SURGEON GENERAL: 1971, at 48–52 (1971); SMOKING AND HEALTH, *supra* note 60, at 60.

63. SMOKING AND HEALTH, *supra* note 60, at 60.

64. *See id.* at 4—67 to 4—77.

65. *Id.* at 4—21, 4—34.

66. McCleskey v. Zant, 580 F.Supp. at 353–55.

67. 107 S.Ct. at 1767.

68. 118 U.S. 356 (1886).

69. 364 U.S. 339 (1960).

70. *Id.* at 340.

71. 107 S.Ct. at 1767–68.

72. *See, e.g.*, Vuyanich v. Republic Nat. Bank of Dallas, 505 F.Supp. 224, (N.D. Texas, 1980), *vacated* 723 F.2d 1195 (5th Cir. 1984); Valentino v. U.S. Postal Service, 511 F.Supp. 917, (D.D.C. 1981), *aff'd* 674 F.2d 56 (D.C. Cir. 1982).

73. 107 S.Ct. at 1768 n.14.

74. 429 U.S. 252, 266 (1977).

75. Furnco Constr. Co. v. Waters, 438 U.S. 567, 577 (1978).

76. *Id.* at 578. *See* Castaneda v. Partida, 430 U.S. 482, 494 (1977) (quoting Alexander v. Louisiana, 405 U.S. 625, 632 [1972]).

77. Castaneda v. Partida, 430 U.S. at 494–97.

78. Texas Dept. of Comm. Affairs v. Burdine, 450 U.S. 248, 253–54 (1981) footnote omitted.

79. Smith v. Texas, 311 U.S. 128, 130 (1940). See also, e.g., Duren v. Missouri, 439 U.S. 357, 363–64 (1979); Taylor v. Louisiana, 419 U.S. 522, 530 (1975); Williams v. Florida, 399 U.S. 78, 100 (1970); Ballard v. United States, 329 U.S. 187 (1946); Strauder v. West Virginia, 100 U.S. 303 (1880).

80. Castaneda v. Partida, 430 U.S. 482, 496 n.16, 497 (1977).

81. 107 S.Ct. at 1767, quoting Village of Arlington Heights v. Metropolitan Housing Dev. Corp., 429 U.S. 252, 266 n.13 (1977).

82. 107 S.Ct. at 1768 n.14.

83. Id. at 1768.

84. Shapiro v. Thompson, 394 U.S. 618, 634 (1969). See generally Gunther, Forward: In Search of Evolving Doctrine on a Changing Court: A Model for a Newer Equal Protection, 86 HAR. L. REV. 1, 8 (1972).

85. 107 S.Ct. 1756, 1766 n.8. See supra note 5. Similarly, in Village of Arlington Heights v. Metropolitan Hous. Corp., 429 U.S. 252, 263 (1977), the Court held that, while a corporate plaintiff had no standing to assert a claim of racial discrimination in zoning since it had "no racial identity," it could complain that the same discrimination violated its rights under the equal protection clause because it was arbitrary and irrational. See supra ch. 3, note 8.

86. E.g., Schweiker v, Wilson, 450 U.S. 221 (1981); Railway Express Agency v. New York, 336 U.S. 106 (1949).

87. 107 S.Ct. at 1767 (emphasis added).

88. This interpretation of McCleskey was suggested by Frederick Schauer, our colleague at the University of Michigan Law School. Professor Schauer pointed out the similarity in this respect between McCleskey and Bowers v. Hardwick, 106 S.Ct. 2841 (1986), in which the Court rejected a constitutional challenge to a Georgia statute making sodomy a crime. In Bowers the Court said, in effect, that although a major line of Supreme Court cases could be read as recognizing a general constitutional right of privacy, see Griswold v. Connecticut, 381 U.S. 479 (1965), Stanley v. Georgia, 394 U.S. 557 (1969), Eisenstadt v. Baird, 405 U.S. 438 (1972), Roe v. Wade, 410 U.S. 113 (1973), in fact these cases merely recognized several specific privacy rights that protect particular types of conduct that are tied to "family, marriage, or procreation," and that is all. 106 S.Ct. at 2844.

89. E.g., 42 U.S.C. § 1981; Executive Order 11,246, 30 FED. REG. 12319 (1965).

90. 42 U.S.C. §§ 2000e–2000e-17.

91. McDonnell Douglas v. Green, 411 U.S. 792, 802–3 (1973); Teamsters v. U.S., 431 U.S. 324, 358 n.44 (1977) (proof of intentional discrimination); Griggs v. Duke Power Co., 401 U.S. 424 (1971) (disparate impact).

92. 100 U.S. 303 (1880).

93. 426 U.S. 229 (1976).

94. 405 U.S. 625, 632 (1972), quoting Hernandez v. Texas, 347 U.S. 475, 482 (1954).

95. E.g., Castaneda v. Partida, 430 U.S. 482, 492–99 (1977) (citing Alexander v. Louisiana, supra, and Hernandez v. Texas, supra); Rose v. Mitchell, 443 U.S. 545, 551–52, 565–66 (same).

96. 106 S.Ct. 1758 (1986). See supra note 47.

97. Id. at 1767.

98. McCleskey v. Kemp, 753 F.2d at 892. See ch. 9, pp. 138–39.

99. 408 U.S. 238 (1972). See supra ch. 1, pp. 5–8.

100. 428 U.S. 153 (1976).

101. 438 U.S. 586 (1978).

102. 462 U.S. 862 (1983).

103. 463 U.S. 939 (1983).

104. 465 U.S. 37 (1984).

105. 107 S.Ct. at 1775–78.

106. Id. at 1775–76 n.30, and cases cited therein. The Court lists cases that prohibit racial discrimination in the exercise of prosecutorial discretion, in jury selection, and in the use of peremptory challenges by prosecutors; that provide for changes of venue in criminal prosecutions that are subject to widespread community bias; that prohibit racially based arguments by prosecutors; and that require voir dire examination on racial bias on behalf of a capital defendant charged with an interracial murder.

107. 107 S.Ct. at 1775.

108. Id. at 1781.

109. Id. at 1779.

110. Id. at 1779 n.38, citing Spohn, Gruhl, & Welch, The Effect of Race on Sentencing: A Re-examination of an Unsettled Question, 16 LAW & SOC. REV. 71 (1981–82); Unnever, Frazier, & Henretta, Race Differences in Criminal Sentencing, 21 SOCIO. Q. 197 (1980).

111. For example, Spohn et al., supra, found no statistically significant direct effects of race on sentencing, but indirect effects mediated through prior record, charge, pretrial status, and type of attorney.

112. RESEARCH ON SENTENCING: THE SEARCH FOR REFORM, vol. 1 at 93 (A. Blumstein, J. Cohen, S. Martin, & M. Tonry, eds., 1983). See also

Hagan & Burmiller, *Making Sense of Sentencing: A Review and Critique of Sentencing Research*, in *id.*, vol. 2 at 1, 31–35.

113. 107 S.Ct. at 1780 n.40, citing Chamblin & Foley, *The Effect of Sex on the Imposition of the Death Penalty*, unpublished paper presented at the meeting of the American Psychological Association, Sept. 1979 (miscited as "Chamblin").

114. 107 S.Ct. at 1780 nn.40–44, citing Steffensmeier, *Effects of Judge's and Defendant's Sex on the Sentencing of Offenders*, 14 PSYCHOLOGY 3 (1977); Cohen & Peterson, *Bias in the Courtroom: Race and Sex Effects of Attorneys on Juror Verdicts*, 9 SOC. BEHAVIOR & PERSONALITY 81 (1981); Hodgson & Pryor, *Sex Discrimination in the Courtroom: Attorney Gender and Credibility*, 55 PSYCHOLOGICAL REP. 483 (1984); Kerr, Bull, MacCoun, & Rathborn, *Effects of victim attractiveness, care and disfigurement on the judgements of American and British mock jurors*, 24 BRIT. J. SOC. PSYCH. 47 (1985); Shoemaker, South, & Lowe, *Facial Stereotypes of Deviants and Judgments of Guilt or Innocence*, 51 SOC. FORCES 427 (1973); Smith & Hed, *Effects of Offenders' Age and Attractiveness on Sentencing by Mock Juries*, 44 PSYCHOLOGICAL R. 691 (1979); Kerr, *Beautiful and Blameless: Effects of Victim Attractiveness and Responsibility on Mock Jurors' Verdicts*, 4 PERSONALITY & SOC. PSYCH. BULL. 479 (1978); Baumeister & Darley, *Reducing the Biasing Effect of Perpetrator Attractiveness in Jury Simulation*, 8 PERSONALITY & SOC. PSYCH. BULL. 286 (1982); Schwibbe & Schwibbe, *Judgment and Treatment of People of Varied Attractiveness*, 48 PSYCHOLOGICAL R. 11 (1981); and Weiten, *The Attraction-Leniency Effect in Jury Research: An Examination of External Validity*, 10 J. APPLIED SOC. PSYCH. 340 (1980).

115. 106 S.Ct. 1758 (1986).

116. 107 S.Ct. at 1791–93.

117. *Id.* at 1792 (quoting Woodson v. North Carolina, 428 U.S. 280, 305 [1976]).

118. 107 S.Ct. at 1792.

119. *Id.*

120. *Id.*

121. 402 U.S. 183 (1971).

122. *Id.* at 207.

123. *Id.* at 206 n.16.

124. *Id.* at 204.

125. *Id.* at 208.

126. Gregg v. Georgia, 428 U.S. 153, 206–7 (plurality opinion).

127. *Id.* at 198, quoting *Furman* 408 U.S. at 313 (White, J., concurring).

128. For an excellent discussion of this line of cases, from *McGautha*

through *Zant* and *Barclay, see* Weisberg, *Deregulating Death,* 1983 SUP. CT. REV. 305.

129. 107 S.Ct. at 1777.

130. *Id.* at 1778.

131. *Id.* at 1777, citation omitted.

132. *Id.* at 1778 n.36.

133. *McCleskey,* 753 F.2d at 899.

134. McCleskey v. Zant, 580 F. Supp. at 365.

135. *See* ch. 9, note 21.

136. Baldus, Pulaski, & Woodworth, *Comparative Review of Death Sentences: An Empirical Study of the Georgia Experience,* 74 J. CRIM. L. & CRIMINOLOGY 661 (1983) at 730. This finding is corroborated by a more qualitative study of capital sentencing in Georgia by Ursula Bentele, *The Death Penalty in Georgia: Still Arbitrary,* 62 WASH. U. L. Q. 573 (1985).

137. *McCleskey,* 753 F.2d at 899.

138. The district court made a similar statement. After holding that the Baldus data were too untrustworthy to form a basis for judicial findings, the court nonetheless purported to rely on these data to conclude that it could reject "any notion that the imposition of the death penalty in Georgia is a random event unguided by rational thought." McCleskey v. Zant, 580 F.Supp. at 365 (emphasis omitted).

139. Gregg v. Georgia, 428 U.S. 153, 206–7 (1976) (plurality opinion); *see also id.* at 220 (White, J., concurring); Proffitt v. Florida, 428 U.S. 242, 259–60 (1976) (plurality opinion). *See* ch. 1, pp. 6–7.

140. Spinkellink v. Wainwright, 578 F.2d 582, 613–14 (5th Cir. 1978) (footnote omitted) ("[I]f a state follows a properly drawn statute in imposing the death penalty, then the arbitrariness and capriciousness—and therefore the racial discrimination—condemned in *Furman* have been conclusively removed."); *see also* Mitchell v. Hopper, 538 F.Supp. 77, 90 (S.D. Ga. 1982), *vacated sub nom.* Spencer v. Zant, 715 F.2d 1562 (11th Cir. 1983), *order aff'd in part sub nom.* Mitchell v. Kemp, 762 F.2d 886 (11th Cir. 1985); McCorquodale v. Balkcom, 525 F. Supp. 431, 434–35 (N.D. Ga. 1981). *But see McCleskey,* 753 F.2d at 890–92.

141. 465 U.S. 37, 54 (1984).

142. 464 U.S. 1027, 1030–31 n.2 (1983) (Powell, J., dissenting) (citations omitted).

143. DiSalle, *Trends in the Abolition of Capital Punishment,* 1 U. TOLEDO L. REV. 1, 13 (1969), cited in Brief for Petitioner at 51, Aikens v. California, *cert. granted,* 403 U.S. 952 (1971), *cert. dismissed,* 406 U.S. 813 (1972) [hereinafter *Aikens* Petitioner's Brief]. (*Aikens* was the

original lead case in the *Furman* litigation, but was dismissed as moot in light of People v. Anderson, 6 Cal. 3d 628, 493 P.2d 880, 100 Cal. Rptr. 152 [1972].) *See also Aikens* Petitioner's Brief at 50–52, 52 n.103; *Furman*, 408 U.S. at 251 (Douglas, J., concurring); *id.* 364–66 (Marshall, J., concurring).

144. *Aikens* Petitioner's Brief at 52 n.101; *Furman*, 408 U.S. at 364 (Marshall, J., concurring).

145. *Aikens* Petitioner's Brief at 52 n.102.

146. Garfinkel, *Research Note on Inter- and Intra-Racial Homicides,* 27 Soc. Forces 369 (1949), *see supra* ch. 2, pp. 17–18 and notes 7–8, *cited in Aikens* Petitioner's Brief at 52 n.102.

147. *Aikens* Petitioner's Brief at 52 n.102.

148. *Id.* at 52–53 (footnotes omitted).

149. *See e.g., id.,* Brief for Respondent at 105, Aikens v. California, *cert. granted,* 403 U.S. 952 (1971), *cert. dismissed,* 406 U.S. 813 (1972) (citing racial statistics for homicide charges and dispositions in California) [hereinafter *Aikens* Respondent's Brief]; *id.* at 106 n.130 (citing national statistics on race and homicide arrests).

150. *See* Bedau, *Capital Punishment in Oregon 1903–1964,* 45 Ore. L. Rev. 1, 11–12 (1965); Bedau, *Death Sentences in New Jersey 1907–1960,* 19 Rutgers L. Rev. 1, 40–46 (1964); *see also Aikens* Respondent's Brief at 108 (citing racial statistics on commutations in California).

151. *Aikens* Petitioner's Brief at 52 n.102, citing *A Study of the California Penalty Jury in First-Degree Murder Cases,* 21 Stan. L. Rev. 1297 (1969), [hereinafter cited as *Stanford Law Review* study]. *See supra* ch. 2, p. 19 and notes 12–15.

152. *Stanford Law Review* study, *supra* note 151.

153. *Furman*, 408 U.S. at 389 n.12 (Burger, C. J., dissenting).

154. Wechsler, in *Symposium on Capital Punishment,* 7 N.Y. L. Forum 247, 255 (1961), quoted in *Aikens* Petitioner's Brief at 54–55.

155. *Furman*, 408 U.S. at 309–10 & n.12 (Stewart, J., concurring).

156. *Id.* at 313 (White, J., concurring).

157. NAACP Legal Defense and Educational Fund, Death Row U.S.A. (May 1, 1988) [hereinafter cited as Death Row U.S.A.].

158. *Id.* at 1.

159. *Compare id. with Aikens* Petitioner's Brief at 52 n.101.

160. Kleck, *Racial Discrimination in Criminal Sentencing: A Critical Evaluation of the Evidence with Additional Evidence on the Death Penalty,* 46 Am. Soc. Rev. 783 (1981). *See supra* ch. 2, pp. 19–20 and notes 19–22.

161. Kleck, *Racial Discrimination,* at 800.

162. These figures are recalculated from Kleck, *id.,* at 798, Table 6.

A parallel analysis using homicide deaths rather than homicide arrests as the denominator produces a comparable result—the relative risk for black defendants increased slightly from :82 before *Furman* to .90 after *Furman. Id.*

163. DEATH ROW U.S.A., *supra* note 157, at 3.

164. FEDERAL BUREAU OF INVESTIGATION, DEP'T OF JUSTICE, UNIFORM CRIME REPORT, CRIME IN THE UNITED STATES 15 (1973), 15 (1974), 15 (1975), 15 (1976), 8 (1977), 8 (1978), 7 (1979), 8 (1980), 7 (1981), 7 (1982), 7 (1983), 7 (1984), 8 (1985), 9 (1986), 9 (1987).

165. Garfinkel, *supra* note 146, at 371, Tables 2, 3.

166. Bowers & Pierce, *Arbitrariness and Discrimination Under Post-Furman Capital Statutes*, 26 CRIME & DELINQ. 563 (1980). See *supra* ch. 2, pp. 20–21 and note 24.

167. *See* e.g., ch. 4, p. 45, Table 4.2.

168. *Supra* note 151.

169. *See* ch. 1, p. 3.

170. 408 U.S. at 389 n.12 (Burger, C. J., dissenting).

171. Fifteen hundred thirty-three defendants were sentenced to death from *Furman* through the end of 1980. Greenberg, *Capital Punishment as a System*, 91 YALE L. J. 908, 918 (1982). An additional 1990 defendants were sentenced to death from 1981 through the end of 1987. Data provided by Tanya Coke, Capital Punishment Information Director for the NAACP Legal Defense and Educational Fund, May 16–18 (*see infra*, ch. 11, note 31). This adds up to a total of 3523 defendants sentenced to death since *Furman.*

172. DEATH ROW U.S.A., *supra* note 157.

173. *Id.*

174. *See* Streib, *Executions Under Post-Furman Capital Punishment Statutes: The Halting Progression from "Let's Do It" to "Hey, There Ain't No Point In Pulling So Tight,"* 15 RUTGERS L. J. 443, 485 (1984).

175. *Id.* at 486.

176. 408 U.S. at 309–10, 313.

177. Gideon v. Wainright, 372 U.S. 335 (1963): see also Argersinger v. Hamlin, 407 U.S. 25 (1972).

178. Miranda v. Arizona, 384 U.S. 436 (1966).

179. Duncan v. Louisiana, 391 U.S. 145 (1968); Taylor v. Louisiana, 419 U.S. 522 (1975).

11 | Conclusion: It's Not Broken Because It Can't Be Fixed

The central message of the *McCleskey* case is all too plain: de facto racial discrimination in capital sentencing is legal in the United States. The Supreme Court hems and haws a bit; it refuses to acknowledge explicitly the fact of discrimination, but neither does it attempt to *deny* the existence of discrimination. However, even the most conservative reading of the Court's analysis is extremely disturbing: although McCleskey presented "a complex statistical study that indicates a risk that racial considerations enter into capital sentencing determinations,"[1] his evidence is legally insufficient to support (let alone compel) an inference of discrimination, and so "it is unnecessary to seek . . . a rebuttal"[2] to his claims. In other words, even a proven risk of racial discrimination in the use of the death penalty poses no constitutional issue, merits no hearing, and requires no response.

Why has the Supreme Court taken this depressingly tolerant attitude toward racial discrimination in capital sentencing? The answer is no mystery; it is apparent from the *McCleskey* opinion and from the legal history preceding it. The Court was afraid of the consequences of a decision to condemn discrimination in the use of the death penalty and to attempt to eliminate it.

There is the problem of boundaries: would the success of this discrimination claim open the door to others, in other contexts? As the dissenters point out, this is not an insurmountable difficulty. Racial discrimination could certainly be singled out as a special problem, and the Court could easily carve out a rule for capital cases only. Long before *Furman* the Supreme Court recognized that "death is different" in ways that have significant constitutional implications,[3] and the entire meandering course of constitutional law on the death penalty since *Furman* is based on that premise. But that might be an uncomfortable position: to hold that a particular pattern proves unconstitutional discrimination in sentencing, but only if the sentence is death.

Still, at worst, the possibility of other claims of discrimination in the criminal justice system is no more than an abstract worry. So far there is little evidence to support any such claims, and there may never be much more. But there is a more pressing and intractable set of problems, the problems of remedy.

First, there is the matter of correcting the consequences of past discrimination. The solution to this problem is straightforward enough, but it is extreme: prohibit the execution of all death sentences pronounced by the system that produced such results. Courts obviously may not correct racial disproportions in capital sentencing by deciding that some killers of blacks who escaped the death penalty at trial should now receive it; to the extent that black victims or the black community may suffer because of inadequate punishment of those who kill blacks, the problem cannot be remedied after the fact. Nor may the courts make things equal by weeding out some arbitrary fraction of those who were sentenced to death for killing whites and leaving the others to their fate. Our system of criminal justice is based on a fundamental assumption that guilt and punishment are judged individually. Aggregate statistics may show that the system is malfunctioning, but no remedy can violate basic rules of individual justice and procedural regularity.

McCleskey suggested a case-by-case approach for reviewing existing death sentences. The Court could have held that the Baldus study created, in effect, a rebuttable presumption of discrimination in white-victim cases—a presumption that could be overcome by convincing evidence that a particular case was so aggravated that race was unlikely to have influenced the outcome.[4] This proposal has the ring of orderliness and moderation, but in operation it would probably have become a procedural knot. If hearings on this issue were made mandatory in white-victim cases, it would be hard to deny them in other racial contexts; and the same complex, shifting, and arbitrary features that make it so difficult to describe the operation of the system and to prove discrimination would stand in the way of any attempt by the state to prove its absence. On the other hand, a general *finding* of discrimination based on aggregate data would translate into a prohibition on the execution of all death-sentenced defendants who were convicted of killing whites. But if that were done, the Court could hardly permit the execution of those who killed blacks, a group that is distinguished by an arbitrary factor and that is, with respect to the identity of its victims, completely racially homogeneous.[5] It would have to wipe the slate clean.[6]

And then what? Dealing with existing death sentences is only one of two remedy problems presented by *McCleskey*, and the easier one at that. If the Court had granted McCleskey's claim it would have had to come to terms with the implications of that decision for the *future* of capital punishment in Georgia (and in any other state for which a similar claim could be proven). But how?

The Court could simply wait and see if the same discriminatory patterns reappear after five or ten years, but that does not seem wise. Phenomena as stable as these are not likely to disappear on their own, and, one way or the other, the Court would have to put capital sentencing on an indefinite constitutional hold while it waited to find out. Perhaps a more practical position is the one advanced by Justice Douglas in *Furman*: that sentencing statutes that produce such results "are pregnant with discrimination"[7] and therefore unconstitutional. But Douglas's position does not lay the issue to rest either. Is the death penalty inherently discriminatory and therefore unconstitutional per se? This is a consistent position with a great deal of historical support, but it is not popular these days with legislatures or with the Supreme Court. If discrimination in capital sentencing is not inevitable, can it be cured by procedural reforms? The last attempt of this sort, initiated by the *Gregg* decision in 1976, provides little basis for optimism.

The roots of this dilemma go back to *Furman* itself. *Furman* might have become the judicial abolition of the death penalty in the United States. It followed a five-year moratorium on executions, it emptied death rows across the country, and it brought the process that fed them to a stop. Many observers saw *Furman* as the end of capital punishment in the United States—a major event, to be sure, but a predictable step in the long-term trend toward abolition of the death penalty in all Western democracies.[8] A second decision officially making the ban permanent would not have been surprising; it might almost have seemed anticlimatic.

It was in this context that the Court decided in *Gregg* to attempt to regulate the death penalty. Regulation was an alternative to the visible and plausible option of abolition. Still, the power to regulate (like the power to tax) is the power to eliminate, and for a lengthy period, from 1976 until 1983, it looked as if matters might be headed in that direction. On the one hand, there were only seven executions in the seven years following *Gregg* (and four of these seven were defendants who had waived one or another form of appellate review),[9] and an extremely successful defense record in the Supreme Court and the federal circuit courts suggested that this near freeze might be maintained.[10] On the other hand, it was becoming apparent that the post-*Furman* reforms did not and could not live up to their billing, and that if the Court truly meant to keep its promise to eliminate discrimination and arbitrariness in capital sentencing it would end up abolishing the penalty piece by piece, if not in one clean stroke.

Abolition is a perfectly practical solution to the problems of capital punishment. Canada, Great Britain, France, West Germany, and Italy, among others—not to mention thirteen American states and the District of Columbia—all do without capital punishment with no apparent difficulty.[11] But abolition is not a serious option in America now. The critical holding in *Gregg* was not the endorsement of "guided discretion" but the decision that the use of the death penalty is consistent with "contemporary values" and "public attitude[s]" toward crime and punishment, and therefore that it is not constitutionally "cruel and unusual."[12] By 1976 the evidence of public endorsement of the death penalty was undeniable. Thirty-five states had reenacted the death penalty in the four years following *Furman*, and hundreds of death sentences had been imposed.[13] The Court was impressed. Despite all the turmoil that has surrounded this issue since *Gregg*, it has never questioned the proposition that capital punishment is not per se unconstitutional, and it is not likely to do so as long as the death penalty remains widely popular. For now that seems safe, since public opinion supports the death penalty more than ever.[14]

Against this background, the sequence of decisions leading up to *McCleskey* seems almost inevitable. If abolition is unthinkable and regulation does not work, the only remaining choice is to tolerate whatever the system produces.

The Court has made that choice, but the justices in the majority seem to be uneasy with their decision to accept a state of affairs that was considered unacceptable at the time of *Furman*. Perhaps that uneasiness explains their repeated insistence that the system is now radically improved.

Just as *Furman* was greeted by many as the abolition of capital punishment in the United States, *McCleskey* has been described as the abandonment of constitutional regulation of the death penalty. Thus, for example, Robert Burt writes that in *McCleskey* "the Court proclaimed the end of its doubts [about the death penalty] and correspondingly signalled its intention to turn away from any continuing scrutiny of the enterprise."[15] Back in 1980 Justice Marshall expressed his hope that eventually the Court would conclude "that the effort to eliminate arbitrariness in the infliction of that ultimate sanction is so plainly doomed to failure that it—and the death penalty—must be abandoned altogether."[16] Under this view, the Court has now accepted Marshall's invitation to give up on the project of ending arbitrariness, but has chosen to keep the death penalty nonetheless.

This interpretation appears undeniable. *Lockett* and *Zant* and *Barclay* and *Pulley*[17] each removed some portion of the restrictions the Court once imposed on the use of capital punishment. Following this sequence, *McCleskey*— "the last broad-based constitutional challenge to capital punishment"[18]—certainly seems to represent a final decision to give up any pretense that the death penalty can be tamed. But if that is so, it should have led to a rapid increase in the rate of executions, as some predicted.[19] To date, however, this prediction has failed.

There were 28 executions in the year following the announcement of *McCleskey* on April 22, 1986.[20] This is an increase over the pre-*McCleskey* rate but not a great one: 21 prisoners were executed in the United States in 1984, and 18 each in 1985 and 1986. The pattern of executions across these twelve months is even more telling (to the extent that trends can be detected in a short period): there were 23 executions in the five months immediately following *McCleskey*, but only five executions in the next seven months after that.[21] It seems that after a short-term bulge of executions that had been stayed pending the decision in *McCleskey*,[22] the pace has settled back to the status quo ante of sporadic deaths.

Has *McCleskey* really changed so little about the use of the death penalty in the United States? So far that appears to be the case, and, while it may be foolhardy to predict anything in this area, the trend seems to be holding steady. How is this possible? Perhaps the practical implications of *McCleskey* are best understood not in terms of its doctrinal content (which includes major revisions of existing law) but in terms of the concrete choice the Court had to make: a racially biased death penalty, or none. The Court chose to keep a biased death penalty, and this was a radical step in itself. But it does not follow that the Court intended to do anything beyond that. In particular, it does not follow that the Court also intended to drastically change the system of capital punishment that existed in the United States prior to April 1987, or to greatly increase the number of executions. Indeed, the conduct of the Supreme Court since *McCleskey* is more consistent with the theory that it intends to maintain the death penalty in approximately the same condition as just prior to that decision.

Even after *McCleskey*, deregulation of the death penalty is not quite complete. A shell of the initial plan, including the procedural apparatus, has been left in place, and, more important, the machinery is still in use. Before the sequence of cases leading up to *Furman* the Supreme Court reviewed few death penalty cases; capital punishment was not a regular part of its workload.[23] Since *Furman* the Court has had, in effect, a death penalty docket that occupies a substantial portion of its time. Contrary to the expectations of Professor Burt and others, *McCleskey* has not changed that.

In the year following *McCleskey*, the Supreme Court decided nine other death penalty cases. This left only one pre-*McCleskey* death penalty case on the Court's docket, but new cases replenished the list. In the same period, the Court agreed to hear nine additional death penalty cases that had not been decided as of May 1988.[24] Most of these cases involve peripheral procedural issues: the content of instructions on mitigating evidence under the Texas death penalty statute;[25] a Maryland requirement that the sentencing jury weigh only those mitigating circumstances on which it agrees unanimously;[26] the use of a subsequently invalidated conviction as an aggravating factor;[27] and so forth. The decisions they produce are unlikely to result in basic changes in capital sentencing one way or the other. On issues of this magnitude the Court has often ruled for the defense in recent years,[28] and *McCleskey* has not changed that. Five of the first nine post-*McCleskey* decisions have gone against the state, and in seven of the nine pending cases the Court granted a capital defendant's petition for review.[29] It is even possible that the decision in *McCleskey* has encouraged the justices in the majority to be particularly scrupulous in considering and deciding these lesser cases. Perhaps they are affected by a lingering sense of uneasiness about racial discrimination, and want to make the process as fair as possible in other respects. Perhaps they take seriously their own statements in *McCleskey* that the death penalty can be made fair by small procedural manipulations.

The fact that the Court keeps taking these cases may be more important than the decisions it reaches. The Supreme Court's continued willingness to play a direct and active role supervising the administration of capital punishment is a signal to the lower courts that the death penalty remains subject to close scrutiny by the federal judiciary, and that they should be careful and thorough in their own death penalty cases. This message has implications far beyond the scope of the few cases that actually reach the high court. For every Supreme Court case there are several lower court cases, or several dozen, that raise the same issue; for every issue that the Court decides there are several issues that it might someday consider. The handful of pending Supreme Court death penalty cases are the tip of a large pyramid of review. Below them are dozens of habeas corpus appeals in the federal circuit courts, hundreds of habeas corpus petitions in the federal district courts, and hundreds more direct and collateral appeals in state courts. Capital cases proceed through this structure in stages: direct review, including, quite often, an initial certiorari petition to the Supreme Court; collateral review in state courts, with, perhaps, another petition to the Supreme Court; federal habeas corpus, ending with yet another Supreme Court petition.[30]

As of February 1, 1988, nearly 40 percent of death row inmates did not yet have decisions on their first direct appeals. Among all those sentenced to death since *Furman* whose direct appeals have been decided, 41 percent had their sentences reversed at this initial review, and an additional 7 percent won reversals in state collateral review proceedings. In the federal courts, capital habeas corpus petitioners have obtained relief in 26 percent of district court cases, and in just over 40 percent of appeals to the circuit courts.[31] All along this route there are delays, remands, and stays. It is probably no coincidence, for example, that the great majority of post-*McCleskey* executions were carried out before the new term of the Supreme Court began in October 1987, since each pending Supreme Court case is likely to hold up executions in at least several other cases that raise similar issues. The overall effect is a process of review that is slow enough so that at any one time few cases are near the end, and exacting enough so that most death sentences are ultimately reversed.

The case of Warren McCleskey himself is a striking illustration of how the system works. On December 23, 1987, eight months after he lost in the Supreme Court, the same federal district court judge who had rejected his discrimination claim nearly four years earlier vacated McCleskey's murder conviction and ordered a new trial.[32] The issue this time is police misconduct in the initial investigation; there is little at stake beyond the outcome of the individual case. Nonetheless, the state has appealed; if it wins (perhaps a year or two hence) there will be another remand, and further litigation, and more delays, and perhaps another reversal. Occasionally this tortuous system of review produces appellate opinions that are important in themselves; *McCleskey v. Kemp* is a conspicuous example. On the whole, however, the process is the product.

The bottleneck is not nearly as narrow as it once was. In the spring of 1983 the Supreme Court not only removed a major restriction on the use of the death penalty,[33] but also authorized the lower federal courts to simplify and speed up the process of review.[34] The result was a quick increase in the rate of executions to the current level of twenty-some a year. That rate may increase again. But even if it were to double or more, execution would remain a rare event in a country of over 230 million, and an unlikely fate for any one of the more than 2000 inmates already on death row[35] or the 280 or so who join them each year.[36]

The Supreme Court, of course, is not the only body that limits the pace of executions. If it left the field entirely, the lower federal courts and the state courts might continue to hold on to capital cases and to dispose of them much as they do now. And if the court system as a whole started clearing large numbers of defendants for execution—two hundred a year, for example, or more—then executive officials might step in. Prosecutors at one end of the process and governors and clemency boards at the other might use their authority to cut the flow down to a rate that somehow seems appropriate.

This scenario depends in large part on the willingness of state officials to drastically limit the use of the death penalty. Is that a realistic possibility? Unlike federal judges, most state judges and prosecutors (and all governors) must stand for election. Considering the popularity of the death penalty, would they not be vulnerable to defeat if they repeatedly spared defendants from execution? In extreme circumstances, apparently yes. In November 1986, Chief Justice Bird and Associate Justices Reynoso and Grodin of the California Supreme Court were defeated in an election that turned primarily on their records in deciding capital appeals.[37] But the lesson of that event should not be overdrawn. The campaign against these justices focused on a single extremely well publicized fact: Chief Justice Bird had voted to reverse each of the sixty-one death sentences that she had reviewed.[38] The only clear message in this is that the electorate in some states may not tolerate judges who are believed to be trying to block *all* executions, at least not when (as in California) no executions in fact take place.

Less extreme but still high reversal rates seem to pose no problem. As of May 1988, several state supreme courts had reversed the convictions or the sentences in the majority of their post-*Furman* capital appeals: South Carolina, 53 percent; Mississippi, 54 percent; North Carolina, 57 percent; Washington and Wyoming, 67 percent each.[39] None of these records has become a political issue. Apparently all the public asks is that some trickle of death cases continue to pass through. If restrictions elsewhere were loosened, state judges and executive officials could probably tighten the valves they control with little or no political risk. Most likely, it would go virtually unnoticed. As things stand, however, their willingness and ability to do so is not being put to a test, since the federal courts have remained at the core of the post-*Furman* regulatory apparatus, and the Supreme Court, even after *McCleskey*, has maintained its role as the central rate-limiting device.

This is a cumbersome and expensive way to keep down the number of executions. The same numerical result might be achieved directly by restricting capital punishment to the most aggravated categories of murders. Justice Stevens suggests this approach in his *McCleskey* dissent as a method of retaining the death penalty without racial discrimination.

> One of the lessons of the Baldus study is that there exist certain categories of extremely serious crimes for which prosecutors consistently seek, and juries consistently impose, the death penalty without regard to the race of the victim or the race of the offender. If Georgia were to narrow the class of death-eligible defendants to those categories, the danger of arbitrary and discriminatory imposition of the death penalty would be significantly decreased, if not eradicated.[40]

Justice Powell, in the final footnote to the majority opinion, argues that this proposal is impractical, for two reasons.[41] First, there would still be borderline cases that would be hard to place, and for which judgments would be hard to justify. Second, prosecutors would find it difficult or impossible to apply such a system "on a case-by-case basis," since they could not have access to the type of information they would need to determine which murder cases fall into categories in which the death penalty is "consistently" applied. These are serious objections, but they are not insurmountable. They could be overcome by restricting the option of capital punishment to uncommon and narrowly defined types of homicides for which the death penalty is almost always sought and imposed upon conviction—mass murders and serial murders, for example. This would eliminate the need for elaborate information or case-by-case judgments, and it would probably eliminate racial discrimination as well. But it would deprive us of something we seem to want: a death penalty that is widely available, and rarely used.[42]

In the last analysis, the discretion that is so highly praised in *McCleskey* is the power to threaten to kill thousands, but to do it only to dozens. Whatever else might be said for the use of death as a punishment, one lesson is clear from experience: this is a power that we cannot exercise fairly and without discrimination.

Notes

1. McCleskey v. Kemp, 107 S.Ct. 1756, 1761 (1987).
2. *Id.* at 1769.
3. *See, e.g.,* Reid v. Covert, 354 U.S. 1, 77 (1957) (Harlan, J., concurring); Williams v. Georgia, 349 U.S. 375, 391 (1955); Stein v. New York, 346 U.S. 156, 196 (1953); Andres v. United States, 333 U.S. 740, 752 (1948).
4. *McCleskey,* Brief for Petitioner at 106–9.
5. The Eighth Circuit discussed this aspect of the problem of remedy in its opinion in Maxwell v. Bishop, 398 F.2d 138, 148 (1968):

> At oral argument . . . counsel for Maxwell . . . [agreed that] his statistical approach would [make it] constitutionally impossible for a negro defendant in Arkansas ever to receive the death penalty upon conviction of the crime of rape of a white woman . . . [but], in contrast, that it would be possible for a white man to receive the death penalty upon his conviction for rape. When counsel was asked whether this would not be discriminatory, the reply was that once the negro situation was remedied the white situation "would take care of itself."

The court found this position completely unsatisfactory: "[E]qual protection is denied if, factually, a member of one race (whether black or white) is subjected, because of his race to a greater or different punishment than a member of another race." *Id.* This doctrine, the court stated, must be guaranteed by the law, not "through assumed and hoped-for day-to-day practicalities." *Id.*

6. Fisher and Kadane discuss a related issue in a different context, the construction of sentencing guidelines based on empirical analysis of past practices in a system that has included discrimination. Fisher & Kadane, *Empirically Based Sentencing Guidelines and Ethical Con-*

siderations, in RESEARCH ON SENTENCING, vol. 2, 184, (A. Blumstein, J. Cohen, S. Martin, & M. Tonry, eds., 1983). For each category of past discrimination a normative, nonempirical judgment must be made: In the future, should all defendants be treated like those who were favored in the past, like those who were disfavored, or somewhere in between? Here, because we are considering past sentences, the normative choice is constrained: Once pronounced, sentences can be reduced, but not increased.

7. 408 U.S. 238, 257 (1972).

8. F. ZIMRING & G. HAWKINS, CAPITAL PUNISHMENT AND THE AMERICAN AGENDA 37 (1986).

9. NAACP LEGAL DEFENSE AND EDUCATIONAL FUND, DEATH ROW U.S.A. (May 1, 1987) [hereinafter DEATH ROW U.S.A.], 4–5.

10. As of 1983, "[o]f the 34 capital cases decided on the merits by [United States Circuit] Courts of Appeals since 1976 in which a prisoner appealed from the denial of habeas relief, the prisoner has prevailed in no fewer than 23 cases, or approximately 70% of the time." Barefoot v. Estelle, 463 U.S. 880, 915 (1983) (Marshall, J., dissenting) (footnotes omitted). One reason for this remarkable reversal rate was the almost unbroken string of victories by capital defendants in the Supreme Court from 1976 through 1982. See, e.g., Gardner v. Florida, 430 U.S. 349 (1977); Coker v. Georgia, 433 U.S. 584 (1977); Lockett v. Ohio, 438 U.S. 586 (1978); Adams v. Texas, 448 U.S. 38 (1980); Godfrey v. Georgia, 446 U.S. 420 (1980); Beck v. Alabama, 447 U.S. 625 (1980); Bullington v. Missouri, 451 U.S. 430 (1981); Estelle v. Smith, 451 U.S. 454 (1981); Eddings v. Oklahoma, 455 U.S. 104 (1982); Enmund v. Florida, 458 U.S. 782 (1982).

11. AMNESTY INTERNATIONAL, UNITED STATES OF AMERICA—THE DEATH PENALTY, at 194, 228 (1987).

12. 428 U.S. 153, 173 (1976) (plurality opinion).

13. Id. at 179–82.

14. For example, in a Gallup survey conducted on January 10 through 13, 1986, 70 percent of a national sample of adults said they "favor" the death penalty in response to the question "Do you favor or oppose the death penalty for murder?" Two Gallup surveys in 1985 found somewhat higher support for the death penalty—72 percent in January and 75 percent in November. From 1936 until 1985 the level of approval of the death penalty on Gallup surveys using this question had always been under 70 percent. In 1972, when Furman was decided, it was 57 percent; and in 1976, when Gregg was decided, it was 65 percent. The Death Penalty, THE GALLUP REPORT, Jan.–Feb. 1986, at 10.

15. Burt, Disorder in the Court: The Death Penalty and the Con-

stitution, 85 MICH. L. REV. 1741 (1987). Professors Baldus, Woodworth, and Pulaski take a narrower view. *"McCleskey* therefore represents, at least for the short run, an end to the scrutiny of the evenhandedness of state death sentencing systems by the federal courts, except in the most obviously gross sort of case." Baldus, Woodworth, & Pulaski, *McCleskey v. Zant and McCleskey v. Kemp: A Methodological Critique,* in Baldus & Cole, STATISTICAL PROOF OF DISCRIMINATION (1980), 1987 Cum. Supp. at 117, 123.

16. Godfrey v. Georgia, 446 U.S. 420, 442 (1980) (Marshall, J., concurring).

17. *See* ch. 10, p. 185.

18. Note, *The Supreme Court 1986 Term,* 101 HAR. L. REV. 119, 150 (1987).

19. *E.g.,* Wicker, *Death and Charity,* N.Y. Times, Sept. 7, 1987, § 1 at 19, col. 4; *Now Come The Executions,* Washington Post, April 24, 1987, § A at 26 (editorial); Note, *The Supreme Court 1986 Term, supra* note 18 at 150, 158. *Cf.* Zimring, *Is The Court Too Split to Sanction Death?* L. A. Times, April 27, 1987, § II at 5.

20. DEATH ROW U.S.A., *supra* note 9, at 5.

21. *Id.*

22. *See* Applebome, *Executions on the Rise as Legal Barriers Fall,* N.Y. Times, Aug. 9, 1987, § 1 at 1, col. 2.

23. Brennan, *Constitutional Adjudication and the Death Penalty: A View from the Court,* 100 HAR. L. REV. 313, 314–15 (1986).

24. *See* DEATH ROW U.S.A., *supra* note 9, at 2–3, and *id.,* Aug. 1, 1987, at 2–3, for lists of the capital cases decided since *McCleskey,* and of those still pending.

25. Franklin v. Lynaugh, No. 87-5546 (review granted October 9, 1987, 56 U.S.L.W. 3287) (argued March 1, 1988).

26. Mills v. Maryland, No. 87-5367 (review granted December 7, 1987, 56 U.S.L.W. 3395) (argued March 30, 1988).

27. Johnson v. Mississippi, No. 87-5463 (review granted January 11, 1988, 56 U.S.L.W. 3459) (argued April 25, 1988).

28. *E.g.,* Skipper v. South Carolina, 106 S.Ct. 1669 (1986); Turner v. Murray, 106 S.Ct. 1683 (1986).

29. DEATH ROW U.S.A., *supra* note 9, at 2–3, and *id.,* Aug. 1, 1987, at 2–3.

30. *See* Greenberg, *Capital Punishment as a System,* 91 YALE L. J. 908 (1982).

31. The unpublished data reported here in the several paragraphs that follow, on the death row population and on the status and disposition of capital review proceedings, were kindly provided by Ms. Tanya Coke,

Capital Punishment Information Director for the NAACP Legal Defense and Educational Fund, Inc., on May 16–18, 1988. *See generally* ch. 3, p. 36 and note 6.

32. McCleskey v. Kemp,—F.Supp.—(N.D.Ga. 12/23/87). [Cite.]

33. *See* Zant v. Stephens, 462 U.S. 862 (1983) (permitting the use of nonstatutory aggravating circumstances in capital penalty determinations); and Barclay v. Florida, 463 U.S. 939 (1983) (same). *See* ch. 1, note 30.

34. Barefoot v. Estelle, 463 U.S. 880 (1983) (approving summary procedures on appeals from the denial of federal habeas corpus petitions in capital cases).

35. DEATH ROW U.S.A., *supra* note 9, at 1.

36. The yearly totals of new death sentences (i.e., excluding reimpositions of previously reversed death penalties) since 1980 have been: 1981, 249; 1982, 296; 1983, 268; 1984, 285; 1985, 292; 1986, 311; 1987, 289. Coke, *supra* note 31. The annual average for this period is 284. (The annual average from 1974 through 1987 is 248. *See* ch. 1, note 3 for the yearly totals from 1974 through 1980.)

37. Clifford, *Voters Repudiate 3 of Court's Liberal Justices*, L. A. Times, Nov. 4, 1986, § I at 1, col. 2.

38. *Id.* The capital appeals reversal records of Justices Reynoso and Grodin were somewhat less extreme—46 of 47, and 40 of 45, respectively—but they received relatively little separate attention. *Id.*

39. Coke, *supra* note 31.

40. 107 S.Ct. at 1806 (Stevens, J., dissenting).

41. *Id.* at 1780–81 n.45.

42. *See generally* Ellsworth & Ross, *Public Opinion and Capital Punishment: A Close Examination of the Views of Abolitionists and Retentionists*, 29 CRIME & DELINQ. 116, 138–39, 164, 168–69 (1983) (attitudes in favor of capital punishment are generally abstract and symbolic, and do not translate readily into decisions to impose the death penalty in particular cases).

Appendix 1

1. Reported Numbers of Homicide Victims, By Source

Georgia

	SHR MAGNETIC TAPE	UCR ESTIMATED TOTALS	UCR ACTUAL REPORTS	VITAL STATISTICS DATA
1976	492	692	517	793
1977	494	593	584	725
1978	551	731	711	749
1979	627	877	843	844
1980	457	743	698	808
Total	2621	3636	3353	3919

Florida

	SHR MAGNETIC TAPE	UCR ESTIMATED TOTALS	UCR ACTUAL REPORTS	VITAL STATISTICS DATA†
1976	841	903	902	980
1977	854	859	859	925
1978	951	949	949	1108
1979	1050	1084	1084	1156
1980	1390	1387	1387	1520
Total	5086	5182	5181	5689

†Includes a small number of homicides attributable to "legal intervention."

Illinois

	SHR MAGNETIC TAPE	UCR ESTIMATED TOTALS	UCR ACTUAL REPORTS	VITAL STATISTICS DATA†
1977	(565)*	(1109)	(1107)	(1264)
1978	1087	1108	1102	1262
1979	1168	1203	1202	1433
1980	1176	1205	1203	1414
Total ('78–'80)	3431	3516	3507	4109

*SHR figures cover period from 7/77 to 12/77 only.

†Includes a small number of homicides attributable to "legal intervention."

Oklahoma

	SHR MAGNETIC TAPE	UCR ESTIMATED TOTALS	UCR ACTUAL REPORTS	VITAL STATISTICS DATA
1976	(83)*	(178)	(178)	(217)
1977	202	241	240	256
1978	229	244	241	272
1979	277	281	279	310
1980	294	299	293	324
Total ('77–'80)	1002	1065	1053	1162

*SHR figures cover period from 8/76 to 12/76 only.

North Carolina

	SHR MAGNETIC TAPE	UCR ESTIMATED TOTALS	UCR ACTUAL REPORTS	VITAL STATISTICS DATA
1977	(344)*	(586)	(570)	(627)
1978	586	600	591	656
1979	583	600	594	658
1980	610	619	611	661
Total ('78–'80)	1779	1819	1796	1975

*SHR figures cover period from 6/77 to 12/77 only.

Mississippi

	SHR MAGNETIC TAPE	UCR ESTIMATED TOTALS	UCR ACTUAL REPORTS	VITAL STATISTICS DATA
1976	179	294	238	306
1977	217	342	259	344
1978	203	302	218	332
1979	201	302	215	347
1980	208	365	255	359
Total	1008	1605	1185	1688

Virginia

	SHR MAGNETIC TAPE	UCR ESTIMATED TOTALS	UCR ACTUAL REPORTS	VITAL STATISTICS DATA†
1977	(303)*	(460)	(460)	(482)
1978	453	452	452	480
1979	444	447	445	501
1980	450	459	458	496
Total ('78–'80)	1347	1358	1355	1477

*SHR figures cover period from 5/77 to 12/77 only.

†Includes a small number of homicides attributable to "legal intervention."

Arkansas

	SHR MAGNETIC TAPE	UCR ESTIMATED TOTALS	UCR ACTUAL REPORTS	VITAL STATISTICS DATA†
1976	171	213	187	191
1977	156	188	177	181
1978	190	199	191	206**
1979	194	198	195	232
1980	202	210	207	250
Total	913	1008	957	1060

**Data from: National Center for Health Statistics: *Vital Statistics of the United States, 1978*, vol. 2, part A. DHHS Publ. No. (PHS) 83-1101. Public Health Service, Washington, D.C.: U.S. Gov't Printing Office (1982).

Sources of Vital Statistics Data

GEORGIA
Department of Human Resources, Physical Health Division
Office of Health Planning & Statistics
47 Trinity Avenue, S.W.
Atlanta, GA 30334
(404) 656-4922

FLORIDA
Department of Health & Rehabilitative Services
P. O. Box 210
Jacksonville, FL 32231
(904) 364-3961

ILLINOIS
Public Health Department
Division of Health Information & Evaluation
525 W. Jefferson Street
Springfield, IL 62761
(217) 785-5254

NORTH CAROLINA
State Center for Health Statistics
Division of Health Services
P. O. Box 2091
Raleigh, NC 27602
(919) 733-4728

MISSISSIPPI
Office of Public Health Statistics
Mississippi State Board of Health
P. O. Box 1700
Jackson, MS 39205
(601) 354-6000

OKLAHOMA

Oklahoma State Department of Health
Public Health Statistics
100 Northeast 19th Street
P. O. Box 53551
Oklahoma City, OK 73152

VIRGINIA

Virginia Center for Health Statistics
P. O. Box 1000
Richmond, VA 23208
(804) 786-6206

ARKANSAS

Arkansas Department of Health
Division of Health Statistics
4815 West Markham Street
Little Rock, AR 72201
(501) 661-2368

2. The Death Penalty Statutes and the Periods of
Study in the Eight States Covered*

GEORGIA. GA. CODE ANN. §§ 17-10-30 et seq. (1982).
Effective 1973.** Study period: 1976–1980.
FLORIDA. FLA. STAT. ANN. § 921.141 (West 1985). Effective
1972. Study period: 1976–1980.
ILLINOIS. ILL. ANN. STAT. ch. 38 § 9-1 (Smith-Hurd 1979
& Supp. 1987). Effective July 1, 1977. Study period: July
1977–1980.
OKLAHOMA. OKLA. STAT. ANN., tit. 21, §§ 701.10 et seq.
(West 1983). Effective July 24, 1976. Study period: August
1976–1980.

*All listed dates are inclusive.
**Statute renumbered from original.

NORTH CAROLINA. N.C. GEN. STAT. § 15A-2000 (1983). Effective June 1, 1977. *Study period*: June 1977–1980.

MISSISSIPPI. MISS. CODE ANN. §§ 99-19-101 et seq. (1972 & Supp. 1986). Effective April 13, 1977. Prior to this statute, the death penalty was available in Mississippi by judicial decree. (See *Jackson v. State*, 337 So.2d 1242 (Miss. 1976) (describing new death penalty procedures and making them retroactive).) *Study period*: 1976–1980.

VIRGINIA. VA. CODE §§ 19.2-264.2 (1983). Effective July 1, 1977.** This statute was applied retroactively to a small number of homicides committed in the months just prior to its effective date. (See *Smith v. Commonwealth*, 219 Va. 455, 248 S.E.2d 135 (1978), cert. denied, 441 U.S. 967 (1979). *Study period*: May 1, 1977–1980.

ARKANSAS. ARK. STAT. ANN. §§ 41-1301 et seq. (1977). Effective 1976. *Study period*: 1976–1980.

Appendix 2

Racial Patterns in Capital Sentencing: Oklahoma, North Carolina, Mississippi, Virginia, and Arkansas*

Table A.1. *Percentage of Oklahoma Death Sentences by Race of Suspect and Race of Victim*

RACE OF VICTIM	RACE OF SUSPECT		
	BLACK	WHITE	ALL VICTIMS
White	16.7% (6/36)	6.6% (34/519)	6.9% (40/581)
Black	1.3% (3/237)	0% (0/13)	1.2% (3/252)
		All cases	4.8% (43/898)

*In the tables in this appendix, entries under the headings "All white victims" and "All black victims" include some cases with suspects who were Asian, American Indian, or of unknown race. As a result, these entries may contain more cases than the corresponding totals of "Black kills white" and "White kills white" cases, or of "Black kills black" and "White kills black" cases, respectively. Similarly, the entries under the heading "All cases" may include some cases with suspects and/or victims who were Asian, American Indian, or of unknown race; as a result, these entries may not correspond exactly to the totals of white-victim and black-victim cases.

Table A.2. *Percentage of Oklahoma Death Sentences by Race of Victim and Suspect, and Felony Circumstance*

	FELONY	NONFELONY
Black kills white	30.8% (4/13)	9.5% (2/21)
White kills white	31.6% (18/57)	3.6% (16/439)
Black kills black	0% (0/14)	1.4% (3/212)
White kills black	0% (0/3)	0% (0/8)
All white victims	30.6% (22/72)	3.7% (18/482)
All black victims	0% (0/17)	1.4% (3/221)

Table A.3. *Percentage of Oklahoma Death Sentences by Race of Victim and Suspect, and Their Relationship*

	STRANGER HOMICIDES	NONSTRANGER HOMICIDES
Black kills white	26.7% (4/15)	9.5% (2/21)
White kills white	22.1% (23/104)	2.7% (11/415)
Black kills black	4.2% (1/24)	0.9% (2/213)
White kills black	0% (0/5)	0% (0/8)
All white victims	21.8% (27/124)	2.8% (13/457)
All black victims	3.4% (1/29)	0.9% (2/223)

Table A.4. *Percentage of Oklahoma Death Sentences by Race of Victim and Suspect, and Number of Victims*

	MULTIPLE VICTIMS	SINGLE VICTIM
Black kills white	0% (0/5)	19.4% (6/31)
White kills white	31.3% (10/32)	4.9% (24/487)
Black kills black	50.0% (1/2)	0.9% (2/235)
White kills black	—	0% (0/13)
All white victims	27.0% (10/37)	5.5% (30/544)
All black victims	50.0% (1/2)	0.8% (2/250)

Table A.5. *Percentage of Oklahoma Death Sentences by Race of Victim and Sex of Victim, Means of Death, and Location of Homicide*

	WHITE VICTIMS	BLACK VICTIMS
Female victim	9.8% (16/163)	1.9% (1/54)
Male victim	5.7% (24/418)	1.0% (2/198)
Killed by guns	6.8% (27/398)	0.5% (1/194)
Killed by other means	7.6% (13/172)	3.6% (2/55)
Rural homicides	6.3% (15/238)	0% (0/80)
Urban homicides	7.3% (25/343)	1.7% (3/172)

Table A.6. *Ratio of Oklahoma Death Sentences by Race of Suspect and Victim and Number of Reported Aggravating Circumstances*

	NUMBER OF AGGRAVATING CIRCUMSTANCES				
	0	1	2	3	TOTALS
Black kills white	0% (0/13)	30.8% (4/13)	20.0% (2/10)	—	16.7% (6/36)
White kills white	1.6% (6/376)	10.6% (11/104)	39.3% (11/28)	54.5% (6/11)	6.6% (34/519)
Black kills black	0.5% (1/202)	6.7% (2/30)	0% (0/5)	—	1.3% (3/237)
White kills black	0% (0/8)	0% (0/2)	0% (0/3)	—	0% (0/13)

Table A.7. *Percentage of North Carolina Death Sentences by Race of Suspect and Race of Victim*

RACE OF VICTIM	RACE OF SUSPECT		ALL VICTIMS
	BLACK	WHITE	
White	7.1% (7/99)	1.9% (14/739)	2.5% (21/850)
Black	0.2% (2/935)	3.8% (1/26)	0.4% (4/966)
		All cases	1.4% (27/1871)

Table A.8. *Percentage of North Carolina Death Sentences by Race of Victim and Suspect, and Felony Circumstance*

	FELONY	NONFELONY
Black kills white	16.3% (7/43)	0% (0/46)
White kills white	11.7% (7/60)	1.1% (7/620)
Black kills black	2.3% (1/43)	0.1% (1/842)
White kills black	50.0% (1/2)	0% (0/23)
All white victims	13.6% (14/103)	1.0% (7/678)
All black victims	4.3% (2/46)	0.2% (2/869)

Table A.9. *Percentage of North Carolina Death Sentences by Race of Victim and Suspect, and Their Relationship*

	STRANGER HOMICIDES	NONSTRANGER HOMICIDES
Black kills white	8.2% (5/61)	5.7% (2/35)
White kills white	6.2% (7/113)	1.1% (7/612)
Black kills black	1.1% (1/95)	0.1% (1/811)
White kills black	10.0% (1/10)	0% (0/15)
All white victims	6.7% (12/178)	1.4% (9/654)
All black victims	1.9% (2/106)	0.2% (2/830)

Table A.10. *Percentage of North Carolina Death Sentences by Race of Victim and Suspect, and Number of Victims*

	MULTIPLE VICTIMS	SINGLE VICTIM
Black kills white	42.9% (3/7)	4.3% (4/92)
White kills white	7.1% (2/28)	1.7% (12/711)
Black kills black	0% (0/3)	0.2% (2/932)
White kills black	—	3.8% (1/26)
All white victims	14.3% (5/35)	2.0% (16/815)
All black victims	0% (0/3)	0.4% (4/963)

Table A.11. *Percentage of North Carolina Death Sentences by Race of Victim and Sex of Victim, Means of Death, and Location of Homicide*

	WHITE VICTIMS	BLACK VICTIMS
Female victim	4.7% (10/215)	1.1% (2/183)
Male victim	1.7% (11/635)	0.3% (2/738)
Killed by guns	1.6% (10/640)	0.3% (2/691)
Killed by other means	5.8% (11/190)	0.8% (2/262)
Rural homicides	3.0% (14/467)	0.4% (2/524)
Urban homicides	1.8% (7/383)	0.5% (2/442)

Table A.12. *Ratio of North Carolina Death Sentences by Race of Suspect and Victim and Number of Reported Aggravating Circumstances*

	NUMBER OF AGGRAVATING CIRCUMSTANCES				
	0	1	2	3	TOTALS
Black kills	0%	3.4%	11.4%	40.0%	7.1%
white	(0/30)	(1/29)	(4/35)	(2/5)	(7/99)
White kills	0.9%	1.4%	20.6%	—	1.9%
white	(5/558)	(2/147)	(7/34)		(14/739)
Black kills	0.1%	0%	4.2%	—	0.2%
black	(1/789)	(0/122)	(1/24)		(2/935)
White kills	0%	0%	100.0%	—	3.8%
black	(0/14)	(0/11)	(1/1)		(1/26)

Table A.13. *Percentage of Mississippi Death Sentences by Race of Suspect and Race of Victim*

RACE OF VICTIM	RACE OF SUSPECT		
	BLACK	WHITE	ALL VICTIMS
White	25.0% (10/40)	4.2% (7/167)	8.2% (17/208)
Black	0.5% (3/621)	11.1% (2/18)	0.8% (5/639)
		All cases	2.6% (22/852)

Table A.14. *Percentages of Mississippi Death Sentences by Race of Victim and Suspect, and Felony Circumstance*

	FELONY	NONFELONY
Black kills white	38.9% (7/18)	18.8% (3/16)
White kills white	27.3% (6/22)	0.7% (1/134)
Black kills black	5.7% (2/35)	0.2% (1/553)
White kills black	28.6% (2/7)	0% (0/11)
All white victims	32.5% (13/40)	2.6% (4/151)
All black victims	9.5% (4/42)	0.2% (1/564)

Table A.15. *Percentage of Mississippi Death Sentences by Race of Victim and Suspect, and Their Relationship*

	STRANGER HOMICIDES	NONSTRANGER HOMICIDES
Black kills white	24% (6/25)	28.6% (4/14)
White kills white	10.3% (3/29)	2.9% (4/136)
Black kills black	4.7% (3/64)	0% (0/550)
White kills black	15.4% (2/13)	0% (0/5)
All white victims	16.7% (9/54)	5.3% (8/151)
All black victims	6.5% (5/77)	0% (0/555)

Table A.16. *Percentage of Mississippi Death Sentences by Race of Victim and Suspect, and Number of Victims*

	MULTIPLE VICTIMS	SINGLE VICTIM
Black kills white	0% (0/2)	26.3% (10/38)
White kills white	22.2% (2/9)	3.2% (5/158)
Black kills black	0% (0/7)	0.5% (3/614)
White kills black	—	11.1% (2/18)
All white victims	18.2% (2/11)	7.6% (15/197)
All black victims	0% (0/7)	0.8% (5/632)

Table A.17. *Percentage of Mississippi Death Sentences by Race of Victim and Sex of Victim, Means of Death, and Location of Homicide*

	WHITE VICTIMS	BLACK VICTIMS
Female victim	11.1% (7/63)	0% (0/127)
Male victim	6.9% (10/145)	1.0% (5/511)
Killed by guns	7.3% (12/165)	0.6% (3/489)
Killed by other means	13.5% (5/37)	1.4% (2/142)
Rural homicides	6.9% (9/131)	0.5% (2/444)
Urban homicides	10.4% (8/77)	1.5% (3/195)

Table A.18. *Ratio of Mississippi Death Sentences by Race of Suspect and Victim and Number of Reported Aggravating Circumstances*

	NUMBER OF AGGRAVATING CIRCUMSTANCES				
	0	1	2	3	TOTALS
Black kills white	9.1% (1/11)	35.7% (5/14)	28.6% (4/14)	0% (0/1)	25.0% (10/40)
White kills white	0.8% (1/125)	6.9% (2/29)	37.5% (3/8)	20.0% (1/5)	4.2% (7/167)
Black kills black	0% (0/527)	1.2% (1/82)	16.7% (2/12)	—	0.5% (3/621)
White kills black	0% (0/4)	0% (0/8)	33.3% (2/6)	—	11.1% (2/18)

Table A.19. *Percentage of Virginia Death Sentences by Race of Suspect and Race of Victim*

RACE OF VICTIM	RACE OF SUSPECT		ALL VICTIMS
	BLACK	WHITE	
White	8.2% (8/98)	1.3% (7/544)	2.3% (15/646)
Black	0.6% (4/703)	0% (0/39)	0.5% (4/742)
All cases			1.4% (19/1389)

Table A.20. *Percentage of Virginia Death Sentences by Race of Victim and Suspect, and Felony Circumstance*

	FELONY	NONFELONY
Black kills white	17.4% (8/46)	0% (0/35)
White kills white	11.1% (5/45)	0.4% (2/458)
Black kills black	7.0% (4/57)	0% (0/611)
White kills black	0% (0/1)	0% (0/38)
All white victims	14.3% (13/91)	0.4% (2/497)
All black victims	6.9% (4/58)	0% (0/649)

Table A.21. *Percentage of Virginia Death Sentences by Race of Victim and Suspect, and Their Relationship*

	STRANGER HOMICIDES	NONSTRANGER HOMICIDES
Black kills white	10.3% (6/58)	6.3% (2/32)
White kills white	5.4% (4/74)	0.7% (3/460)
Black kills black	1.8% (1/57)	0.5% (3/636)
White kills black	0% (0/18)	0% (0/21)
All white victims	7.6% (10/132)	1.0% (5/496)
All black victims	1.3% (1/75)	0.5% (3/657)

Table A.22. *Percentage of Virginia Death Sentences by Race of Victim and Suspect, and Number of Victims*

	MULTIPLE VICTIMS	SINGLE VICTIM
Black kills white	20.0% (2/10)	6.8% (6/88)
White kills white	5.0% (1/20)	1.1% (6/524)
Black kills black	7.1% (1/14)	0.4% (3/689)
White kills black	—	0% (0/39)
All white victims	9.7% (3/31)	2.0% (12/615)
All black victims	7.1% (1/14)	0.4% (3/728)

Table A.23. *Percentage of Virginia Death Sentences by Race of Victim and Sex of Victim, Means of Death, and Location of Homicide*

	WHITE VICTIMS	BLACK VICTIMS
Female victim	4.6% (9/195)	1.7% (3/178)
Male victim	1.3% (6/451)	0.2% (1/564)
Killed by guns	1.5% (7/463)	0.4% (2/507)
Killed by other means	5.0% (8/159)	0.9% (2/224)
Rural homicides	2.1% (6/287)	0.4% (1/236)
Urban homicides	2.5% (9/359)	0.6% (3/506)

Table A.24. *Ratio of Virginia Death Sentences by Race of Suspect and Victim and Number of Reported Aggravating Circumstances*

	NUMBER OF AGGRAVATING CIRCUMSTANCES				
	0	1	2	3	TOTALS
Black kills white	0% (0/29)	4.5% (1/22)	14.6% (6/41)	16.7% (1/6)	8.2% (8/98)
White kills white	0% (0/425)	4.4% (4/90)	10.7% (3/28)	0% (0/1)	1.3% (7/544)
Black kills black	0% (0/594)	2.4% (2/82)	8.0% (2/25)	0% (0/2)	0.6% (4/703)
White kills black	0% (0/21)	0% (0/17)	0% (0/1)	—	0% (0/39)

Table A.25. *Percentage of Arkansas Death Sentences by Race of Suspect and Race of Victim*

RACE OF VICTIM	RACE OF SUSPECT		
	BLACK	WHITE	ALL VICTIMS
White	12.3% (7/57)	1.8% (6/339)	3.3% (13/396)
Black	0.5% (2/388)	0% (0/10)	0.5% (2/398)
		All cases	1.9% (15/798)

Table A.26. *Percentage of Arkansas Death Sentences by Race of Victim and Suspect, and Felony Circumstance*

	FELONY	NONFELONY
Black kills white	12.0% (3/25)	15.4% (4/26)
White kills white	10.2% (5/49)	0.4% (1/270)
Black kills black	7.7% (2/26)	0% (0/350)
White kills black	0% (0/1)	0% (0/9)
All white victims	10.8% (8/74)	1.7% (5/296)
All black victims	7.4% (2/27)	0% (0/359)

Table A.27. *Percentage of Arkansas Death Sentences by Race of Victim and Suspect, and Their Relationship*

	STRANGER HOMICIDES	NONSTRANGER HOMICIDES
Black kills white	12.5% (4/32)	12.5% (3/24)
White kills white	10.4% (5/48)	0.3% (1/291)
Black kills black	3.0% (1/33)	0.3% (1/355)
White kills black	0% (0/4)	0% (0/6)
All white victims	11.3% (9/80)	1.3% (4/315)
All black victims	2.7% (1/37)	0.3% (1/361)

Table A.28. *Percentage of Arkansas Death Sentences by Race of Victim and Suspect, and Number of Victims*

	MULTIPLE VICTIMS	SINGLE VICTIM
Black kills white	100% (1/1)	10.7% (6/56)
White kills white	15% (3/20)	0.9% (3/319)
Black kills black	0% (0/11)	0.5% (2/377)
White kills black	—	0% (0/10)
All white victims	19.0% (4/21)	2.4% (9/375)
All black victims	0% (0/11)	0.5% (2/387)

Table A.29. *Percentage of Arkansas Death Sentences by Race of Victim and Sex of Victim, Means of Death, and Location of Homicide*

	WHITE VICTIMS	BLACK VICTIMS
Female victim	4.1% (5/121)	0% (0/91)
Male victim	2.9% (8/273)	0.7% (2/307)
Killed by guns	3.8% (11/287)	0.3% (1/321)
Killed by other means	1.9% (2/106)	1.4% (1/74)
Rural homicides	3.3% (7/209)	0.5% (1/200)
Urban homicides	3.2% (6/187)	0.5% (1/198)

Table A.30. *Ratio of Arkansas Death Sentences by Race of Suspect and Victim and Number of Reported Aggravating Circumstances*

	NUMBER OF AGGRAVATING CIRCUMSTANCES				
	0	1	2	3	TOTALS
Black kills white	0% (0/16)	26.1% (6/23)	5.6% (1/18)	—	12.3% (7/57)
White kills white	0% (0/249)	3.0% (2/67)	5.3% (1/19)	75.0% (3/4)	1.8% (6/339)
Black kills black	0% (0/332)	2.4% (1/42)	7.1% (1/14)	—	0.6% (2/388)
White kills black	0% (0/6)	0% (0/3)	0% (0/1)	—	0% (0/10)

Appendix 3: Methodology and Further Analyses

A. Statistical Significance

We report two sets of probability values in the text in conjunction with the tables that classify homicides along a scale of aggravation (see Tables 4.22, 4.23, 4.27, 4.29, and 4.31). These two sets of figures were calculated by different procedures.

1. Column p-values

The p-values at the foot of each column in the tables that classify the homicides by race of victim but not race of suspect reflect the probability that the observed number of death sentences, or a greater number, could have been imposed in white-victim cases by chance, given the total number of death sentences imposed at the specified level of aggravation, and given the numbers of black-victim and of white-victim homicides that occurred at that level of aggravation.

For the tables that classify homicides by race of suspect as well as by race of victim, the situation is slightly more complex. These tables include four racial categories: black-kills-white, white-kills-white, black-kills-black, white-kills-black. If neither the race of the suspect nor the race of the victim had an effect on capital sentencing, then one would expect the death sentences imposed at each level of aggravation (*i.e.* in each column) to be distributed roughly in proportion to the number of homicides occurring in each racial category. If racial biases against both black suspects and the killers of white victims were operating, however, then one would expect blacks who kill whites to be treated more severely than whites who kill whites, who in turn would be treated more severely than blacks who kill blacks, who finally would be treated more severely than whites who kill blacks. Indeed, these racial categories could be ranked along a scale in that order. The *p*-values reflect the probability that a distribution of death sentences as skewed towards the upper end of this racial scale as the observed distribution, or more skewed, could have occurred by chance in a particular column, given the number of homicides occurring in each racial category and given the total number of death sentences imposed at the level of aggravation specified by the column.

The probability values for both sets of tables were calculated by a randomization test[1] and hence depend on fewer assumptions than standard statistical tests. Using the definition of racial bias given above, we determined the number of possible distributions of death sentences as racially biased or more racially biased than the observed distribution, and divided that number by the total number of all possible distributions of death sentences across racial categories. The calculations were performed by a computer algorithm designed by Robert Mauro.

2. Overall p-values

The "overall *p*-values" reported in these tables were derived from odds ratios that were calculated by the modified Woolf's estimator of the odds ratio.[2] For the tables that include race of suspect as well as race of victim, these odds ratios compare the odds of receiving the death penalty for the killing of a white to the odds of receiving the death penalty for the killing of a black, controlling for the level of aggravation and the race of the suspect. For the tables that include only the race of the victim, the odds ratios compare the odds of receiving the death penalty for killing a white to the odds of receiving the death penalty for killing a black, controlling for the level of aggravation.

B. Logistic Regression

In analyzing the relationship between a single outcome or dependent variable (y) and several predictor or independent variables (x_1 through x_n), the technique of choice is usually some variant of ordinary least squares (OLS) multiple linear regression. Multiple regression produces a linear equation in the following form:

$$Y = a + b_1 x_1 + b_2 x_2 + \ldots + b_n x_n + u.$$

The quantity u in this regression equation represents the discrepancy between the values of the outcome variable predicted by the equation and the observed values; it is called the "random disturbance." In multiple regression, the parameters (a, b_1, b_2, $\ldots b_n$) are estimated so as to minimize these discrepancies. This produces a set of coefficients (b_1, $\ldots b_n$), which (if certain assumptions are held) are valid estimators of the actual parameters defining the linear relationship between the dependent variable and the independent variables.

Ordinary least squares multiple regression is designed to deal with continuous outcome variables (such as age) that can assume any number of values. Logistic multiple regression is a variant of multiple regression that is designed to deal with the special features of regression analysis with a dichotomous outcome variable that can take only two values, 0 or 1. In this study the outcome variable is assigned a value of 1 for every homicide in which the death penalty was imposed, and a value of 0 otherwise.

In logistic regression, the parameters of the following model (or its equivalent) are estimated:

$$Ln(p(y)/(1 - p(y))) = b_1x_1 + b_2x_2 + ... b_nx_n + u$$

The quantity $p(y)$ is the probability of the outcome y; the quantity in the parentheses on the left—$(p(y)/(1 - p(y)))$—is the familiar odds ratio of the outcome y, and the symbol Ln means that we are considering the natural log of that quantity. (The "odds ratio" is equivalent to the commonly used betting odds; odds $= p/(1 - p)$, where p is the probability of the event in question. Thus if the probability of an event is .5 the odds ratio is 1, or "1 to 1"; if the probability is .6 the odds ratio is 1.5, or "3 to 2," etc.) Therefore, each b_i reflects the amount of linear change in the natural log of the odds ratio of the outcome resulting from a change in the related independent variable x_i. In this study, all the independent variables are dichotomous, hence each b_i reflects the change in the log of the odds of a death sentence resulting from the presence of a particular potentially aggravating circumstance or racial characteristic.

If both sides of this equation are converted to exponential form, the following result is obtained:

$$p(y)/(1 - p)) = e^{(b_1x_1 + b_2x_2 + ...b_nx_n + u)}$$

or:

$$p(y)/(1 - p(y)) = (e^{b_1x_1})(e^{b_2x_2}) ... (e^{b_nx_n})(e^u)$$

Thus, the effect of an independent variable can be expressed as a multiplier of the odds ratio of the outcome variable. Each x_i in this study has only two possible values: 1 if the particular circumstance is present and 0 if it is absent. Therefore, the quantity (e^{b_i}) represents the factor by which the odds of the outcome are multiplied when the circumstance is present. For example, the effect of a variable with a coefficient of .2 will be to increase the odds of the outcome by a factor of ($e^{.2}$), which is equal to 1.2, and a variable with a coefficient of 1.2 will increase the odds of the outcome by a factor of ($e^{1.2}$), or 3.3.

The estimation of the parameters of a logistic regression model is a somewhat more complex task than the estimation of the parameters of a linear regression model. Several methods of estimation are possible. We used a maximum likelihood estimation procedure that relies on an iterative fitting algorithm embodied in the logistic regression procedure available in the BMDP programs developed at the Department of Biomathematics, University of California, Los Angeles.[3]

Some of the variables that we considered are interaction variables. These variables represent the effect that a particular underlying variable has in the presence of another variable or variables. For example, it is possible that the use of a gun is an aggravating factor in felony homicides but not in nonfelony homicides, or that its aggravating impact is greater among felony homicides. An interaction variable representing the effect of the simultaneous presence of a felony circumstance and the use of a gun will enable the regression equation to capture such conditional effects.

Note, however, that when interaction variables are used the interpretation of the associated regression coefficients is not straightforward. To evaluate the increase in the log-odds ratio resulting from the simultaneous presence of two variables, the contributions of each variable and of the interaction variable must be summed. If the coefficient associated with the interaction variable is negative, then the increase in the log-odds caused by the simultaneous presence of both variables is less than the sum of the effects of each variable acting alone. This does not mean that when both aggravating circumstances occur the suspect is less likely to receive the death penalty. In most cases the increase in the likelihood of receiving the death penalty will be greater than the increase that would have occurred if only one aggravating circumstance were present, but smaller than one would expect if the increase were predicted by simply adding the effects associated with each aggravating circumstance. For example, if the commission of a contemporaneous felony increases the log-odds of the death penalty by .4, and the killing of multiple victims increases the log-odds of the death penalty by .2, the interaction coefficient representing the effect of killing multiple victims during a felony might be $-.1$. This would indicate that the increase in the log-odds of receiving the death penalty for the killing of multiple victims during a felony is .4 + .2 + $(-.1)$ = .5. The increase in the log-odds resulting from the combination of the aggravating circumstances (.5) is greater than that resulting from either factor acting alone (.4 and .2 respectively) but less than the sum of the effects of the individual factors (.4 + .2 = .6).

Another problem in interpreting logistic regression coefficients is caused by the fact that the relationship between increases in the log of the odds ratio and increases in the probability of an outcome (e.g., a death sentence) is not linear. A given increase in the log of the odds ratio results in increases of different sizes in the probability of the outcome depending upon the probability level prior to the increase. The mathematical relationship between these two quantities is displayed in Figure 1. The presence of a particular circumstance may increase the log of the odds ratio of a death sentence (measured along the horizontal axis) by a given amount, a. This change, however, increases the probability of a death sentence by a greater amount—p^1—when the initial probability of a death sentence is in the middle range, and by a smaller amount—p—when the initial probability is either very low or very high.

In the present context this relationship reflects the common sense notion that when a homicide is moderately

Figure 1. *Relationship Between Probability and Log-Odds*

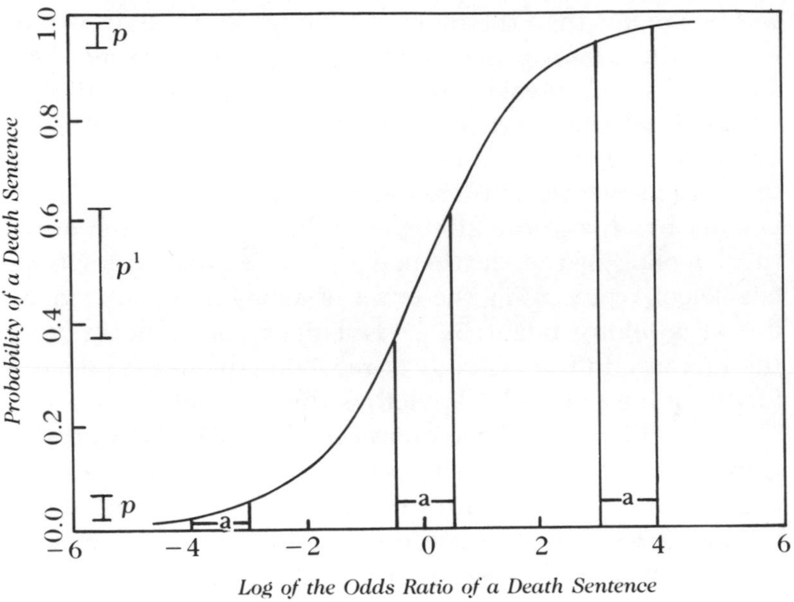

Log of the Odds Ratio of a Death Sentence

aggravated, and the probability of the defendant receiving the death penalty is therefore moderately high, the presence of an additional aggravating factor may have a large effect. If, however, the homicide is particularly heinous and therefore the probability of the defendant's receiving the death penalty is initially very high, then the presence of yet another aggravating circumstance will result in a smaller additional increase in the probability of a death sentence. Similarly, if the initial probability of a defendant's receiving the death penalty is very low, the presence of a single aggravating circumstance will not move the case into a category in which death sentences are fairly common and therefore will have a relatively small effect on the probability of the defendant's receiving the death sentence.

C. Cell-by-Cell Analysis

While logistic regression provides a useful summary of the interrelationships between predictor variables and the outcome variable, it is also useful to examine how each separate combination of predictor variables affects the outcome. By doing so one can obtain a different view of the interrelationships than the one provided by summary statistics. Furthermore, when the theoretical assumptions upon which an inferential statistic are based are not completely fulfilled in the data, such a detailed analysis can warn of potential problems in interpreting the inferential statistics.

To examine more closely the effect of the victim's race on capital sentencing, we first divided the homicide cases in each state into groups that are identical on all of the legitimate and potentially legitimate aggravating circumstances that we considered (the presence of contemporaneous felonies, the number of victims, the sex of the victims, whether a firearm was used, and the relationship of the offender to the victim), and that involve victims of the same race. We then compared each of these groups to the group of cases that matched it on all of the legitimate and potentially legitimate factors but differed on the race of the victim. A full presentation of this analysis would consist of the complete multiway frequency table created by all the possible combinations of the variables considered. Since such a table is rather unwieldy, we have summarized these comparisons below. For each state the following information is reported: (1) The number of nonempty groups; (2) the number of matched pairs of nonempty groups; (3) the proportions of all cases included in these matched groups; (4) the number of groups in which death penalties occurred; (5) the number of matched pairs of groups in which death penalties occurred; (6) the proportion of all death penalty cases included in the matched groups; and (7) the proportion of matched groups in which death pen-

Table A.31. *Cell-by-Cell Analysis of Death Sentencing by Race of Victim*

	GEORGIA	FLORIDA	ILLINOIS	OKLAHOMA	MISSISSIPPI	NORTH CAROLINA	VIRGINIA	ARKANSAS
1. Number of nonempty groups	45	54	58	38	38	42	46	41
2. Number of matched pairs of nonempty groups	19	24	27	14	15	17	20	17
3. Proportion of cases in matched pairs	$\frac{2110}{2118}$	$\frac{3308}{3486}$	$\frac{2984}{3080}$	$\frac{766}{898}$	$\frac{799}{852}$	$\frac{1758}{1871}$	$\frac{1374}{1389}$	$\frac{775}{798}$
4. Number of groups in which death sentences occur	36	42	34	31	15	23	19	16
5. Number of matched pairs in which death senences occur	17	18	16	12	6	10	9	7
6. Proportion of death sentences included in matched pairs	$\frac{76}{79}$	$\frac{107}{128}$	$\frac{39}{45}$	$\frac{32}{43}$	$\frac{18}{22}$	$\frac{20}{27}$	$\frac{18}{19}$	$\frac{12}{15}$
7. Proportion of matched pairs with white-victim DP rate > black-victim DP rate	$\frac{15}{17}$	$\frac{15}{18}$	$\frac{13}{16}$	$\frac{11}{12}$	$\frac{5}{6}$	$\frac{8}{10}$	$\frac{8}{9}$	$\frac{5}{7}$
p	.002	.005	.012	.004	.109	.055	.020	.226

alties occurred in which the proportion of death sentences among white-victim cases was greater than that among black-victim cases. (See Table A.31).

In each state, the great majority of the comparisons between matched groups reveals a higher proportion of death sentences among white-victim cases. The proportions reported above are statistically significant (by a sign test) in Georgia (p = .002), Florida (p = .005), Illinois (p = .012), Oklahoma (p = .004), and Virginia (p = .020), nearly significant in North Carolina (p = .055), and not significant in Mississippi (p = .109) and Arkansas (p = .226). The latter two proportions failed to reach conventional levels of statistical significance primarily because of the small number of matched groups being compared, 7 in Arkansas and 6 in Mississippi.

Notes

1. *See* E. S. Edington, Randomization Tests (1980).

2. *See* Gart, *Alternative Analysis of Contingency Tables*, 28 J. Royal Statistical Soc'y, Series B 164–79 (1966).

3. Further information on this procedure is available in Jennrich & Moore, *Maximum Likelihood Estimation by Means of Non-Linear Least Squares*, 1975 Am. Statistical Ass'n, Statistical Computing Sec. 57–65.

Index of Cases

257

General Index